Nicholas Poppe

REMINISCENCES

Edited
by
Henry G. Schwarz

Center for East Asian Studies, Western Washington University

Studies on East Asia, Volume 16
REMINISCENCES, by Nicholas Poppe

The Center for East Asian Studies publishes scholarly works on topics relating to China, Japan, Korea, and Mongolia.

Editor:
Professor Henry G. Schwarz

Nicholas Poppe

REMINISCENCES

Edited
by
Henry G. Schwarz

Western Washington

Library of Congress Cataloguing in Publication Data

    Poppe, N. N. (Nikolaĭ Nikolaevich), 1897–
       Reminiscences

      (Studies on East Asia; v. 16)
      Includes index.
        1. Poppe, N. N. (Nikolaĭ Nikolaevich),
    1897–   . 2. Altaists—Biography.
    I. Schwarz, Henry G., 1928–   II. Title
    III. Series
    PL1.P65 1982 410'.92'4   B   82-4544
    ISBN 0-914584-16-2   AACR2

In Memory of

Nataliya and Edith,

my faithful companions and helpers

Acknowledgments

The photograph of Gordon Hall in Tientsin has been reproduced, with the courteous permission of the Fleming H. Revell Company, Old Tappan, New Jersey, from the book *The Siege in Peking* (New York and Chicago, 1900) by W. A. P. Martin. The photographs of Koenig and the Alexander Koenig Museum have been obtained, through the courtesy of Professor Dr. Martin Eisentraut, Director of the Alexander Koenig Museum in Bonn, now retired, from his book *Alexander Koenig und sein Werk, Biographie eines Bonner Ehrenbürgers* (Bonn, 1973). The nine lines from Alexander Pushkin's "Ruslan and Lyudmila" in Walter Arndt's translation have been taken, with the courteous permission of the Ardis Publishing House in Ann Arbor from Alexander Pushkin, *Ruslan and Ludmila* (1974). I express here my gratitude to the two publishing houses and to Professor Dr. Martin Eisentraut.

The following photographs have been taken from old publications which are not copyrighted:

Johann Georg Koenig and his wife, Elisabeth, née Weber, from Julia Koenig, *Johann Georg Koenig und sein Haus, Dem Demütigen gibt Gott Gnade, 1785-1885* (St. Petersburg (1885));

Ferdinand Morawitz, from the necrology by Andrei Semenov, "Ferdinand Ferdinandovich Moravits † 5 dekabrya 1896," *Trudy Russkago Entomologicheskago Obshchestva v St.-Peterburge* 31 (1898), i-x;

Oskar Fredrik Hultman, from Hugo Pipping, "Oskar Fredrik Hultman, Minnestal vid Finska Vetenskaps-Societetens sammantrade den 14 April 1930," *Societas Scientiarum Fennica, Årsbok-Vuosikirja* VIII B, no. 6 (Helsingfors, 1930), 1-17;

Professor Shternberg, from N. I. Gagen-Torn, *Lev Yakovlevich Shternberg* (Moscow, 1975).

The remaining photographs are reproductions of photographs in the Poppe family album, snapshots made by me and photographs in my possession.

Preface

The idea of writing this brief life story has not come from me. I have never thought to write one, not because I am, in principle, opposed to the idea but simply because it has never occurred to me. I should add that I never thought that such a story might be of any interest to others, not to mention that I am not so ambitious as to yearn for fame. I have done only what I wanted to accomplish in order to satisfy my own curiosity. Besides, in order to write a complete autobiography, one must have ample materials, such as notes and diaries. I had kept a diary before the revolution of 1917 but not after it, although the period following the revolution was in many respects the most interesting one. Diaries became very dangerous after the October revolution, as the Soviet secret police, when raiding people's homes, was especially eager to confiscate diaries. Information in diaries, such as the names and addresses of various persons, could have dire, sometimes fatal, consequences for a diary's author and for the persons mentioned in it. Later, when I lived in war-time Germany, I did not keep a diary because living conditions were so harsh that keeping a diary would have been the last thing on one's mind. Besides, I had already forgotten long before then that there is such a thing as a diary.

The idea of writing down my reminiscences has come from my friends in the United States, Europe and Japan. Listening to some episodes of my life, such as my travels in Siberia and Mongolia and my activities in the Soviet Union and war-time Germany, they urged me to write everything down so that it could be read by people. I agree that this is a good idea, especially in view of the fact that I have met many interesting people and witnessed events not experienced by people outside places where these events took place. I am aware of the fact that I know some details of generally known events which are unknown to most persons and which are not found in the literature.

I finally agreed to record my reminiscences about people and events I witnessed or learned about from reliable sources. Of course, I had to inform the readers in brief about myself and my family. I have omitted details concerning life in our family, my everyday routine activities, birthday celebrations, and vacations. I have confined myself to the most essential. The result is a rather thin book, quite different from the multi-volume biographies of great celebrities in whose company I certainly do not belong.

The reader should be told in advance that this book contains only what I have personally experienced, along with some commonly known facts which form the background. One should not expect to find here detailed descriptions of events such as the October revolution or the civil war in Russia, nor should one expect to find analyses of such events.

My main source is my memory which is, on the whole, quite good. Information about my ancestors has been obtained from several publications cited in Chapter 1, and dates of births and deaths of some scholars were obtained from their obituaries or articles in encyclopedias.

Some events mentioned in this book took place long ago, like the October revolution, the civil war in Russia, and Stalin's era with all its atrocities and violations of fundamental human rights. Times have changed, and many aspects of life in the Soviet Union today are different from those of long ago. However, I do not speak about the Soviet Union of today but of the time when I lived in that country. If I skipped the purges and deportations, I would paint an utterly false picture of that country. Thousands of persons who witnessed the events of Stalin's era would rightfully criticize my reminiscences as biased.

I have put together all the necessary facts, either by record-ing on tape or in writing, in the form of a rough continuous text, with numerous handwritten additions. I take pleasure in expressing my heartfelt thanks to my friend, Professor Henry G. Schwarz, of Western Washington University, for not only editing the manuscript of this book but for practically rewriting the entire original text. Professor Schwarz is also the one who most urgently insisted that my reminiscences be put down in writing and eventually published.

The text contains numerous Russian personal and place names. They are rendered in a simplified English transcription. The following symbols should be pronounced as indicated:

A, a are English <u>a</u> as in f<u>a</u>ther

E, e are <u>ye</u> as in English <u>ye</u>t

È, è are English <u>e</u> as in <u>e</u>bb and b<u>e</u>d

I, i are English <u>i</u> as in <u>i</u>n and p<u>i</u>n, and after a vowel like
       English <u>i</u> as in o<u>i</u>l, or <u>y</u> as in Ma<u>y</u>

ii is a diphthong approaching the English <u>ee</u> in s<u>ee</u>m

Kh, kh are Gaelic <u>ch</u> as in lo<u>ch</u>

Y, y before a vowel are English <u>y</u> as in <u>y</u>ard and <u>y</u>olk and
       after a consonant like English <u>i</u> as in w<u>i</u>nter

Zh, zh are English <u>s</u> in plea<u>s</u>ure.

Nicholas Poppe

Contents

Illustrations

1 Childhood and Youth

I was born in Chefoo in the Chinese province of Shantung on August 8, 1897 and baptized there in the Anglican church. My father, Nicholas Edwin Poppe (1870-1913), was secretary of the Imperial Russian consulate in Tientsin. He had graduated from the Oriental Department of St. Petersburg University where he had studied the Chinese, Manchu, and Mongolian languages and various other Oriental subjects including East Asian history. He was the son of a tailor, Gottfried Maximilian Poppe, and the latter's wife, Maria née Tromberg, of Estonian extraction. His father, although a simple man, understood the importance of education, and all three of his children graduated from high school and later studied at the university. My father's brother Vasilii graduated from the Law School of St. Petersburg University and later became a lawyer, and his sister Maria graduated from the women's university (Vysshie Zhenskie Kursy) in St. Petersburg—at that time there were no co-educational universities in Russia—and became a teacher.

My mother, Elisabeth (Elizaveta), 1878-1955 (Illus. 1), was the daughter of Ferdinand Karl Joseph Morawitz (1827-1896), a well-known entomologist and vice-president of the Imperial Russian Entomological Society, who also held the degree of medical doctor (Illus. 2). The Morawitz family deserves special attention. My maternal great-grandfather Ferdinand Joseph Kaspar Morawitz (1796-1844) migrated from Altenburg in Saxony to Russia during the Napoleonic wars at the beginning of the nineteenth century. He was

1

Illus. 1. Elisabeth Poppe, née Morawitz Illus. 2. Ferdinand Karl Joseph Morawitz

a blacksmith by profession and a skillful builder of coaches. As
these were practically nonexistent in Russia at that time he
managed to accumulate quite a fortune. Of his four sons there
were, besides my grandfather Ferdinand, August, who was the
curator of the entomological division of the Museum of Zoology of
the Imperial Russian Academy of Sciences; Nicholas, professor of
anatomy at Kiev University, and Alexander, who died when he was
still a high school student. There was also a daughter, Amalia Maria
Josepha, who married a Finlander, Frithiof H. Hultman. Her son was
Oskar Fredrik Hultman (1862-1929) (Illus. 5) who became a well-
known scholar of the Swedish language and professor at Helsinki
University. Thus all immediate descendants of Ferdinand Joseph
Kaspar Morawitz were scholars or parents of scholars.

My maternal grandmother, Wilhelmine Emilie Karoline née
Boetz (1854-1919), was the daughter of a baker, Wilhelm Boetz
(1819-1885), who had married Elisabeth Koenig. The Koenigs were a
well-known family in old Russia. Elisabeth's parents were Johann
Georg Koenig (1785-1856) (Illus. 3) and Gertrud Elisabeth Koenig,
née Weber (Illus. 4) who migrated from Germany to Russia where he
became a well-known sugar manufacturer and owned many sugarbeet
plantations and factories. His family's fame was further enhanced
by his grandson Alexander Koenig (1858-1940) (Illus. 6) who was the
son of Leopold, brother of the above-mentioned Elisabeth, my
maternal great-grandmother. This Alexander Koenig studied
zoology, became a well-known and wealthy scholar who founded the
Alexander Koenig Zoological Museum in Bonn, Germany which still
exists (Illus. 7).

As grandson of the empire builder "Sugar Koenig" and son of
the latter's eldest son and heir to old Koenig's enormous wealth,
Alexander was in a position to finance his zoological expeditions to
various countries and the construction of the museum, all this
entirely with his own money. To explain more clearly the
relationship between Alexander and myself, let it be said that he
was the nephew of my maternal great-grandmother, or he was the
first cousin of my maternal grandmother or cousin once removed of
my mother. One of Johann Georg Koenig's sons, Emanuel, became a

3

Illus. 3. Johan Georg Koenig   Illus. 4. Gertrud Elisabeth Koenig, née Weber

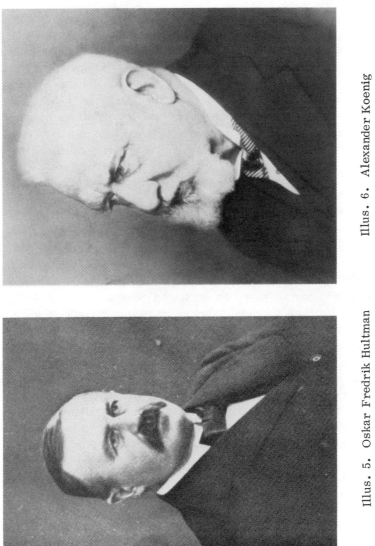

Illus. 6.   Alexander Koenig

Illus. 5.   Oskar Fredrik Hultman

first-rate painter, and some of his paintings were exhibited in art museums.

There is no doubt that the Koenig family was gifted. My mother, Elisabeth, was a talented woman. She knew many languages and spoke fluently not only Russian, German, French and English, but also Italian and Chinese. Later, when we spent our summers in Finland, she also learned to speak Finnish. She was a good painter, too, probably having inherited the talent from her great-uncle Emanuel, and I remember some of her paintings hanging in our apartment.

I do not remember anything of my early childhood in China. I have only a vague recollection of being in a large room with French windows. Outside the house large trees cast shadows and made the room rather dark. I was sitting on a chair, and somebody was play-ing with me and patting me. It was my amah's son. My amah's name was Mrs. Wang and I loved her dearly. She was my first language teacher for at that time I spoke only Chinese, even with my mother. As for my pranks I had a bad habit of running off and disappearing which caused no end of worry to my mother, the amah, and servants. Search parties would be organized, and sometimes it took several hours before they would find me at the market or near some temple, conversing with the Chinese and often calling them, to their delight, various names I had picked up from our servants.

In 1900 we were in Tientsin during the Boxer uprising, and my mother and I as well as the dependents of all the other employees of foreign consulates were besieged in the British municipal building called the Gordon Hall (Illus. 8). We were sitting in a basement behind chests and sacks, while the rebels tried to get in, probably with the intent to massacre us. That event left its mark on my young impressionable mind, because throughout my life I have suffered from a recurrent nightmare in which I am sitting in a dark room while somebody dangerous is trying to get in and harm me. Fortunately the joint allied expeditionary force lifted the siege and liberated us. Because of the chaotic conditions prevailing after the Boxer uprising, my father decided in 1901 to send my mother and me to St. Petersburg. We went first to Port Arthur by train where we

Illus. 7. The Koenig Museum in Bonn

Illus. 8. Gordon Hall in Tientsin

boarded a coastal steamer bound for Japan. The ship's departure was delayed by a storm, and we had to wait a few days. One day we went to some friends' house where a birthday party for their daughter was to take place. During the celebration, quite unexpectedly, their otherwise very friendly dog became aggressive and bit one of the children. It was evident that the dog was rabid, and I still remember the ensuing pandemonium. The child attacked by the dog went on with us to Japan since that was the nearest country where anti-rabies shots could be had. There the child underwent medical treatment and returned home. After transferring to an ocean-going ship in Nagasaki, I embarked on my first long voyage, traveling through the Pacific and Indian Oceans, the Red Sea, the Suez Canal, the Mediterranean and Black Seas to Odessa. Whereas my mother suffered from seasickness most of the trip, I did not feel any ill effects. On the contrary, as my mother told me some years later, I took advantage of being left alone and amused myself by throwing various objects, such as toothbrushes, combs, and slippers through the porthole into the stormy ocean. The last leg of our journey was by train across Russia north to St. Petersburg.

In St. Petersburg we moved in with my maternal grandmother, Wilhelmine Emilie Karoline Morawitz, who was still living in the house which had belonged to her late husband. He had died in December 1896, less than a year before my birth. The house was located at 33 Voznesenskii (Ascension) Prospekt, near the Ascension Cathedral. I had a hard time adjusting to life in St. Petersburg. I missed my amah, her two sons, and the Chinese in general. St. Petersburg was quite different from Chinese cities, and the climate was atrocious. I spoke only Chinese, now a useless language, even when conversing with my mother, but I soon learned Russian. However, I never felt quite at home in St. Petersburg and, strange as this may sound, I always wanted to leave the city and move to another country. This is probably why later I decided to study Oriental languages and go as a consular employee to China or some other East Asian country. Although I believed for some time that this was my most ardent desire, the real thing which I subconsciously wanted was, as we shall see later, to be a scholar.

Illus. 9. The Author at the Age of Four.

In 1902, after my mother and I had lived in St. Petersburg for about a year, my father returned from China to spend more than a year with us while assigned to the Foreign Office. I was put in care of a German governess from Latvia named Christine Ozol. She taught me German and soon I became fairly fluent in that language. On August 6, 1903 my sister Elisabeth (Elizaveta Nikolaevna) was born. Almost immediately after her birth my father had to return to China to assume his new post of consul in Tsitsihar in Heilungkiang province. We followed him a short time later. We traveled from St.

Petersburg to Moscow and there boarded a train of the Trans-Siberian Railroad which had only been opened to traffic a short time before. When we took it, the train went only as far as the western shore of Lake Baikal. Steep mountains, descending straight into the lake, delayed the construction of a rail line around the lake for several years. When the project was eventually completed, it included more than fifty tunnels of various lengths. We stayed for several days in Irkutsk, some forty miles west of Lake Baikal. Irkutsk, the major city in that part of Siberia then as it is now, commanded my youthful attention from the very start. I found it picturesque and rather different from St. Petersburg and Moscow. Most houses were built of wood, the streets were wide, and everywhere one could see spruce trees in the backyards. The hotel where we were staying was rather primitive; I remember that it had neither a toilet nor even an outhouse. When we inquired about a toilet, we were told matter-of-factly that there was none and that guests were to relieve themselves behind a shed in the hotel's backyard. I was glad that my initiation into this aspect of Siberian life did not take place during winter!

From Irkutsk we took a train to Lake Baikal and crossed the lake by steam ferry. The train was put on that ferry without a locomotive and brought to the other shore where another locomotive was waiting. From there we went via Chita and Manchouli to Tsitsihar. My father had prepared everything for our arrival, and the greatest surprise for my mother and me was that he had sent from China for my former amah, Mrs. Wang, to come and be my sister's amah. I could still speak some Chinese, but my vocabulary was, of course, that of a three-year-old child and therefore my conversations with the amah were very limited, and it proved absolutely impossible for me to have a real conversation with her.

Tsitsihar was a typical Chinese city, with narrow, winding streets and many temples.[1] The consulate was located outside the city in the steppe, in a large park of elms and surrounded by a wall made of adobe bricks. We had a detachment of Cossacks for our protection. These were the Ussuri Cossacks, so named after the river that forms part of the eastern frontier of Manchuria. They wore dark blue uniforms with yellow stripes on their trousers and matching yellow shoulder boards. They had a large number of handsome but ferocious Siberian dogs which they used as watchdogs because the steppe teemed with bandits, whom the local inhabitants called *hung hutzu* (red beards). I remember those Cossacks very well, in particular the two I befriended, named Loginov and Portnyagin. The consulate was very near the Nonni, a very wide and mighty river. The area around the consulate was uninhabited but from time to time one could see Mongol caravans passing by. These caravans made a deep impression on me, and it is possible that my interest in Mongolian languages and folklore is partly due to the childhood sight of those Mongols traveling to and from remote places, leading their heavily laden camels.

There was a shed not far from the consulate grounds in which chicken feathers were stored, probably for export. One day when my mother and I were out for a walk, we passed that shed and saw that some beggars had camped out there. One of them, who was naked except for a mat made of burlap, ran out toward us, kowtowed and begged for money. We were so terrified by his appearance that my mother gave him far more than the usual amount beggars got, and we quickly retreated into our consulate park. The poverty of those wretched human beings was utterly terrifying. I have never seen anything like that again. In all my later travels I never saw beggars stark naked in the winter, in snow, and the temperature far below freezing. I imagine that many of them perished.

Another interesting recollection from those times is of the execution grounds not far from the consulate, where bandits and other criminals were put to death. Of course we did not attend any executions and had no intention of doing so, but from time to time on our walks in the consulate park we came across human bones brought in by dogs. I remember how on one occasion I discovered a skull lying under a bush.

The Cossacks were inveterate hunters and they often brought pheasants, hares and other game for our dinner. This, of course, excited me very much and I wanted to hunt also, so I constructed some snares and carefully placed them all over the consulate park.

To my great surprise I always found a pheasant or a hare in my snares. What I did not know at the time was that the kindly Cossacks placed the animals in my snares to please me.

The consulate was housed in a large brick building. We had numerous servants who did all the chores around the house. The cook only bought food in the market and prepared our meals. He had two assistants, one to help him with his own tasks and the other to do the dishes. Another servant was in charge of splitting and sawing logs in the backyard, and yet another brought the firewood into the house and heated the stoves. One servant had as his sole duty the dusting and sweeping of the house. A boy served at the table. I don't remember how many servants we had but there were probably about twenty at any given time. We lived in a manner entirely comparable to that of other Europeans in Asia, like the British in India or the French in Indochina.

The city of Tsitsihar was, as I already said, a typical Chinese city. There were no Russians except for the consular employees, the Cossacks, soldiers and occasional travelers passing through. I therefore wonder why a consulate had been established at all; and this question also puzzled my father because he had hardly anything to do in the way of consular business. Months passed by and no Russian showed up to have his passport extended or to get bailed out of trouble with the Chinese authorities.

The soldiers mentioned represented a large Russian military unit, the 128th East Siberian Infantry Regiment, and the officers of that regiment often visited us, sometimes staying for dinner. I still remember a few names. The commander of the regiment was Colonel Andro-Ginglyat, who was of French descent. He was a well-educated man. Like most of the other officers who could not afford being officers in the better regiments of European Russia, and also because of his debts, he had ended up in that East Siberian infantry regiment. In fact, most of the officers had terrible debts which accumulated as a result of gambling losses.

When we arrived in Tsitsihar in 1903, it was autumn, but soon winter was upon us and the daytime temperature, usually close to minus twenty degrees Centigrade, would quite often plunge even lower. At Christmas time the officers, some of whom had their families living with them, arranged a children's party at their club complete with a Christmas tree. My only recollection of that memorable event was that I attended it with a splitting headache, one of many such headaches that I would have to endure often during my later life.

Our life in Tsitsihar came to an end sooner than we had expected. In February of the following year the war between Japan and Russia broke out, and the Japanese troops advanced so rapidly through Manchuria that it looked as if they would soon reach Tsitsihar. My father therefore made arrangements to send us back to Russia. Tsitsihar was not exactly on the railroad line but about ten miles from Khurkhira station on the Chinese Eastern Railroad. As it turned out, our return trip to Russia was rather uneventful. When we arrived at Lake Baikal it was frozen solid and the ferry did not operate. Instead, railroad tracks had been laid across the lake directly on the ice. Ties had been put on the ice, covered with snow and sprayed with water to freeze them solidly in place, and then individual railroad cars were pushed across the lake. The remainder of the trip back to St. Petersburg was slow because the Trans-Siberian Railroad was only a single track at that time, and since military trains crammed full of soldiers and supplies had the right-of-way, we had to spend much time waiting at train stations and on sidings.

I never saw my father again after we left Tsitsihar. The Russo–Japanese War, the revolution of 1905 in Russia, and his greatly expanded duties as a consul–general in Mukden and Harbin prevented my father from returning home. He died, or more exactly, he was murdered in 1913. He had always been very careless about his personal security and never locked doors or closed windows. One night in April 1913 while he was in his apartment in the consular building in Harbin, a burglar climbed through a window of his apartment. When my father heard something in the room next to his, he went to investigate and was fatally stabbed. His body was brought to St. Petersburg for burial in the Smolensk cemetery.

The greatest event in my youth came late in 1904 when a teacher began to come to our home several times a week to teach me the three R's. Lina Grigor'evna Chebulaeva was a student at the women's university. She was a good teacher and a nice person. At that time we spent our summers in Finland near the railroad station Raivola, about sixty kilometers from St. Petersburg, where we rented a summer cottage. Miss Chebulaeva stayed the entire summer with us and was sometimes visited by one of her male friends who I believe was her fiancé. His name was Aleksandr Fedorovich Shishmarev. He came two or three times that summer of 1904 and then disappeared. He was said to have been arrested by the Tsarist police because of some involvement in anti-government activities. He might have been a member of the Social Democratic or some other party which were all outlawed in Russia. Poor Miss Chebulaeva was very unhappy. Our German governess, Christine Ozol, had left because she married a Latvian officer in the Russian army by the name of Timmermans. Later she had several children and they lived somewhere in Latvia. Timmermans himself died before World War I and I do not recall what happened to his family.

My sister was a weak child who was frequently ill. My mother was unable to nurse her and therefore the physician recommended a wet nurse, Vasilisa Moiseevna Mikhailova, who hailed from the Novgorod region which is not far from St. Petersburg. Vasilisa was a very interesting woman. She knew many fairy tales and all kinds of ancient legends and was very superstitious. She believed in the evil eye and in evil words. She did not allow me, for instance, to pour water out of the window of our summer cottage because, as she put it, "That is a very bad sin because you pour water on your ancestors' heads whose spirits dwell here." She told stories such as one about a lake near her home village in Valdai *uezd* (county) where a creature lived which was part man and part horse—a kind of centaur. Each time someone was about to die in that village, the creature would come out and announce that person's name. Once Vasilisa's mother passed by the lake when the centaur suddenly emerged and shouted, "Martin, Martin, Martin." Three days later, Martin, the woman's neighbor, died. I regret very much that at that time I knew nothing about collecting folklore and folk beliefs, otherwise I would have

14

collected all her tales about supernatural creatures. Vasilisa lived many years with our family and later became our cook.

Vasilisa's family was very poor. One day when my mother entered the kitchen she met Vasilisa's brother who promptly bowed low before her. My mother learned later that the brother came to visit Vasilisa because he was in dire financial straits. He needed ten rubles to pay the annual head tax for himself and his family, altogether five persons. Vasilisa gave her brother the money out of her savings, but had she been unable to do so, his only horse or cow would have probably been sold by the village head to satisfy his tax obligation. Still more revolting was the fact that while this poor peasant was obliged to pay income tax, we as a government official's family paid property taxes but no income tax, and the very rich paid no taxes of any kind. This was one aspect of the "good old days" in pre-revolutionary Russia.

The Russo-Japanese war was a complete disaster for Russia both on land and on the high seas. Much of it was due to almost unimaginable incompetence. As the Japanese armies advanced into Manchuria and the world press announced the names of town after town occupied by the victorious troops, Russian commanders could not even locate these towns on their own staff maps, let alone defeat the enemy. It turned out, as my mother told me later, that before the war Russian army topographers went across Manchuria and would ask the local inhabitants in Russian for the name of their villages and towns. The answer, naturally enough, was quite often "Putung" (I don't understand) which was then formally entered on the Russian staff maps. The result was "Putung I," "Putung II," and so on. The Russian fleet fared no better. It had no wireless and all signals between ships were relayed by flag signals. As the Russian fleet approached the Straits of Tsushima where the Japanese had been waiting, they had no trouble reading the messages and therefore knew every Rusian maneuver beforehand. Moreover, the Russians did not yet have smokeless powder so that after the first few salvoes, the Russian naval gunners could no longer see their targets which, of course, were constantly changing their positions.

These failures were symptomatic of rot that had set in all the

15

way to the top of the chain of command. For example, it was an open secret that while Russian soldiers were fighting in Manchuria wearing boots with cardboard soles, the ballerina Mathilda Kshesinskaya, the Tsar's mistress, had great influence on the Grand Prince Sergei who was one of the highest military officials. She persuaded him to place a large order for uniforms and footwear with a particular company. After the deal had been completed, the owners of that company presented Kshesinskaya with a very expensive diamond necklace.

The Russo-Japanese war demonstrated that Russia was backward and absolutely incapable of coping with modern problems. It was inevitable that the 1905 revolution broke out. I felt that revolution only indirectly, and I remember only one event of that time. While I was walking with my grandmother down the street, about one hundred yards from us some people suddenly threw a bomb into a coach. They were anarchists holding up an armored truck which was transporting money between two banks. The driver and one of the accompanying soldiers were either killed or badly wounded, and a large group of spectators had gathered around the demolished truck. I remember the police taking two or three men into custody, and these men were probably executed later. One result of the revolution was the establishment of a kind of parliament, called the Duma, which the Tsar granted to the people. The Duma turned out to be quite ineffective, however, because each time an important decision was to be taken, it was dissolved and new elections were held to elect other members who were more docile and agreeable to the Tsar's government. It is a pity that the results of the revolution of 1905 were so meager, otherwise the October revolution would have never occurred.

In 1907 when I was ten years old, I enrolled in a gymnasium, the Latin division of the École des Églises Réformées de St. Pétersbourg. It belonged to the Swiss, German, and Dutch Presbyterian churches in St. Petersburg. In Russia the Presbyterian church was called "Reformed Church." My school was for boys only. Later, in 1913, a girls' school was attached to it, but the two schools remained separate as there was no coeducational school anywhere in Russia at that time. The students were German, Swiss, French, Dutch, and a few English and several Finns as well as many Russians whose parents were anxious to have their sons learn German and French in which all subjects were taught. Only courses in Russian language, literature, and history were taught in Russian.

I suppose entering the gymnasium marked the end of my childhood, although it is impossible to say in what month of a particular year one ceases to be a child and becomes a youth. I am speaking here about the mental development of young human beings. I do not believe I am mistaken when I say that I was no longer a child at the age of twelve, for by that time I was no longer interested in toys such as tin soldiers, houses, trains, and boats. Instead, I began to prefer books. I was interested in other countries, other peoples, their histories and even their languages. I began to note the differences in speech of Finns and Russians living in different areas. I was only fourteen when I already knew that in Parikkala a special Finnish dialect was spoken, actually one of the subdialects on the border of the Savo and Karelian dialects. I knew that the words *mehtä* "forest," *tehas* "factory," *tahon* "I want," *kaho* "look," *moahaa* "into the earth," and others were regular correspondences of Literary Finnish *metsä, tehdas, tahdon, katso,* and *maahaan,* respectively. I, therefore, could easily transform dialectal forms into literary forms. Likewise, I noticed that our Russian servants from the villages of Novgorod province would say *kupivši* "bought" instead of Literary Russian *kuplen* or *ne xvataj rukam* "do not touch with your hands" instead of *rukami.*

I was also very fond of movie projectors and films, and the dream of my life was to have an outboard motor, an object that had just come on the market. In summer I was mostly busy with water sports. Finland has many lakes and rivers and also a long coastline stretching from the border of Sweden to the Russian frontier. I had, however, to wait several years before I could afford an outboard motor.

In 1911 I bought a movie projector with money I had saved. I also bought used films which had been discarded by movie theaters. Many of them were cultural films, featuring trips around the world.

I remember one film was about Niagara Falls and Quebec City. Another showed the fountains of Versailles Park. At that time I had no idea that I would ever even be near those places later in my life. I also had films of comedies and even short dramas. One of them took place during the French revolution and was about a young revolutionary officer who freed an aristocrat whose daughter he loved. The officer was sent to the guillotine for disobeying orders. Another drama was a color film which certainly must have been hand-colored as color photography did not exist at the time. The film was called "The Love of a Slave Girl." It was a story about a young man in ancient Rome, son of rich parents, and his love for a slave girl. Unable to marry, the lovers, like Romeo and Juliet, took their own lives.

At that time I also liked animals and, in fact, I am still fond of them. I had rabbits and guinea pigs and green lizards, a turtle, a dog, a cat, a lamb, squirrels, and a hedgehog. I actually owned a small private zoo.

When I turned fourteen in 1911, I entered fifth grade in our school, the École des Églises Réformées. We had much Latin, six hours a week, and we had a full day of classes on Saturdays. As a result, in fifth grade I already knew that French *homme* had developed from Latin *hominem*, and French *cheval* was the same as Latin *caballus*. We had Greek seven hours a week, with two hours on Saturdays, as well as German, Russian, French, algebra, geometry, trigonometry, history, geography, art history, singing, and sports. School days lasted six hours, from nine to three, and discipline was severe.

We had a deep respect for our director, Arthur Brock, Master of Arts and former professor at the prestigious Nezhin Lyceum, who was our Latin teacher in the senior grades. We read Horace and Cicero with him and had to learn many passages by heart. I still remember Cicero's Phillippics against Catilina ("Quousque tandem abutere, Catilina, patientia nostra?") and Horace's contempt for the ignorant crowd ("Odi vulgus profanum et horreo!"), both of which are probably now banned from the high school curricula in the "people's democracies." Among our other teachers, a particularly good one was Erich von Voss who taught German and Greek in different grades. Our class had only Greek with him, reading the *Iliad*, the *Odyssey* and Plato. Voss was a philologist with a Ph.D. from Leipzig University. His doctoral dissertation had been on a Sanskrit subject. He was an excellent philologist and taught us philological methods. For example, we learned the art of precise translation with thorough analysis of each grammatical form occurring in the original text.

Another interesting teacher and an excellent scholar was Oskar Waldhauer, a specialist in ancient art. He was one of the part-time teachers at our school, his main occupation being the custodianship at the Hermitage Museum. He had a vast knowledge of Greek and Roman art and had assembled a huge card file on art objects preserved in various museums around the world and another file of those objects still in Greece, Rome and those countries which had been under Roman domination. After the revolution the Soviet secret police conducted a search of his house and discovered his card files. They took the cards with them and never returned them to him so he felt his life work was wasted. He became so frustrated that he started to drink and died of alcoholism. After the revolution, Director Brock, mentioned earlier, became professor of German literature at the Gertsen Pedagogical Institute in Leningrad. At the time of the Great Purge in 1937 he was arrested and exiled to Kazakhstan where he died very soon thereafter. It is one of fate's ironies that in 1927 he and his wife had received exit visas and had visited their son in Latvia. Instead of remaining there, they returned to Leningrad, not knowing what awaited them in Russia ten years later.

Whereas Brock, von Voss and Waldhauer were excellent teachers, some other members of our faculty were not. The mathematicians, for example, never explained anything. They simply called the best student to the blackboard and had him solve a theorem while the rest of us watched, not understanding how the boy solved the problem. As a result, many of us were rather poor at mathematics. As I was one of them, my mother hired a tutor, Andrei Ivanovich Gershun, who had graduated from our school and was now a student at the Institut Putei Soobshcheniya (Institute of

Communications Engineering) in St. Petersburg. He was a nice man and excellent mathematician who explained everything to me that our teacher should have taught us to begin with.

The winter of 1911–1912 was very difficult for me. I was sick most of the time. First I caught the German measles. After that I had several bouts with the flu and missed so many classes that I could not catch up and had to remain in the same grade for the second year. I spent part of the next winter in a small Finnish town on the Vuoksi River called Antrea, about one hour by train from Viipuri (Viborg in Swedish). Antrea is now part of the Soviet Union, having been conquered during World War II. I recovered there very well and the following year I repeated fifth grade. My tutor continued to coach me in mathematics as well as in Greek and Latin. Going through fifth grade the second time around had its unexpected rewards, for I found my new classmates much more likable than those in my former class. I made many new friends and graduated with them in 1916. I will mention here only a few of them who were particularly close to me. One was Victor von Striedter, the son of the leader of the nobility in the Novgorod area. Victor's father was a high official in the office which managed the imperial court's affairs, something akin to an Imperial Household Agency. Another student was a certain Sergei Lipskii, a Russian and a very pleasant boy, who also was the best student in our class. A third friend was Georgii Prokofiev, the son of a famous painter, who later became a well-known scholar in the field of Samoyed linguistics and ethnography. Another good friend of mine was Dmitrii Wentzel who later became professor of mathematics at the Artillery Academy. I visited all of these friends often and they came to see me. Later we founded a kind of club where we discussed various historical, philosophical, and religious subjects. Occasionally we also invited our favorite teachers to participate in our discussions and afterwards we had parties with cookies, cakes, and snacks.

During summer vacations, which lasted from June 1 to September 1, my family at first went to Antrea, and after 1911 to Parikkala, a beautiful town on Lake Simpele in the eastern part of the country (Illus. 10). Its railroad station is now on the line between Lappeenranta and Savonlinna. We stayed in a fine villa which my mother first rented and later bought (Illus. 11). On my trip to Finland in 1976, I visited that area again and saw our former villa which we had sold after the revolution, through the Finnish consulate, to a friend of ours who lived in Finland. My summer vacations in Finland greatly influenced me because to a certain degree they formed my view and understanding of the surrounding world. I spoke Finnish so fluently that many people thought that I was Finnish and even related to my many Finnish friends. They could not distinguish the difference between their and my pronunciation. There in Parikkala I began my love affair with Finland and the Finns, and I still have a very high regard for the people and their beautiful land.

The part of Finland where Parikkala is located is called Southern Karelia and has been inhabited since ancient times. Before 1813 Parikkala was called Koitsanlahti and before that, Joukio. Joukio appears in old Russian documents of the Novgorodian period, to be exact, in the fourteenth century, where it is written "Evgija" which stands for Yowgia. The village of Joukio still exists near the present border between Finland and the Soviet Union.

Rural Finland was rather conservative in the years before World War I, and in Parikkala many old customs and superstitions were still alive. Thus when the old church was destroyed by fire, it was believed that the disaster had been foretold by the woodpeckers which always pecked at the outer walls of the church. A more likely explanation is that the wooden structure had been infested by dry rot and so its timbers housed insects which attracted the woodpeckers in the first place. People of both sexes still used the same sauna together, and one frequently saw both men and women run stark naked from the sauna to their houses or to the lake where they would plunge into the ice-cold waters.

Folksingers often came from other parts of Karelia. Once two men came to our house. They used an eastern Karelian dialect spoken in Russia, and one of them had a *kantele*, a stringed folk instrument. They straddled a bench, facing each other, and started to sing. Their song was from *Kalevala*, the Finnish national epic, and told how the epic's main character, Väinämöinen, built a boat.

21

Illus. 10. Lake Simpele

Illus. 11. The Villa in Parikkala

Their performance made a deep impression on me. After they had left, I asked my mother to get me a copy of the *Kalevala*. She presented me with one, and I read it with great fascination. No detective story or Wild West adventure yarn could have intrigued me as much. The visit of these two Karelian folksingers may have been a decisive factor in my life, because after that my interests turned to the history of the Finns and other Finno-Ugric peoples. I read Yrjö-Koskinen's *History of Finland*,[2] and later Castrén's description of his travels in Siberia and his ethnological lectures on the Altaic peoples.[3] I decided to study the languages and folklore of the Finns and other peoples including the Mongols and Turks who Castrén regarded as being linguistically related.

Finland was a very clean country, whereas Russia was filthy and its villages were very unkempt. Finnish roads were excellent; in Russia they were hardly more than mud paths, impassable in spring and fall. In Finland there were telephones and telegraphs everywhere, and well-stocked stores, physicians and pharmacies were found in every *pitäjä*, i.e. township. For the Russians all this was absolutely unknown, and it was common to travel from a village to the nearest town, sometimes seventy or eighty kilometers away, on absolutely wretched roads in order to find a physician. The Finns were very industrious and honest, but Russians generally were not. In Russia when people started to work they often just leaned on their shovels, debating just how a particular job should be done. Besides, there was much theft in Russia. It was impossible to leave anything unguarded for even a moment. If, for instance, after entering a store one put his briefcase down, one could find it gone when ready to leave. In Finland I had a bicycle and I often rode it to the edge of the forest, parked it against a tree, entered the forest to pick mushrooms or berries, and came back after a few hours to find the bicycle still standing under the same tree. This would have been absolutely impossible in Russia. In Finland when we left our villa to take a walk in the fields or forest, we never locked our doors. The windows and doors were always open. Silverware, including real silver spoons and other valuables were left lying on our dining room table, and no one ever entered the house and stole anything.

However, not all was well in Finland. In spite of an excellent climate and general cleanliness, tuberculosis was rampant. One cause was unpasteurized milk from tubercular cows. Another cause was unsanitary conditions in village homes. Their sealed double-paned windows could never be opened, causing the air inside to be heavily polluted with tobacco smoke and various household odors. I remember several young people who died of tuberculosis. Yrjö Loikkanen lost both his brother, Emil, and his younger sister, Helmi, to tuberculosis. Another victim was a certain Pekka Kanahentä, a strong and healthy boy, who caught tuberculosis and died in less than a year.

In Parikkala I made the acquaintance not only of youngsters my own age but also of some adults. I remember a certain man whose last name was Möltsi, who was an engineer at a sawmill which belonged to a Mr. Helenius. Möltsi was a Social Democrat and due to his influence I began to realize that some social democratic ideas were good and that they should be put into effect. This Möltsi may later have participated on the Red side during the civil war in Finland, and it is possible that he perished in it. Among my numerous young Finnish friends, my best friend was Yrjö (George in English) Loikkanen, whom I just mentioned. He was the son of a bricklayer and an intelligent and very nice boy who was slightly younger than I. Very often we went by motorboat—I already had an outboard motor—from island to island in Lake Simpele, and he taught me a great deal about Finnish living conditions. I knew many farmers and I often went to their homes so I knew them personally and became familiar with their way of life.

From my Finnish friends I learned about a resistance movement against Russian domination. Even as early as 1909–1910, when we were still vacationing in Antrea, there was an incident I remember very clearly. One day, while walking with my mother in a forest, I was walking ahead when at a distance I saw a group of men sitting and talking seriously to each other. As soon as one of them saw me approach, they all jumped up and disappeared in the underbrush. They were too well dressed to be vagabonds, so I surmised that they were workers or intellectuals engaged in some revolutionary activity. I also learned that in a particular place not far from Parikkala, the Finns had stashed away arms for use in a possible uprising against the Russians. This cache was hidden in a forest near Ojajärvi, a railroad station between Viipuri and Elisenvaara, which is now part of the territory annexed by the Soviet Union after the war against Finland in 1939-40. It is interesting to note that the Russian authorities never discovered the arms cache, and it is likely that these weapons were used later, in 1917-18, when the Finns were fighting their war of liberation against the Reds. Some of the inhabitants of Parikkala became later prominent freedom fighters against Russia. One of them was Yrjö Fagerlund, who was an excellent hunter and marksman and owned a big farm not far from our villa. Years later I read an article about him in the Finnish encyclopedia and instantly recognized his photograph.

Parikkala was not only a place greatly endowed with natural beauty, it was also an important cultural center. There was a co-educational high school, something that did not exist in any part of Russia, and important musicians and artists very often came to Parikkala. The musicians included the famous composers Oskar Merikanto (1868-1925) and Toivo Timoteus Kuula (1883-1918), and the latter's wife, the singer Alma Silventoinen (1884-1944). My mother knew many of these people and we often visited each other. The well-known Finnish philologist Onni Hannikainen, director of the Lycée in Kuopio, spent his summers at a place not far from our village. The son of the well-known writer Minna Canth lived in a beautiful house in Parikkala and also had a farm about three kilometers from our place. Thus I had the opportunity not only to relax in summer but also to get a very good knowledge of the Finnish country, people, and culture. By the time I was a teenager I already had a very good knowledge of Finnish literature, having read Juhani Aho, Alexis Kivi, Frans Eemil Sillanpää, Minna Canth and the works of other writers.[4]

Soon after the assassination of the Austrian Archduke Franz Ferdinand at Sarajewo in June 1914, all the St. Petersburg newspapers started to carry frightening news of an imminent war, but in the weeks immediately before the outbreak of World War I, my family was not affected at all. I finished my school year and we went to Parikkala and a seemingly normal summer began for me. But soon it turned out to be neither a normal nor happy summer at all. In fact, it marked the end of the only period in my life when I was happy.

When the war began on August 1, the Finns were enthusiastic. The Finnish policeman at the railroad station Elisenvaara expressed the general feeling among the Finns by openly boasting to all passengers that now Russia would at last be thoroughly defeated. All Finns believed this, and the thought made them happy. The same sentiments were later expressed by Yrjö Fagerlund, the intelligent and educated rich landowner I mentioned above, so this sentiment must also have been common among Finnish intellectuals.

From its very beginning the war was disastrous for Russia, and this was a direct result of Russia's backwardness and unpreparedness. Both the military leadership and the general public were convinced that a world war could not last for more than three or four months. This opinion, however, was not shared by my paternal uncle Vasilii, the lawyer. He was convinced that the war would last seven years. His prophecy turned out to be correct; the world war and the subsequent civil war lasted exactly seven years. Unfortunately, Russia had weapons and ammunition for only a few months. It soon became clear that the war would not be over that quickly and without Allied help Russia would be unable to continue fighting Germany and the other Central Powers. American and British war supplies could not reach Russia because the Baltic Sea was controlled by German warships. The Black Sea was unusable because Turkey, one of the Central Powers, had closed the Dardanelles. The only access available to the West was from the White Sea and the Arctic Ocean in the north. Unfortunately, there was no railroad linking the only ice-free port, Murmansk, to the interior. The Russians, therefore, started to build the Murmansk Railroad which branched off from the trunk line between Petrograd, as St. Petersburg had been renamed, and Vologda.

The Finns were not drafted into the armed forces. Formerly, they had their own army but the Russians disbanded it in 1900, imposing a special tax on the Finns in lieu of conscription. In addition to this, the Finns, like many minority peoples in Russia, especially the Kirghiz, Kazakhs and Uzbeks, had to perform corvée in wartime. They pushed construction projects, such as the Murmansk Railroad, through swamps, lakes, and across rivers. Many workers perished from standing all day long in cold water which was always up to their knees and sometimes up to their chests. Many Finns who had returned from construction jobs told me that the mortality rate was particularly high among the Uzbeks, Kazakh, Kirghiz, Buryats and other people of Siberia and that at least 100,000 of them met their death in the subarctic swamps. This was the main cause of the general uprising in Russian Central Asia and Kazakhstan in 1916, an uprising never mentioned in the Russian press at that time and cruelly suppressed by the Tsarist government. In addition to the 100,000 deaths in the swamps in Northern Russian, at least 250,000 Turks were killed in Turkestan by punitive units of the Tsarist army. The 1,500 kilometer-long railroad had been built so quickly that by late 1915 or early 1916 it started operating and began to carry the much needed war supplies shipped from Great Britain.

The opposition to the Russians was very strong in Finland. Workers, farmers, intellectuals, and businessmen were united in their desire to see their country freed from Russian domination. No sooner did the war begin than young men in Finland started to "disappear." First, one of the neighbors' sons stopped showing up at our house, then another young man disappeared from our village, and eventually we learned that they had gone across the border to Sweden, Denmark and finally to Germany, where they joined the German army in order to fight against the Russians. Very soon a Finnish division was formed. At the same time Pilsudsky, the future leader of independent Poland, was organizing Polish regiments to fight under the German army against Russia.

As for the events at the front, it should be said that by the summer of 1916 the German army occupied all of Russian Poland and a large portion of the Baltic area, including the city of Riga. In light of these stunning German victories, the Tsar's granting of independence to Poland was truly ridiculous. I still remember the speech made in the Duma by Chkheidze, a Social Democrat, who called the Tsar's generosity "mustard after dinner." It was clear that Russia was losing the war. Although the Allies were sending weapons and other supplies to Murmansk, everything was in short supply and by the middle of 1916 bread lines had even formed in larger cities. Actually, there was enough food in Russia, especially in the Volga, Kuban, and Western Siberian regions, but the railroads were disorganized and soon a shortage of railroad cars became noticeable as well. This shortage was caused by the fact that the railroads leading into Rumania were single-tracked so that as soon as a supply train arrived at the Rumanian front, it was unloaded and pushed off the track to make room for the next train. Before long enormous car cemeteries cropped up in different parts of Rumania.

We all knew that everything was in short supply at the front and that only every other soldier was armed with a rifle. When the soldiers were ordered to attack, half of the unit would stay behind to wait until some of their comrades would fall, leaving their rifles lying on the ground. The other half of the unit would then jump up, run out to collect those rifles and join the remaining troops at the command, "Forward, collect rifles, proceed!" The widespread shortages caused an immense number of casualties and, of course, many defeats. Another cause of defeat was the incompetence of the commanding generals. At the very beginning of the war, as the German army approached Paris, the Russians sent a large army under the command of General Samsonov and another under the command of General von Rennenkampf into East Prussia. Both armies perished there in the battle of Tannenberg, and an additional blow was that the Rennenkampf army had included the best Guards regiments. In spite of terrible losses, in 1916 the government continued to disseminate news that the situation was good. In that year's summer, one of the Petrograd newspapers carried the headline: "Great is the God of Russia," followed by a long article about the complete annihilation of the German fleet in Riga Bay. Many years later when I visited in Germany in 1973 my friend Wilfried Strik-Strikfeldt, the author of the well-known book *Against*

Hitler and Stalin,[5] showed me a copy of that newspaper which he had saved. He had lived near Riga at that time, and he assured me that no such battle ever took place—in fact, that no German fleet had ever entered Riga Bay. All that had actually happened was that a German minesweeper appeared at some distance in the bay, the shore batteries opened fire, and the minesweeper steamed away. Strik-Strikfeldt added that he felt very sad telling me the true story, because everything that happened later was partly the result of the incompetence and backwardness of the Russian system.

This kind of war propaganda was actually criminal because young men were enthusiastic from the very beginning of the war anyway, and many of them volunteered for military service. I remember a certain boy in our class named Nikolai Shmidt. Despite his German name, he was Russian, and in fact hated the Germans. He was one of those many young men who, duped by the government's criminal propaganda, believed in a quick and decisive victory over Germany. He left school to join the army because he was afraid that the war would be over before he could be graduated. As it turned out, he fought for several years in the war against Germany but was later killed during the civil war. Another example was the son of our director Brock. He volunteered and after a mere three months' training at an officer's school, he was sent to the front. Just as he disembarked from the troop train, a stray bullet struck him in the head and he was killed instantly. His life was wasted through the incompetence of the Russian military commanders who should never have allowed the train to come so close to the German lines.

It was not only young army volunteers who suffered, but many segments of the civilian population also were burdened. There were many people of German descent in Russia. Some of them were still German citizens, but many others were Russian subjects, and even their parents and grandparents had been Russian subjects. In Parikkala there was a baker of German descent. He and his wife had been born and raised in Finland and could not even speak German. However, they did not have any papers proving their Finnish citizenship. Therefore, the Russian authorities evicted them and

29

exiled them to Siberia. Alexandra Boetz, my uncle's widow, and her daughters Alexandra and Lydia were banished to the Volga area. During this exile my aunt got breast cancer and died in a village where there was no doctor nor a hospital. Lydia, too, died in exile, very soon after her mother. After the revolution Alexandra returned to Leningrad where she studied and became a teacher. She died of tuberculosis in 1933.

All of the above-named were Russian subjects, and it is incomprehensible that they had been exiled simply because they had German names. One of my aunts, Maud Boetz, had a brother who owned a saddle factory in Moscow. When the war began, his factory and office were demolished during an anti-German pogrom, even though he himself was not German. After this he could no longer manufacture saddles, which was ironic because he had manufactured most of the saddles used by the Russian cavalry.

The war also heightened the government's natural suspicious-ness, and this resulted in the rapid growth of the secret police. Alexander Boetz, another cousin, was in Arkhangelsk during the war. One day he and a friend were walking in the street. They were conversing animatedly and even laughed a few times, when suddenly they were arrested by the police who claimed they were laughing because the Germans had just won a battle! Both of them were exiled to Siberia, and they did not return until after the war was over. I met Alexander's daughter again in Stuttgart in the 1970s, and she told me many details of the hardships her parents suffered. My paternal uncle, Vasilii, was a lawyer with the Crédit Lyonnais Bank as well as some other firms. During the war one of these companies ordered a huge dredge from Sweden, and the Swedish firm delayed its delivery. The dredge was urgently needed for the construction of the Murmansk Railroad, as no dredges were made in Russia and were very scarce. My uncle sent a telegram to Sweden with the anxious question: "When will dredge arrive?" He was promptly arrested, only to spend months in jail waiting for a trial which was never held. An investigation revealed that the secret police had suspected "dredge" was the name of a German agent whom my uncle was expecting. My uncle was eventually released from jail, but he quit

30

working for the company and vowed never again to have anything to do with firms that ordered machinery from other countries. All these cases are from my personal environment and my immediate family. It is, of course, shameful that the Russian government should have committed such blunders, which damaged their own war efforts, and even crimes against humanity.

In this connection I should mention that many Russian citizens of German descent were loyal subjects of the Tsar who fought at the front like everyone else. Moreover, during the entire war not a single case of treason among Russian citizens of German origin was known, whereas the most sensational case of German espionage involved an ethnic Russian on the Russian General Staff, Colonel Myasoedov. This Myasoedov frequently visited the defense minister's wife, Mrs. Sukhomlinova, and stole papers lying on her husband's desk to be photographed and sent to the Germans.

It is unfortunate but true, as I was to learn later in life, that even countries I admired for their democratic institutions could commit crimes against their own citizens that were no different from the crimes of the Tsarist government. For instance, during the second world war the United States forced many of its citizens of Japanese descent into detention camps. These Americans were deprived of their farms and other worldly goods, and most never got their farms back again. It did not matter at all that these hapless victims had, of course, nothing to do with Pearl Harbor or any other action of the militaristic clique of Japan. I have come to the sad conclusion that under certain circumstances it matters little whether a country calls itself a democracy, like the United States, or an absolute monarchy, like Tsarist Russia. Any country has the potential to become oppressive under similar circumstances; certainly in this case the United States and Tsarist Russia behaved exactly alike.

In the spring of 1916 I graduated from high school and received my diploma with a silver medal. This award was only on paper, and the medal was never handed out. At that time I was interested in linguistics and folklore, especially that of the Finno-Ugric peoples, such as the Finns, Estonians, and Mordvinians.

However, since my early childhood I had also been reading books on the Altaic peoples of Siberia and I now wanted to study subjects dealing with them. Of course, we were uncertain as to what kind of job might be obtained after studying such subjects, because in Russia well-paid academic positions were difficult to come by. This was one reason why I was persuaded by my mother and aunt to study natural sciences and medicine and follow the path of my maternal grandfather and my granduncle, Alexander Koenig. In any event, my relatives were dead set against Oriental languages or anything connected with East Asia after my father had been murdered in Harbin. The Boxer Revolt and the unhappy war with Japan had reinforced their antipathy to East Asia. And so I enrolled at the medical school of Petrograd University which had only been opened at the beginning of the war. Together with my friend Victor von Striedter, who was later to become a medical research scholar, I set out to become a doctor of medicine.

2 My University Years

Victor von Striedter and I attended anatomy classes taught by Professor Tonkov who served concurrently as professor at the military medical academy. We took courses in biology from Professor Shimkevich, but these were very boring because he simply read aloud from his book and showed us slides which were nothing but reproductions of illustrations in his book. We also had courses in chemistry given by the well-known scholar Chugaev, and studied physics under Ioffe who later became a member of the Academy of Sciences.

News from the front was very bad, and in Russian cities food shortages resulted in the formation of long lines in front of stores that were almost empty inside. Those who at the beginning of the war had thought that a modern war would last only a few months realized that they had been badly mistaken. In December 1916 a very important event occurred. The notorious thaumaturge Rasputin, always a subject of rumors and discussions among the people, was assassinated. This act generated more rumors which were extremely damaging to the Tsar and his family. It was clear to everyone that things could not continue going on as they had. University students were, in general, a discontented lot, and many belonged to various revolutionary organizations. We medical students did not join such groups, however, because we had so much work to do, and falling behind meant expulsion.

Illus. 12   Petrograd University

I was still attending the university in February of 1917 when the revolution took place. On March 15 the Tsar abdicated. I must confess that the magnitude and worldwide importance of this event was completely obscured by what was to me a personal tragedy. My dog, a fox terrier, having apparently eaten a poisoned mouse, died a few days before the revolution, and I was inconsolable. This shows how immature I was at the age of nineteen! I later regarded my dog's death as an omen foreshadowing the tragedy which was to befall the nation and the dissolution and ruin of my own extended family. It was as if someone wanted to say: "Be prepared! The real tragedies lie ahead!"

A new government was formed by A. F. Kerenskii, and for a short time order was restored and the war continued. The revolution in Petrograd seemed comparatively uneventful, and there were relatively few casualties. This was one reason why many newspapers called the revolution the least bloody in human history. This was a great mistake, for only eight months later the Bolsheviks staged another revolution, and the following civil war brought devastation and bloodshed without parallel in history.

My University Years

My first year at the university ended in May 1917, and we went as usual to spend the summer in our villa in Parikkala. That summer in Finland, goods were very scarce, for there was a food shortage and it was very difficult to buy anything in the stores. I rented my motorboat to a Mr. Fettig who was the director of one of the banks in Petrograd. He and his young wife lived in a very beautiful rented villa on Lake Simpele. They hired my friend Yrjö Loikkanen to operate the motorboat and to act as their pilot because Yrjö knew the lake and all the submerged rocks and shallow places. Meanwhile, the news from Petrograd was very bad. On June 3, 1917 a real battle took place in the streets of Petrograd between the Bolsheviks and the Kerenskii troops. This so upset Fettig that he liquidated all his property in Petrograd and transferred his money to a bank in Sweden. He stayed in Parikkala until the end of the summer. One day he came to say goodbye to us as he and his wife planned to leave for Sweden the next day. We never saw them again, and soon we realized how right he was in deciding to leave Russia.

Fettig foresaw the coming disaster, but the Kerenskii government did not. Instead of concluding a separate peace with Germany and proceeding to vitally needed reforms such as agrarian reform and labor legislation, it went on fighting a war which only brought defeats.

Summer was coming to an end. In August 1917 the Russian troops of the Viipuri garrison mutinied and drowned their officers in the Gulf of Finland. This was a very frightening event. In September we returned to Petrograd because my sister had to continue in high school and I had to resume my studies at the university. But as the university was hardly functioning at all, I quit attending classes, was promptly drafted, and found myself in the Semenovskii Regiment, one of the infantry regiments founded by Peter the Great.

Order still reigned in the regiment. We marched, went through our drill formations, and were to be sent to the front right after basic training. Our dispatch orders, however, were not carried out because on October 25, 1917 (i.e., November 7 according to the present Gregorian calendar) the Bolsheviks seized power in Petrograd. The night before this takeover, our regiment had been ordered to occupy all bridges across the Neva River and not to let anyone across. I was standing guard at the Troitskii Bridge (named "Trinity" after a nearby church) which several platoons of our company were to defend against the Bolsheviks. We heard some gunfire in the distance, but as nothing happened around the bridge, we were sent back to our barracks. Soon thereafter, I was assigned as a clerk to regimental headquarters. My new duties exempted me from basic training, but I found the work extremely boring. I resolved at that point in my life never to work in a bank, office, or store. Any work would be better than that!

Finally, in 1918 the old army was disbanded. When we went to get our discharge papers, the line was so long that I did not bother to wait to get mine. In the end this turned out to be a stroke of luck because my name never appeared on any list of former Tsarist army members. Thus I could always state on questionnaires that I had never been in military service. I must say that this kind of deception was unavoidable with the coming of the Bolsheviks. In order to survive, people had to conceal facts, to lie about their ethnic origin, their father's occupation, and many other personal details.

After my short and inglorious military career I decided to resume my studies at the university, but now realized that medicine was not for me. I was determined that no matter how grim the job market might turn out to be, this time I was going to enroll in the Department of Oriental Languages.

I had always been interested in languages, especially in the Finno-Ugric ones, but these were only taught at the universities in Helsinki and Budapest. By that time, however, Finland was embroiled in a civil war instigated by the Russian Communists. The Reds seized Viipuri, Helsinki, and many other cities, but the new Finnish government established itself in Vaasa, a relatively small town on the Gulf of Bothnia, and resisted. It was soon greatly strengthened by the Finnish volunteers that had been fighting with the Germans against Russia, and who now returned to defend their homeland. They were well disciplined, well armed, and had been tried in battle during years of service with the German armed forces. Most Finns were opposed to Communism, and these returning troops were joined by large numbers of volunteers. The Finns living in the northern part of the country were especially hostile to Communism because most of them were Revivalists and regarded Communism as an anti-Christian movement. In the spring of 1918 the Germans sent a brigade under the command of General von der Goltz. He landed in Southern Finland and, together with the Finns under the command of Marshal Mannerheim, defeated the Reds.

Finland's newly won independence proved to be my loss. I was now prevented from going to Helsinki to study. Since I was not quite sure what to do, I went to Petrograd University at the end of March or early April 1918 to consult Professor Rudnev, a professor of Mongolian. Because he had married a Finn, spoke Swedish, and knew Ramstedt very well, I regarded him as someone who could give me proper advice. I discussed my situation with him and, in view of the alleged affinity of Finno-Ugric and Altaic languages, I decided to compromise and make Mongolian my primary field of study.

Rudnev was a very pleasant man. Unlike many professors who treated their students in a polite but cool manner, he received me very cordially. From the very beginning he addressed me in the familiar form and, even though I was twenty years his junior, he addressed me as Kolya, a diminutive for Nikolai, and asked me to address him in the familiar form. Of course, I addressed him in the more formal way as Andrei Dmitrievich (i.e., Andrew, son of Dmitrii). He was very pleased to learn that I spoke Finnish and obviously realized that I was a promising student. He gave me his book on Mongolian grammar and told me to read it, memorize as much as I could, and to return exactly one week later. There was no time to waste so I immediately set to work. I mastered his grammar and learned the Mongolian alphabet. When I returned a week later, Rudnev asked me to read and translate a rather difficult tale. I still remember its title, *Jayidang qar-a ere üker-tü köbegün-ü tuɣuji* (The Boy Riding a Black Ox). It was a Buddhist legend where the boy turned out to be a sage engaged in a philosophical disputation, answering all questions brilliantly. It was a very difficult text and, of course, many passages of my translation were incorrect. Such was the beginning of my Mongolian studies.

Rudnev was satisfied with my performance, and I regarded
him as a good teacher, for he did not lead his students by the hand
but forced them to do much of the work themselves. Rudnev had
two other students at that time. One of them was N. R. Pallisen,
who wore a naval officer's uniform, but he soon dropped out and
went to Southern Russia where the White armies, i.e. anti-Communist forces, were being formed to fight against the Communists.
I never met Pallisen again, but I later learned that he had been in
Yugoslavia, and after World War II moved to Germany and became a
librarian at Marburg University, remaining there until his death in
the early 1950s. The other student was A. A. Kolpakov. I was very
thankful to him because he managed to find a job for me. Since
scholarships were non-existent in those days, I had to find some
means to keep body and soul together. I would have preferred
working in the evenings so that I could pursue my studies during the
day. Kolpakov worked at the Office of Supply which distributed
food to the population of Petrograd, supervising the issue of ration
cards and the transportation of flour, grain and other foodstuffs
from various parts of Russia into Petrograd. In the job which
Kolpakov had secured for me, I was to keep track of grain trains
coming from Siberia and the Ukraine. I monitored a constant flow
of telegrams which specified freight car serial numbers, the nature
of their cargo, and their location at any given time.

Unfortunately, soon after my initiation into Mongolian
studies, events occurred which separated Rudnev from me. One
weekend Rudnev took the train to Viipuri, as was his custom, to visit
his family. That happened to be the very weekend Mannerheim's
armies cut the railroad line, and Rudnev could not return to Petrograd. I never saw him again. Many years later, when I was already
in Germany, I wrote him a letter and got a very friendly answer
from him. After my move to the United States we continued to correspond until his death in 1958. Rudnev could not teach Mongolian
in Finland because there were simply not enough students interested
in Mongolian; but since he was also an excellent musician, he
became a professor of piano at the conservatory. When he died I
was very sorry. He was a good friend and a fine person.

Anyway, in 1918, with Rudnev unable to return to Petrograd, I had to search for another teacher. I had heard of Boris Yakovlevich Vladimirtsov. Shortly after he returned from Southern Russia, I went to see him. The Kalmucks, who lived north of the Caspian Sea, had formed their own government and had invited Vladimirtsov to become their minister of education but he refused. That turned out to be fortunate for him, for after the anti-Communist governments in various parts of Russia had been toppled, collaborators were seriously punished by the victorious Bolsheviks.

Vladimirtsov was an interesting man. First I will describe his outer appearance. He was extremely nearsighted, had a very unhealthy, grayish-yellow complexion, and he looked a little bit swollen rather than merely corpulent. He stuttered slightly and had a nervous tic. He frequently made sudden jerking movements of his head. As a scholar he was superior to Rudnev. He knew Sanskrit, Tibetan and Turkic, but only spoke Mongolian moderately well, a far cry from Rudnev who spoke it brilliantly. He was also well versed in the Western literature on Oriental subjects. He had graduated from the university in 1909 and had first gone to Mongolia and later to Paris to study under Édouard Chavannes, Paul Pelliot, the Abbé Rousselot, and the famous linguist Antoine Meillet. After a year in Paris, he shifted to London, where he was a frequent visitor to the British Museum, and personally knew Denison Ross and other famous British scholars of that time. He was witty and entertaining and had many interesting stories to tell about his experiences in Mongolia, Paris and London. I remember how one day he warned me never to assume that no one would understand you if you spoke in a rare foreign tongue. He illustrated this point by the following incident. He was standing in a crowded streetcar in Paris when it suddenly stopped and he was almost hurled down to the floor. After he let loose a stream of extremely vulgar Mongolian invective, a lady gently invited him, in Mongolian, to sit down in some space she had made for him. It just so happened that she had spent some time in Mongolia, probably as a missionary's wife, and Vladimirtsov felt mortified that she had understood his obscenities.

At the university we read Mongolian texts, and the first one was the biography of the Mongolian saint Neyichi Toyin. He was a sixteenth-century Mongol, son of a prince, and had become a Buddhist monk and missionary as a result of the following occurrence. When Neyichi Toyin was about fifteen years old, he went with his father to hunt the wild horses which still roam across the Mongolian plains. These were not domestic horses that had become wild, but wild horses which had never been domesticated. His father shot an arrow at a pregnant mare and she collapsed. The arrow had pierced her belly and a foal fell out. The wounded mare kept licking and cleansing her newborn foal until she died. The foal did not survive, either. This made such an impression upon Neyichi Toyin that he decided to resign from this world and become a monk.

Rudnev was a full professor but Vladimirtsov was only a *dotsent*, something like an American associate professor. He was, in my opinion, much more scholarly than Rudnev, but he was younger and therefore could not be promoted, especially as there was no vacancy open for a full professor. On the other hand, Vladimirtsov was not as accurate and disciplined as Rudnev. He seldom adhered to his schedule and was always late to his classes. If he had a class at ten o'clock, he would arrive at eleven or even later, and instead of ending at twelve so that students could attend some other professor's lecture, he would go on lecturing until two so that his students often missed their next class.

Very soon I became familiar with his private life. While a *magistrant*, i.e. a candidate for the master's degree, doing research in Mongolia in 1909, he fell in love with a Mongolian girl and wanted to marry her, but a certain Burdukov, who was a merchant living in Mongolia and spoke Mongolian very well, dissuaded him. He pointed out that the nomad girl from a tent in Mongolia would be very unhappy living on the third or fourth floor of an apartment house in Petrograd, seeing only asphalt pavement all around, not to speak of the fact that her mentality made her absolutely unsuitable for marriage to a Russian professor. Vladimirtsov later fell in love with a young girl, Kapitolina Vasil'evna Vyatkina and wanted to marry her. This Vyatkina became an anthropologist and research scholar at the Museum of Anthropology and Ethnography of the Academy of Sciences. For some reason she did not accept his proposal, and he remained single until 1919. In 1919 he married a graduate student from the women's university, Lidiya Melioranskaya who, incidentally, was not related to the well-known Turcologist P. M. Melioranskii. She later told me about how he had proposed to her. In 1919 the Academy of Sciences and the Hermitage Museum organized a Buddhist art exhibition in Petrograd. Various Buddhist images, statues of Buddha and art objects were exhibited, and lectures were given by such famous Buddhologists as Ol'denburg on Buddhist art, Shcherbatskoi on Buddhist philosophy, Otton Rozenberg on Buddhism in Japan, and Vladimirtsov on Buddhism in Mongolia and Tibet. The exhibition drew many people who were interested in Buddhist art and among those admiring the exhibits was Lidiya Melioranskaya. Vladimirtsov did not know her at all, but he looked at her, liked what he saw, approached her and said, "Excuse me, would you marry me?" She was taken aback by his forward manner and at first could not respond at all, but then for some reason said, "Well, of course!" After they had a chance to become acquainted, they actually did marry and later had two daughters and a son.

Vladimirtsov's lecture on Buddhism in Mongolia and Tibet was later published as a brochure. Its title read in Russian, *Buddhism in Mongolia and Tibet: A Lecture Held on September 31, 1919*. September has, of course, only thirty days. This error was typical of Vladimirtsov who was a very sloppy proofreader. Most of his works contain numerous misprints, but he always seemed more amused than chagrined when he discovered one. "Oh, here's another misprint!" he would happily exclaim. Another example of a misprint is his article on the Mongolian legends about Amursanaa, the famous rebel leader of the mid-eighteenth century. The name of one of the heroes meant, literally, Iron Heart. This name is usually translated into Russian as Iron Thought, but in Vladimirtsov's article it appeared as Iron Mouse, the Russian words for mouse (*mysh'*) and thought (*mysl'*) resembling one another. He never detected this misprint while reading the proofs, and his readers, of course, could never have guessed that the hero's real name was Iron Heart.

41

Although Vladimirtsov became my teacher and I was very thankful to him for everything he did for me, I cannot help but mention that he was in one respect very different from Rudnev and all my other teachers. Everyone else supported and welcomed my plans of writing articles and presenting papers, but Vladimirtsov was not very pleased with such projects and always tried to dissuade me. When I published my article on Old Mongolian literary language in *Asia Major* in 1924,[1] Vladimirtsov was very displeased with its appearance, and even said that he had planned to write an article on this subject himself. I must say that even if he had such a plan, the subject is so vast that as many as twenty articles could have been written with no adverse effects on any of the authors. Science develops as a result of competition among different interpretations of the same subject, and out of this competition emerges the truth. Surely no single person could have done it all in one article.

Once later when I was working at the Asian Museum of the Academy of Sciences, my job being to register and catalog Mongolian manuscripts, I discovered some interesting materials which I laid aside in order to study them later at my leisure. Vladimirtsov came in and asked me where a certain manuscript of Saghan Sechen's history of the Mongols was. I answered, "It's right here. I've put it aside so that I can investigate its archaic language." Oh, I'm sorry," he said, "but you can't do that because I need it for my current work." Of course I handed the material over to him, but he obviously never touched it for he never wrote or published anything on that subject.

A still stronger example follows: One day in the early 1920s a Dagur by the name of Erdem Bilig came to Petrograd in order to study. The Dagurs are a Mongolian tribe speaking a very archaic, conservative dialect which resembles Middle Mongolian, spoken in the thirteenth to sixteenth centuries. I wanted to study the Dagur language which had never before been investigated, so I asked Vladimirtsov if I should do work with that student. "Oh," he said, "I would advise against it. It is a very uninteresting mixture of Mongolian and Manchu words. I already did some work with this man but gave it up." Consequently I never started working with Erdem Bilig.

Several years later, during my second trip to Mongolia in 1927, I met the well-known Mongolian scholar Tsyben Zhamtsarano who was a Buryat originally from the Aga district and who had been a lecturer in Mongolian at St. Petersburg University during Tsarist times. Around 1910, however, he was stripped of his Russian citizenship and exiled to Mongolia. By 1927 he became the secretary of the Mongolian Learned Committee which later, in 1961, was renamed the Mongolian Academy of Sciences. Zhamtsarano told me that a group of Dagurs was living in Ulaanbaatar, the capital of the Mongolian People's Republic, and added, "These people speak a very archaic Mongolian language, and I think it would be a very good idea if you investigated it." I started work with those people without any qualms, feeling that I could not hurt Vladimirtsov since he had no connection with this group of Dagurs. I collected some very interesting materials which I published in 1930.[2] I gave Vladimirtsov a complimentary copy, and a short time later he told me, "It is an extremely interesting language. I would never have expected it to be so archaic." I thought to myself: "When I wanted to investigate that language back in the early twenties, was it not you who told me that Dagur was an uninteresting mixture of Mongolian and Manchu? Did you tell me the truth then?" Vladimirtsov, indeed, did not tell me the truth, and what his purpose actually was is anyone's guess. I cannot help but think that he was simply jealous that I might have written something as a result of my work with Erdem Bilig.

So this is how it was with Vladimirtsov. He was a brilliant scholar, but he also had his faults. Later on in 1929 he was elected a member of the Academy of Sciences, but he enjoyed his new position for only two years. He died at the age of 47 on August 17, 1931, when I was in the Selenga region of Buryatia. His sudden death was caused by his first and only heart attack. I must say that this was not too surprising, because Vladimirtsov led a very irregular life. He did not start his work day until ten or eleven at night and then worked until four or five in the morning. In order to stay awake he drank large quantities of very strong coffee laced with rum or brandy. He got up around ten every morning and around noon he went to the university or to the Academy of Sciences. He returned

43

home for dinner around five. He was also a chain smoker, smoking up to two packs, each containing twenty-five papirosi. He also liked very hot, Japanese-style baths. While sitting in a bathtub filled with near boiling water, he would drink a bottle of hot port in order, as he used to say, to warm up from within. Such a life style eventually killed him. When I warned him of the dangers, he brushed my criticisms aside by saying, "Life itself is bad for our health."

Aleksei Vasil'evich Burdukov, whom I mentioned earlier, was a man with a very limited formal education, but he had read very much and had a great interest in anthropology, folklore, and languages. He collected Mongolian stories, songs and other materials, and was a self-taught researcher. He sent his materials to Kotwicz and other well-known scholars in Petrograd, and some of his articles were even published in the journal *Zhivaya Starina* (Living Antiquity), the official organ of the Russian Ethnographical Society. After the revolution Burdukov moved to Petrograd and became a teacher of colloquial Mongolian, which he spoke fluently, at the Institute of Oriental Languages. In 1933 or 1934 when there were great shortages in Leningrad, he gave about two ounces of gold dust which he had brought from Mongolia, to a lady whom he knew quite well and who was on her way to Siberia to procure food. While she was buying food and paying with the gold, she was arrested by the police that were investigating black market operations. Under interrogation she revealed that part of the gold had belonged to Burdukov. Soon thereafter Burdukov was arrested in Leningrad and was told by the secret police that he would be released the moment he handed over all the gold in his possession. As he kept maintaining that he had no more gold, he remained in jail and soon his wife was also arrested. Eventually they decided to tell the police where the gold was hidden, and they wrote a letter to their daughter, Taisiya, telling her where to find the gold and asking her to hand it over to the man sent by the secret police. The daughter, who later became my secretary at the Academy of Sciences, did as she was instructed and her parents were released from jail. When World War II began, however, everybody who had ever been arrested was taken in again, so Burdukov was arrested by the secret police in July 1941 and this time disappeared forever. Many years later, after Stalin's death, Taisiya published her father's memoirs, and in the preface she described what had happened to him.[3]

To return from this excursus on Burdukov, who was closely associated with Vladimirtsov and later with me, I will finish characterizing my university professors. Another of my teachers was the Polish scholar Władysław Kotwicz. I took Manchu and Oirat, including Kalmuck, from him. He was quite different from Vladimirtsov, for he was very quiet and spoke with such a low voice that one could hardly hear him. He was sickly by nature, a hypochondriac, and missed many classes. One day I asked his daughter Maria, the librarian at the Institute of Oriental Languages, whether her father would come that day to the university, and she answered, "No. Yesterday Father stepped into a puddle of water and got his feet wet, and today he imagines he has a cold." This sort of thing happened quite often. Kotwicz lived like a hermit in a large unheated apartment, and his only companion was his daughter. Kotwicz's wife had died of alcoholism, and Maria had had an unhappy childhood. Kotwicz was a great scholar but a strange bird, as one might say, and I wonder how he managed to bring up his little daughter. Everything was very strange in his apartment. One day I was at his apartment, with a blanket on my shoulders because of the extreme cold, and we were reading an Oirat text, probably an epic. I do remember reading one with him but perhaps not on that occasion. At any rate, I suddenly heard a loud noise above my head. I looked up and saw a crow sitting on the stove. "Oh, that crow," Kotwicz said, "I found him in the street. The poor thing was dying so I picked him up, brought him here and now he is living with us." Kotwicz left Russia in 1923 to return to his native Poland. He died in Vilnius in 1944, soon after the Soviet army had occupied the city.

My professor of Turkic languages was Aleksandr Nikolaevich Samoilovich, of Ukrainian origin and a descendant of the hetman Samoilovich. He was jovial, debonair and friendly. He was fond of good food and wine, and he told many jokes. All in all, he was the exact opposite of Kotwicz. Kotwicz did not speak Mongolian or Kalmuck at all, and Vladimirtsov spoke Mongolian rather poorly, but

Samoilovich had a perfect command of Turkish. He also spoke Uzbek and Crimean Tatar, and had a thorough knowledge of Turkmenian. His works were numerous,[4] and he was an excellent and very pleasant teacher. With him I read the Altai Turkic texts collected by W. Radloff,[5] the history written by Abu'l Gazi Bahadur Khan in the Chagatai language,[6] and the memoirs of Emperor Babur which were published in a facsimile edition by Annette Beveridge.[7]

I also began to read Orkhon Turkic texts with him, but unfortunately Samoilovich was at that time hired by Karakhan, the deputy commissar of foreign affairs, and sent to Turkey. Later Samoilovich was also sent to Turkistan to help develop the culture of the Uzbeks and other nationalities of Central Asia. During the Great Purge in 1937 Karakhan was arrested and executed, along with such Uzbek leaders as the government chairman, Faiz'ullah Khodzhaev and the secretary of the central committee of the Communist Party in Uzbekistan, Ikramzade. These officials were accused of being traitors, nationalists, and collaborators with fascist organizations. In the summer of 1938, Samoilovich was also arrested and disappeared. This happened in the health resort Kislovodsk in the northern Caucasus where my family and I were also staying. In fact, we had visited him several times. One day when we went to visit him again, he was not there, and some other vacationers living in the same health resort told us that he had been taken at night by the secret police. He must have died soon thereafter. In 1978 a memorial volume for Samoilovich was published under the title *Tyurkologicheskii sbornik 1974* (Turcological Symposium 1974) which contains, among other things, Samoilovich's biography. It informs the reader of many details of his life but does not mention where, when, and how he died. It is indeed strange to read what he was doing in this or that year and note abruptly that in 1938 he died. Unfortunately, this has happened frequently in the Soviet Union. Rehabilitated victims of the Great Purge are often honored with memorial volumes which omit the last year of their lives or the circumstances of their deaths.

I owe Samoilovich a great deal. I wrote my first book, a Yakut grammar, because he had asked me to write it. The Yakut publishing house had wanted a grammar and originally asked him to write it, but since he was too busy, he asked me to do it instead. The book appeared in 1926.[8] Samoilovich was also the one who suggested that I read a paper at the first Turcological Congress in Baku in 1926. He was quite different from Vladimirtsov, who never encouraged me to write anything or to present papers at meetings of learned societies. I liked Samoilovich very much, and I missed him greatly after his disappearance.

My other teacher of Turcology was Sergei Efimovich Malov, the son of a Russian Orthodox priest. Malov was in his forties, much older than Vladimirtsov. He spoke Turkic languages fluently but with an atrocious pronunciation. Vladimirtsov used to ridicule him by saying a bear had stepped on Malov's ears. Malov, however, had a perfect theoretical grasp of the Turkic languages. He was a long-time co-worker of and the aide to the famous Turcologist Radloff. Malov knew Ancient Uighur better than anyone else in the world. He wrote excellent works about the languages of the Yellow Uighurs and other nationalities.[9] He spoke a Northern Russian dialect which pronounced the unstressed o (= ə) as o whereas in most parts of Russia, educated people do not pronounce it this way. He was also rather eccentric. He never used the telephone because he was afraid of it, explaining that "something could suddenly jump into my ear." When he left a room where the lights were on, he would say, "Let's blow out the electricity," as if it were a candle. When he was at somebody's home, he drank wine only at the very beginning of the party because he explained, "My wife might notice that I had some wine and would command, 'Open your mouth and breathe out, you old devil! You certainly have been at it again!'" With Malov I read Ancient Uighur, specifically *Altun Yaruk* (The Sutra of the Golden Beam) as well as Modern Tatar texts. Malov died in 1957 when I was in the United States.

My third teacher of Turcology was P. A. Falev, a young man with whom I studied Osmanli Turkic and Nogay, the latter being a language he had personally investigated. I also read with him the Kazakh epic *Edige* which had been published in Arabic script. Unfortunately these studies did not last very long because he died of

47

spotted fever after a journey to Turkistan in 1921. This disease was widespread in Russia at that time. Falev had gone with a group of students to Turkistan where the students were to do practical work under his supervision. He caught the disease on his return to Petrograd and died.

I also studied Tibetan under the famous Sanskritologist and Tibetologist Fedor Ippolitovich Shcherbatskoi.[10] I read with him the Tibetan text of the Sanskrit work Bodhicaryāvatāra, written by Śāntideva. He was a very learned man and a good teacher, though perhaps a bit too demanding. His great weakness was women. He was a notorious ladies' man and behaved toward them in a brutal way, quite contrary to what one would expect of such a great scholar. I suppose that all women were just objects to him, and he had no other use for them. Once the permanent secretary of the Academy of Sciences, Ol'denburg, sent a lady stenographer to Shcherbatskoi's home to do some work with him. In no time at all she came running back, disheveled and crying that she would never go there again. A lady friend of my first wife, Nataliya, told her that once she was sitting at a dinner party next to Shcherbatskoi when he started to paw her legs and thighs. Only after she whispered to him, "Leave me alone or else I'll scream," did he stop.

Shcherbatskoi was, however, a courageous and honest man and he never hid his true beliefs. He hated everything that the Soviets called democracy. I remember that at a meeting of the Oriental Society of the Soviet Union, which bore the name of the Collegium of Orientalists, Professor Konrad, the well-known Japanologist, was presenting a paper on democratic institutions in ancient Japan. During the subsequent discussion Shcherbatskoi asked him, "Tell me, Professor, what do you call democracy?" Konrad replied, "When people have the right to meet and discuss matters, and to vote and elect," to which Shcherbatskoi retorted, "Indeed! So any fool was permitted to say whatever was on his mind." The effect of his remark was that of an exploding bomb, and everyone was afraid that Shcherbatskoi would be arrested. It is worth noting, though, that outspoken people like he were never touched by the secret police. Another man with this kind of courage was the great physiologist Pavlov. He was very religious and in his institute refused to treat every fifth day as a day of rest and instead insisted on celebrating Sundays.[11] He had even an icon hanging on the wall of his laboratory. The Soviets could do nothing against him because he was so famous.

Another professor I remember from my university years was the Semitologist Pavel Konstantinovich Kokovtsov. He was undoubtedly a great scholar and a very honest man. In 1911 a trial took place in Kiev in which a certain Mendel Beilis, who was Jewish, was accused of having committed a ritual murder of a Christian boy by the family name of Yushchinskii. Kokovtsov announced that he would like to participate in the trial as an expert on Judaism. Whereas all the other witnesses insisted on Beilis's guilt, Kokovtsov rose to declare that the Jews never committed ritual murder and indeed that their religion forbade any kind of murder. He stated that no blood was ever put into the dough for matzohs because blood would contaminate the matzohs, making them unkosher. He demanded a thorough investigation. The blood traces on the wallpaper in Beilis's room turned out to be simply filth, and the most important witness against Beilis was a prostitute, named Vera Cheberyak. She had been intimidated by the police who threatened to force her out of business if she did not testify against Beilis. The investigation also revealed that among the boy's real murderers were a member of a reactionary group and a customer of Vera Cheberyak.

In the anti-Semitic climate of Russia Kokovtsov's action demonstrates that he was a courageous, honest and decent man. He was, however, also a rather odd person. For example, when he was young he went to Palestine to study, but turned back as soon as he reached Istanbul. His excuse was that in Istanbul he had seen branches from trees lying on the streets where the wind had blown them down. He reasoned that "if such things happen in Istanbul, just think what it must be like farther on in Palestine." On another occasion, Vladimirtsov met Kokovtsov on a bridge crossing the Neva River in Petrograd. Kokovtsov was wearing one hat and carrying another in his hand. Vladimirtsov asked, "Have you bought a new hat, Professor?" "No," Kokovtsov replied, "this is an old hat but several days ago I saw a man walking here and the wind carried off his hat. I thought that the same could happen to me, so I now carry a spare hat with me." Kokovtsov was a bachelor and he was very much against marriage. In his opinion, a scholar should not marry because marriage interferes with his work. Thus when his student M. N. Sokolov wanted to marry, Kokovtsov said, "Don't get married. If you really need a woman, you can always go to a brothel." Sokolov, however, disregarded his advice, married, and was consequently in Kokovtsov's disfavor for a long time. Sokolov, incidentally, as well as another of Kokovtsov's students, A. P. Alyavdin, were the sons of Russian Orthodox priests, and this might be the reason why both of them were arrested in 1937 and disappeared forever. Kokovtsov tried to have them freed but without success. Kokovtsov died at an advanced age during the winter of 1941-42 while Leningrad was under siege.

One man who did not have too many eccentricities was the famous Orientalist Vasilii Vladimirovich Bartol'd.[12] He was a fine scholar and known all over the world but he was most unattractive in his appearance, being crosseyed and lame. He had once fallen from a horse while riding in Turkistan and broken his leg. The leg had not been set properly, and he remained lame for the rest of his life. Moreover, he stuttered very badly and it was almost impossible to understand him, a fact that could lead to disaster during examinations. He would flare up in rage whenever anyone asked him to repeat a question. When I was taking my final examination in the history of Oriental Studies in January 1921, he asked me three questions. I answered the first two instantly and very well, but when he asked me the third question, he began to stutter so badly that I could not possibly understand what he was saying. I dared not ask him to repeat it, so I pretended to be thinking it over and then finally said, "I'm sorry, sir, but I can't answer this question. I don't know." He then smiled and explained to me the route which Rubruck had taken in 1253 to 1255 from Europe to the Great Khan in Mongolia. I already knew all the places on Rubruck's itinerary, had even made a map of his trip, and could have answered the question easily. Still, I passed the examination with flying colors. I learned that knowledge and ability alone will not always lead one to his goal, but often skillful diplomacy is also needed. Later I shall mention other means which I had to use in my life, such as lying to the Soviets and Nazis.

One of the great scholars and outstanding servants of the nation was Sergei Fedorovich Ol'denburg, the Permanent Secretary of the Academy of Sciences (Illus. 13). I had first met him in 1919 when I attended the Orientalist meetings which he often chaired.[13] I have already noted some of the strange characteristics of other Orientalists and brilliant scholars, but I must say that Ol'denburg did not have such eccentricities. There was nothing strange about him except perhaps that he was absolutely incapable of appreciating a joke or anecdote. Whenever anyone finished telling a joke, Ol'denburg would ask, "And what happened then?" because he had, as usual, missed the point.

When Lenin was alive, i.e., until 1924, Ol'denburg's authority was fully recognized by the Soviets. He met Lenin on a few occasions, such as discussions of the Academy's budget and food supplies for scholars, many of whom were starving. Lenin always listened to him attentively and whenever possible, Lenin always fulfilled Ol'denburg's entreaties. In 1922 Ol'denburg and Shcherbatskoi were permitted to travel abroad and organize the exchange of information and publications. There, in Paris, Ol'denburg met his son, Sergei Sergeevich, who had played an important role in the Constitutional Democratic Party (commonly abbreviated in Russian as KD) and who had emigrated after the seizure of power by the Bolsheviks. After his return from Paris, Ol'denburg again met Lenin. After they had concluded their business, Lenin asked him: "Did you visit your son while in Paris?" and when Ol'denburg said that he had, Lenin replied: "I fully understand you." This episode shows how immensely more human Lenin was than Stalin who would have severely punished Ol'denburg.

Another excellent scholar and teacher was Lev Vladimirovich Shcherba, a general linguist with a specialty in Russian languages and its history.[14] He was a friendly person who often invited his colleagues, graduate students, and promising undergraduates to parties held at his home to celebrate Tat'yana's Day (January 18) on which day St. Petersburg/Petrograd University had been founded in 1818. Like Samoilovich, Ol'denburg and Bartol'd, Shcherba seemed to be well disposed toward me.

Illus. 13. Sergei Fedorovich Ol'denburg

One of the first scholars I met, right at the beginning of my university studies, was Nikolai Yakovlevich Marr, who was famous as an excellent philologist and connoisseur of the Armenian and Georgian languages.[15] The son of a Scottish gardener and a Georgian woman, he spoke Georgian like a native, because it was his mother tongue. Later in the twenties he became famous as the creator of his "new linguistics," according to which the vocabulary of all languages in the world consisted of various combinations of four original elements. At the beginning of this craze, Vladimirtsov attended most meetings of Marr's seminar and I joined Vladimirtsov. Later, however, both of us realized that Marr's seminar had nothing to do with linguistics. It was merely a forum for his own ravings, so we stopped attending these meetings. In spite of this, I remained on friendly terms with Marr who was certainly a gentleman and a decent and honorable person. His followers and adepts were, however, mostly scoundrels who denounced as counterrevolutionaries and anti-Marxists those who disagreed with Marr. It is greatly to Marr's credit that he himself managed to extricate quite a number of people from the clutches of the secret police. As a half-Georgian and speaker of excellent Georgian, Marr got acquainted with Stalin and conversed with him in the latter's native tongue. He was certainly in Stalin's great favor.

Another of my teachers was Lev Yakovlevich Shternberg, the professor of ethnography. He was to play yet another role in my life which I will discuss in more detail later on.

These were the great persons in whose shadow I was working at the university. Unfortunately, there were also some people who were not so good. To this category of human refuse belonged Evgenii Dmitrievich Polivanov, a brilliant linguist and author of first-rate works on Japanese, Turkic, comparative Altaic linguistics, and other subjects.[16] Immediately after the October Revolution he became the deputy minister of foreign affairs under Trotskii. One of Polivanov's first acts was to evict two very elderly professors from their homes at the official residence apartments of the Ministry of Foreign Affairs. These two unfortunate men were V. A. Zhukovskii, professor of Iranian studies and director of the School of Oriental Languages at the Foreign Ministry, and Professor N. I. Veselovskii, an Asian historian. Veselovskii was old and in poor health and, having been literally thrown out into the street during winter and having been forced to leave all his personal property in that apartment, he very shortly caught pneumonia and died. Zhukovskii also died soon after his eviction. Polivanov's colleagues regarded these evictions as acts of personal revenge. Polivanov was also an opium addict, an alcoholic, and a dissolute person. When living in the university dormitory he often caroused and brawled and once tried to break into the bedrooms of female students. There was a lot of yelling and screaming while he was trying to get past the barricaded door of the girl's section of the dormitory. The Russian novelist Veniamin Kaverin, who at that time was a student of Oriental languages, described Polivanov as the prototype for the main character in his novel *Skandalist* (The Scandalmonger).[17] Later Polivanov moved to Uzbekistan and eventually for some time did research and teaching in Moscow. There he collided with Marr's followers, attacked Marr's theory in his publications, before returning to Uzbekistan. He was arrested there in 1937 and died in jail, unable to withstand being suddenly deprived of drugs. His death was a severe loss to the scholarly world, for in spite of his evil habits, his atrocious behavior, and cruelty toward several people, he was an excellent scholar. I once compared him to a jewel dropped into a cesspool: even when it becomes filthy and polluted, a jewel is still a jewel.

Having discussed some of my professors, I shall now proceed to describe the living conditions after the revolution.

3 The Period of War Communism & the New Economic Policy

The most important public events of 1918 were the beginning of the civil war and the murder of the Tsar and his family by the Bolsheviks. The Tsar had abdicated in 1917 and under the provisional government lived with his family in the palace in Tsarskoe Selo, a small town near Petrograd. Tsarskoe Selo was similar to Versailles in France and Potsdam in Germany as being the Tsars' palace town. The head of the provisional government, A. F. Kerenskii, foresaw danger for the imperial family and soon after the February Revolution in 1917 approached the government of Great Britain seeking political asylum for the Tsar and his family. The British must have known the unstable situation in Russia and consequent danger for the Tsar. But even though the Tsar was a cousin of the British king, they refused to help. The reply was that the British government did not regard the time as appropriate for the Tsar's journey. I regard this as unforgiveable. It would be interesting to know what time could have been more appropriate, considering the imminent civil war, general chaos, murder, and looting everywhere in Russia.

Kerenskii then removed the Tsar and his family to Tobolsk in Western Siberia which was at the time still relatively peaceful. However, when Kerenskii's government fell and the Bolsheviks seized power, the local soviet in Tobolsk took over the management of the Tsar's household. It transferred the Tsar, the Tsarina, and all five children to Ekaterinburg where they were all shot in the summer of 1918. To murder a woman and her children was a heinous crime, and only the killing of the Tsar could have been justified as an act of revolutionary justice, though first he should have been tried and condemned to death if found guilty. How much more civilized the Germans were who permitted Kaiser Wilhelm II who had abdicated to move to the Netherlands.

The revolution of February 1917 has been called the "unbloodiest revolution in human history" but it soon turned out to be the most devastating as far as loss of human lives, property, and cultural values were concerned. In 1918 civil war was started. An anti-Communist army formed by Admiral A. V. Kolchak achieved some early victories, temporarily occupying all of Siberia and the lands east of the Volga river. Eventually, however, it was defeated, and Kolchak himself was taken prisoner and executed in 1920. Another anti-Communist army led by General A. I. Denikin operated in Southern Russia. A third army under the command of General N. N. Yudenich advanced from Estonia and almost took Petrograd in 1919, and a fourth army headed by General Baron P. N. Vrangel began its operations in the Crimea and occupied parts of Southern Russia in 1920. All of them were initially successful but later suffered identical fates: they were defeated and their leaders were either executed or escaped abroad. In my opinion, there were three reasons for their defeat. The anti-Communist armies failed to coordinate their movements and instead fought *seriatim*. As one army was defeated, another took to the field. Second, the anti-Communist armies were always numerically inferior to the Bolshevik forces. The third and most important reason was the lack of a clear political program. The Soviets promised that land would be expropriated from the large landowners and redistributed among the peasants. The anti-Communist armies and their civilian administrations, however, did not make such promises. Would the peasants get land? There was no official answer to this question. Moreover, it remained unclear what kind of government Russia would have in the event of an anti-Communist victory. Would it become a monarchy or a republic? If a republic, would it be capitalist or social democratic? As a result of this vagueness, the anti-Communist movement had little support from the peasants and even less from the industrial workers. The peasants expected to get land from the Communists but, of course, they did not suspect that ten years later, in 1929, collectivization would deprive them of their newly won property.

As for my own experiences during this period of war communism, I can only say that the year 1918 was very difficult for my family. My mother obtained a job at the main post office in Petrograd, and I attended courses at the university in the mornings and worked at the Commissariat of Supply at nights, as I have already described. I received a small salary which was insufficient because everything was enormously expensive. We had lost everything in 1918 when the banks were nationalized. My cousin Alexander Boetz, who had been arrested in Arkhangelsk in 1914 and spent several years in exile in Siberia, returned and got a job at the bank where our safe was. He was on good terms with the commissar of the bank. This commissar offered to return the contents of all safes to their owners if they would share them fifty-fifty with him. Alexander told my grandmother about this proposal, and although she was highly indignant, she could not make up her mind. She asked her brother Wilhelm, who had been a stockbroker and was considered a financial expert, for advice. He told her, "Don't do it. The Bolsheviks will be here and gone tomorrow. You'd be crazy to give them half the contents." The safe contained stock certificates of foreign companies, jewelry and many other valuables. If Grandmother had listened to Alexander, she would have saved half her fortune of foreign stocks and bonds, and she would have been able to sell them at a later time.

The house we lived in was taken over by the city. It had belonged to my grandfather, and my mother had been born there, but since my mother was the widow of a consul-general of the Imperial government, the revolutionaries made her life difficult indeed. She and my grandmother were branded as parasites, assigned to the "exploiter" class and were given ration cards of the very lowest category. At first their daily bread, mixed with moss and sawdust, was rationed at eight ounces. Later they got four and finally only two. Sometimes, in order to stave off hunger, we bought ordinary oats for horses on the black market. After boiling the oats and grinding them in a meat grinder, we added a bit of water, and ended up with a kind of porridge that contained much chaff. In January and February 1919 it was 29 degrees Fahrenheit in our apartment, but we had no firewood for our stove. After dark I needed light in order to do my homework, but the supply of electricity was so erratic that I had to go to the black market to buy two small lamps and some high-priced kerosene. These lamps were nothing more than small bottles with wicks in them, and they gave off a feeble light, more or less like Christmas tree lights. If I set them up on each side of my book there was just enough light to read by.

Another event took place in 1918. My grandmother had a sister, Charlotte Diederichs, the widow of an accountant or bookkeeper and the mother of two boys, Max and Willi. Willi had served as a captain in an engineering regiment during the war and stayed with us after his return. He had just married and, having no other place to stay, lived with his young bride in our living room. She had worked as a nurse at one of the military hospitals during the war. One summer night a group of armed men suddenly burst into our apartment. They were members of the Red Guards, the paramilitary organization of the Bolsheviks. Willi was arrested and, together with other former officers, he was to be taken on a barge to the Gulf of Finland and drowned. This is exactly what they had done in Viipuri in August 1917. Willi's brother Max knew, however, the German ambassador, Count Mirbach, whom he asked to intercede on Willi's behalf. Count Mirbach ordered his secretary to draw up a letter declaring that Willi Diederichs was a German citizen and should be released immediately. Max took the letter to where the unfortunate officers were being held, presented it to the authorities and Willi was promptly released. A day or two later Willi and his wife left for Germany.

This same Count Mirbach was murdered soon thereafter by a member of the Social Revolutionary Party, Yakov Blyumkin, whose motive was simply to provoke war between Germany and Soviet Russia. Although the Soviets promised the German government that Blyumkin would be shot, I actually met him in 1926 in Ulaanbaatar where he was working as the station manager for TASS, the Soviet news agency. He did not escape a bitter end, however, for during the Great Purge in 1937 he was shot, having been found guilty of being a former member of the Revolutionary Socialist Party and possibly also because he was Jewish. He was not being punished for the murder which he had really committed but was sentenced to death for having been a member of a political party. In the Soviet Union this was a greater crime than murdering a non-Communist!

After Willi's departure his room was confiscated and the housing office placed a family in it. Christmas 1918 was grim. We had nothing at all. During the night of December 31, 1918 my grandmother died of malnutrition and a broken heart. While she was lying dead in her room, a meeting of the Revolutionary House Committee was conducted in one of the rooms of our apartment. The committee members were drinking, dancing and singing at the top of their voices. I will never forgive them for this. They behaved like scavengers around a dead body, celebrating their New Year, sitting in our apartment on furniture that did not belong to them and maybe even drinking wine bought with money confiscated from our bank account.

A certain Mr. Mikhelson, who had a mechanical workshop in our house, paid my grandmother's funeral expenses. We did not even have money to bury her, and my uncle Ferdinand's financial position was as bad as ours. Ferdinand was a very nice man but a good-for-nothing. When my grandfather died, Ferdinand was fifteen. He immediately dropped out of school and when he was twenty-one he demanded from his mother, that is my grandmother, his share of his father's fortune. According to law, his mother retained one-half and the other half was divided among the children. Being the only son, Ferdinand received six-sevenths of that half, and my mother got only one-seventh, or one-fourteenth of the total fortune. Ferdinand started squandering money on women and expensive hunts. For these he had a pack of thirty dogs which he housed in a special kennel where they were taken care of by a hunter and his wife. The only good thing his money brought him was his wife Nina, a real beauty. Ferdinand happened to meet her somewhere, learned that

59

she was married and, with the help of a lawyer, he bought her from
her husband. He gave Nina's husband a large sum of money so that
he would divorce her, allowing Ferdinand to marry her. The husband
agreed to the deal because he was poor and needed the money.
When war came and Ferdinand was to be drafted, one of our porters
who had connections with the draft board told Ferdinand that a bribe
of 25 rubles, about $12.50, would buy a deferral. Ferdinand was
indeed not sent to the front. He remained in Petrograd where he
worked as a clerk in one of the military offices, but soon found this
work boring and volunteered for the front where he caught pneumonia. After the Bolsheviks seized power in 1917, Ferdinand once
came to his mother with whom we were living and mocked her, "You
saved and took good care of your property but where is it now? The
Bolsheviks took everything. But I have already squandered everything. I haven't got a penny to my name but I had an excellent life
with lots of beautiful women and entertaining company." I must
admit that this point of view was not entirely wrong; perhaps it was
just as well after all that he had squandered all his money and left
nothing for the Bolsheviks. In 1921, Ferdinand died of tuberculosis
on a train to a sanatorium in Southern Russia.

I should also say a word about my paternal uncle, Vasilii
Poppe. Soon after the Bolsheviks had seized power on November 7,
1917, he and his wife came to say goodbye. He said the Bolsheviks
would rule Russia for a long time, perhaps a whole century, and
therefore he was leaving in a few days for Riga, Latvia. Riga was
occupied by the Germans, and from there he went to Germany where
he died in 1927. His widow, now in her eighties, is presently living in
Germany, and their son Vasilii, a doctor of chemistry, in his fifties,
lives near Chicago.

The year 1919 had a sad beginning. Of all of us, the one who
was best off was my fifteen-year old sister Elisabeth. Her former
nurse Vasilisa, whom I mentioned earlier, was a faithful soul who had
stayed on with us even though we were unable to pay her. She often
went to her native village from where she brought eggs, flour,
potatoes, sometimes even pork or a chicken. One half of the food
she bartered on the black market for textiles and clothes, which she

then took to her village to pay for the food. The other half of the food she gave us free of charge. She took my sister to her own village. Elisabeth lived for several months in a warm peasant house and had plenty of food, and that probably saved her life. Vasilisa's own daughter, Masha, was a very pretty girl. She married a Finnish gentleman by the name of Alfred Walle who was the son of a pastor in Uukuniemi. In 1920 Vasilisa followed them to Finland. Many years later when I already lived in the United States, I wrote a letter to Finland to inquire about them and learned that Mr. Walle was still alive, but that Masha and Vasilisa had both been dead for quite some time. Masha reportedly died of a tumor and Vasilisa of diabetes.

In April 1919 I went to the outskirts of Petrograd to buy some milk and potatoes. The area was too close to the Finnish border, so I was arrested by border guards and brought back to the office of the county administration *(uezd)*. Fortunately, the manager of the supply office where I worked interceded on my behalf, and I was released in May.

A second disaster befell me in 1919. A new anti-Communist army under the command of General Yudenich was approaching Petrograd from Estonia, and most able-bodied men, including students like myself, were drafted by the Communists. I felt terribly unhappy for two reasons. First of all, I hated military service, especially the idle hours when one was forced to sit around and listen to other soldiers telling dirty jokes. I also hated the thought of being sent to fight against those who wanted to liberate us from Communism. One morning while I was in the barracks compound, I heard a cheery voice. "Kolya! It's you! How come you are here?" Our family physician, Dr. M. D. Grinberg had been drafted as the regimental surgeon. After listening to my story, he said, "Listen, come to my office tomorrow. One of my colleagues will be there and the two of us will certify you as unfit for military duty." When I went to the infirmary the next morning, Dr. Grinberg examined me and told his colleague, "This man has an advanced stage of tuberculosis. Would you care to examine him?" "No," said the other physician, "I'm too busy. Write everything down and I will sign it." Armed with a medical certificate, I marched to the regimental headquarters and was promptly discharged. I owe a great debt to our good Dr. Grinberg who in subsequent years remained our family doctor and was even the doctor of both my sons when they were little. Dr. Grinberg died in 1935 and we mourned for him very much.

Hunger was the greatest calamity in 1919-20. Food rations were miserably small, and everything was extremely expensive on the black market which was conducted only by barter. I remember that I exchanged my golden tie pin adorned with a small ruby, a diamond, and a sapphire for two pounds of bread and a few pounds of potatoes. To make things worse, in 1920 our apartment was burglarized when everyone was at work. The burglars took clothes, silver spoons, a clock and some other things. We had already suffered other losses. My mother had taken her sable coat, some other furs, and her remaining jewelry to a "commission store," i.e., a store specializing in second-hand merchandise. A certain percentage of the money earned from the sale of an item was kept by the store. That particular store was run by a woman whom my mother knew. The store was burglarized, or was said to have been burglarized, and my mother's furs and jewelry were among the goods stolen.

Thefts and burglaries occurred at an alarming rate. In addition, bandits with garrots hid behind fences or in gateways along the dark snow-covered streets at night. Some robbers fixed springs to their boots to make very long jumps. There was no escape from them. Later I saw some kids jumping with such springs in the United States, and I reflected how these gadgets were used in revolutionary Petrograd for far less innocent purposes. An interesting case deserves mention. A man belonging to the upper classes, wearing an expensive furcoat, was held up. It was winter and very cold. The robbers took his coat and suit and left him in underwear in minus 20 degrees Centigrade. He begged the bandits to give him at least one of the filthy old greatcoats the bandits were wearing. They gave one to him and he went home. His wife took the greatcoat and ripped it apart in order to wash it and later perhaps make something else out of it for her husband. Between the lining and the coat she found several American hundred-dollar bills. The greatcoat had probably belonged to an officer murdered by those bandits who had not suspected the true value of his coat.

Numerous crooks and swindlers did a thriving business in counterfeit exit visas and foreign passports. Counterfeit foreign currency was also for sale on the black market. I remember, in summer 1918, when the Finnish Red Guards were defeated, many of them roamed the streets of Petrograd, offering Finnish money for exchange into rubles. As a matter of fact, the Finnish government in Vaasa had declared all paper money issued by the Reds invalid. Petrograders, however, did not know this and eagerly bought those worthless bills. There were no police on the streets, and people were at the mercy of bandits and swindlers. However, when people caught a criminal, he was killed on the spot. Sometimes innocent people were lynched. Once in the black market area of town I saw an elderly woman suddenly start to scream that somebody had stolen her purse. The person nearest to her was immediately suspected and, without even attempting to search him, the mob literally tore the man to pieces. Before long, the "victim" exclaimed: "My God! I have found my purse. I put it into the wrong pocket." Then the mob dashed upon her and tore her to pieces, yelling: "We've killed an innocent man because of you!"

Everyone was demoralized by dire poverty, hunger and hopelessness. A frightening example was a gentleman in his late forties who begged in the streets. His son, a youth of about eighteen began to pimp for his own sister, a girl of no more than sixteen. In the late evenings when returning home from work I often saw him soliciting for her. This was the ultimate level of degradation. Others did not physically become prostitutes, but they were morally no better off. One person who fell into this kind of depravity was a certain Lenochka (diminutive form of Elena, English: Ellen), the daughter of a well-known Petrograd physician. She was engaged to a certain Vladimir Voronin, my friend and son of my mother's class-mate. Having no home of his own, he occupied a room in his future father-in-law's apartment. Vladimir was the son of a rich textile manufacturer who had some commercial dealings with foreigners. His father had escaped to Western Europe where he had some money

Chapter 3

in a bank, and before leaving Petrograd, the father and one of his
faithful workers buried all their jewels in the garden behind the
house where they lived.   A couple of years had elapsed since the
father's escape, when one day the worker came to tell Vladimir that
the jewels should be removed as construction on the site was about
to begin.   One night they went to the garden and dug up the jewels.
Vladimir took them home, laid them out on his bed and called
Lenochka to come in and look.   She came and gasped at the sight.
Vladimir had to go on an errand, and when he came back a few hours
later, he entered his room and saw the jewels were not there.   He
thought Lenochka had taken them to a safe place and asked her
about them.   "What jewels?" she answered, "I don't know of any
jewels."   Vladimir soon moved out and Lenochka returned his ring.
Later she married someone else in a lavish wedding, and the
newlyweds equipped their apartment with expensive furniture.   The
jewels had been very valuable and were worth at least half a million
American dollars.

At that time of hunger, unheated homes, general hopelessness
and despair, a strong belief in the supernatural spread among the
people who eagerly listened to stories filled with mysticism.   One of
them became particularly popular.   As the story goes, a little girl
entered the crowded waiting room at a doctor's office.   Paying no
attention to the patients waiting for their turn, she went straight to
the doctor's office and asked him to go immediately to her mother
who was gravely ill.   There was something in the girl's appearance
that made a deep impression on the doctor.   He asked his patients to
wait until he came back and went to the address the girl gave him.
It was a dilapidated house in a remote street where only poor people
lived.   The woman was, indeed, seriously ill, and the doctor went to
a public telephone to call an ambulance to take her to a hospital.
After the ambulance arrived, the doctor prepared himself to return
to his office when the woman thanked him and asked, "How did you
know, Doctor, that I am ill and where I live?"   The doctor answered
that her little daughter had come and asked him to see her.   "But,
Doctor, my little girl died two years ago," replied the woman and
started crying.   It was the girl's soul which had gone to the doctor's
office.

In their misery and despair, people even invented news about severe defeats inflicted upon the Bolsheviks by the White armies. Once I heard that the notorious bandit Nestor Makhno, who with his army of many thousands of bandits was indiscriminately killing Bolsheviks and innocent bystanders alike and was looting towns and villages, was none other but the Tsar's brother Mikhail, the name Makhno being an acronym for Mikhail Aleksandrovich, khranitel' nashego otechestva (Michael Alexandrovich, the Keeper of our Homeland).

In 1919 at least one good thing happened: I got a job at a research institute. It was very difficult to keep up my studies which required serious homework every evening, when I had to sit in an office and work at night. Therefore, my professor of anthropology and ethnography, L. Ya. Shternberg, gave me a job as assistant research scholar at the Geographical Institute which had two departments, one for geography and the other for ethnography. Professor Shternberg knew that I had a good knowledge of Finnish and its dialects and so assigned me the task of drawing an ethnographical map of the Finnish population of the Petrograd region. I made trips to various villages, studied the local Finnish population, and marked the different dialect groups with different colors on the map. My investigations of the ethnic composition of the Finnish population brought me into many villages. One was Izhora (Finnish: Inkeri). The local Finnish pastor was Siitonen, the maternal uncle of Yrjö Fagerlund in Parikkala, whom I mentioned previously. When I mentioned the name of that pastor in the village, everything became very simple for me. The Finnish peasants said that they could easily tell that I was a "White Finn" from Finland, but I could rest assured they would never tell this to the Russians. I felt very flattered because my Finnish must have impressed them. Still it was a dangerous situation.

Later, in 1920, Professor Shternberg got money for an expedition to study the Karelians of the Tver' region, specifically those of Vyshnii Volochok county. I went there with several students of the Geographical Institute. I visited the Karelians in several villages, particularly in Tsybul'skaya Gorka. It was a relatively small village

Illus. 14. Lev Yakovlevich Shternberg

of about thirty households located near a small lake with pitchblack water and mossy, swampy shores. The local Karelians were very superstitious and believed in mermaids, water kings, forest ghosts and the like. They also believed that a certain Ilmineine lived in the lake and when someone was ill, he or she went to the lake and spoke an incantation roughly as follows: "Old man Ilmineine, old man and old woman, having golden eyes and wearing silver caps, come and take your goods (i.e., the illness) and give me back my health." Ilmineine is the Karelian name for the "king of water" which corresponds to Finnish Ilmari, the name of the god of air, and Votiak (Udmurt) Ilmer, "God." There were many victims of this sort of superstition and quacksalvery. For example, there was an old woman who lived in the neighboring house who was blind because when she had an eye disease, the local witch doctor had treated her eyes with powderized pumice "to rub out the illness."

The Karelian peasants were suspicious of strangers, and for the first few days of our stay in the village the peasants mistrusted us. On the first Sunday all of us went to church in the next village, about two kilometers away, and after that we became honored guests in all homes. Some peasants even suggested that I marry a woman whose husband had not returned from World War I. She had a house, a few cows, and a field, and she badly needed someone who could help her to run the farm!

I could understand the local Karelians very well, but they did not always understand what I said, because I used Finnish expressions unfamiliar to them. In general, the Finnish language has many synonyms, but most of these synonyms are lacking in Karelian. Sometimes the Finnish words had different meanings, and this caused funny misunderstandings. In one village when I was accommodated in a peasant's home, he asked me in Karelian how long I intended to stay. I said, "One week," but he understood this as "one generation's time." The Karelian word for "week" is a Russian word, but the Finnish word for "week" is of Germanic origin. Finnish *viikko* is the same as English *week* which sounds similar to Russian *vek* which means "one century" or "one generation's time," English *week* and Russian *vek* being etymologically unrelated. It goes without saying that the man was horrified to learn that I planned to stay in his home for a whole century.

Professor Shternberg was working at the Museum of Ethnography and Anthropology of the Academy of Sciences, and was also a professor at both the Geographical Institute and the university. He was good-natured and kind. In his youth he had belonged to a revolutionary group and was exiled to the island of Sakhalin north of Japan. There he investigated the Gilyaks and wrote a book about them.[1] He was released from exile due to the good offices of Wilhelm Radloff, the famous Turcologist and the director of the museum, who had many other political exiles returned to their homes. Radloff knew the Empress Dowager who was the Danish princess Dagmar, the mother of Tsar Nikolai II. Each time Radloff appeared for an audience with Her Majesty, she asked him, "And who is it this time, my dear professor?" Then she would add, "All right, I'll ask my son."

Although Professor Shternberg was a kind man, or perhaps because he was a kind man, he had to suffer much from the intrigues of others who tried to undermine his position. He was so accustomed to the people he helped turning against him that once he told me, speaking about one of those people, "It is strange that he is undermining my position and intriguing against me, because I have never done anything to him." Shternberg was a revolutionary of the old school, which held freedom to be the most important tenet of all, and he was suffering in spirit under the Soviets. He died in 1927. Had he lived longer he would probably have been arrested and left to die in a concentration camp.

I had much free time at the Geographical Institute and I could always do my homework and prepare myself for classes. The students of the Geographical Institute were intelligent and well prepared, and many of them became well-known scholars. One of them was my schoolmate Georgii Prokofiev who became a specialist in the northern peoples of Russia, particularly the Samoyeds. He studied the Samoyed language and dialects and published a number of important linguistic works including a description of the Yurak-Samoyed and Ostyak-Samoyed languages.[2] For a while he was a professor at the Institute of the Peoples of the North, but in 1937 he was fired. His position was very difficult and he lived in dire need. Eventually he was reinstated, but he died of starvation in besieged Leningrad in 1942. Vera Tsintsius, of Latvian origin, became an outstanding scholar in the field of Tungus languages and published a number of excellent works.[3] She, too, was temporarily detained sometime between 1937 and 1940 but was later released. Her candidate's (master's) thesis was so brilliant that Shcherba, the professor of linguistics, and I recommended that she keep it for her future doctoral dissertation and present something less important for her master's thesis. She still lives in Leningrad and enjoys the respect of all who know her. G. M. Vasilevich was also a student of the ethnographical department of the Geographical Institute. Like Tsintsius, she became an outstanding scholar in the field of Tungus linguistics and the author of excellent Tungus dictionaries.[4] She died at an advanced age in 1974 or 1975. I should also like to mention my classmate Oskar Wiesel. He was interested in India, but he could not finish his studies as he was arrested and exiled to Central Asia. He died there soon after his arrival. His younger brother Emil had died of tuberculosis in Leningrad several years before that. Their father was a well-known professor at the Academy of Arts.

One of the most brilliant students was Nadezhda Petrovna Dyrenkova who was to become a well-known scholar in the field of Turkic studies.[5] She was intelligent, friendly and helpful, and the two of us became good friends. I learned her life's story. She was one of the two daughters of rich parents who owned several estates, one of which was near the railroad station Batetskaya, not far from Leningrad. Her mother lived there in the early 1920s and still owned the estate, but she was about to be expropriated. This prompted Nadezhda to marry a certain G. K. Sadikov, an officer in the Soviet Air Force who had been decorated with the Order of the Red Banner for valor in the war against Poland in 1920. It was a marriage of convenience because both of them believed that because of his position in the armed forces she would be able to keep the estate. In 1923, however, other people were already living in most parts of the large manor and only a few rooms had been left to the family. Later the marriage was dissolved, and Sadikov married somebody else. Nadezhda invited me to stay there for a month in the summer of 1923. She was a passionate archeologist and had already made excavations of many Russian graves of the twelfth to fourteenth centuries. I also knew something about archeology and had participated in field work, and while helping her in her research I used the opportunity to help her salvage some of their family things. In the attic there was a huge and expensive rug which perhaps was fifty feet long. That rug was to be taken secretly out of the attic and the house. Of course, this was an impossible task because of its tremendous weight, so I cut it into many smaller pieces, using a razor blade, and my heart bled while I was cutting up this precious rug. I loved this Nadeshda Dyrenkova very much and she also had affection for me, but she was not ready for marriage as she wanted to devote herself to scholarly work. We remained good friends until the end. In the late 1920s or early 1930s she met with great misfortune. During one of her trips to Siberia to study one of the Turkic tribes, I think the Shor, she was badly burned by the sun. She had a very beautiful complexion with tender, light skin, but her face was completely burned and she developed a kind of skin cancer. Later, when she returned to Leningrad she went to a physician who diagnosed her disease as lupus. Even if the disease were curable, it was probably too late to do anything about it, so she remained with her face completely ruined. She died of starvation at the beginning of 1942 in besieged Leningrad.

So this was the Geographical Institute. It was an interesting establishment and there were many talented and valuable people. I remember them with a certain tenderness.

Professor Shternberg was greatly interested in the Karelians of the Tver' region. These Karelians had migrated at the beginning of the seventeenth century from Finnish Karelia to the Tver' region and were supposed to have preserved many ancient customs. Therefore, he obtained funds for field research and invited me to participate. I conducted my research among the Karelians of the Tver' region in the summer of 1920 and returned to Petrograd with a rich collection of materials containing numerous women's laments, e.g., a woman crying for her dead child or mother, cries of mothers for their daughters being given into marriage and also songs and some tales. These materials were quite interesting because the Tver' Karelians had been investigated very little, and I hoped to add to these materials and to publish them later on. They remained, however, unpublished in my apartment in Leningrad when I left the city in the summer of 1941 in order to join my family in the northern Caucasus.

Besides my work at the Geographical Institute, I was soon given another job. During the summer of 1920 the Institute of Living Oriental Languages was founded. It began as a practical educational estabishment. Oriental languages, literatures, history, and related subjects had been taught at St. Petersburg/Petrograd University even as early as the 1860s but on a purely scholarly basis. Graduates from the university's Oriental department either became research scholars or diplomats to the Orient. The need for a practical school of Oriental languages was great, and although there had been such an academy in St. Petersburg before the revolution it had not been well organized. Therefore a group of scholars including Ol'denburg, Vladimirtsov and Kotwicz decided to found a special institute which would answer the demands of their time, that is to train Russians interested in the Orient for some specific vocations such as consular employment. Kotwicz was the most active scholar and he was the institute's first director. Another section of the institute admitted students from the non-Russian parts of the Soviet Union and from Oriental countries, such as Tibet and Mongolia, to train them in Western-style management and administration. Given the low state of education in those parts of the world, these students had first to be placed in preparatory courses, and Kotwicz had hired me to teach Russian, elementary mathematics and other basic subjects to a group of Mongols and one Tibetan from Lhasa. The institute was not far from where I lived, and I walked there and back almost every day.

The Mongols and the Tibetan had a very difficult time learning Russian. Russian is phonologically and grammatically quite different from their own languages and has many exceptions to general rules, so that it is often difficult, even impossible, to know beforehand how a word is to be declined or conjugated. My students could not pronounce initial consonant clusters and always inserted vowels between consonants. They could not pronounce the initial r, either, and put a vowel in front of it, as in "aradio" instead of "radio."

71

Worst of all, neither the Tibetan nor the Mongols could get adjusted to Petrograd's cold and clammy climate. The Tibetan died very soon, about four or five months after his arrival. Some of the Mongols lived longer, but almost none survived. There were also three Kalmucks who had enrolled in 1920. They were better adjusted to the climate, graduated from the institute, and returned to the Kalmuck country.

One of my students was Bardym Man'yarovich Zamatkinov, a Buryat of the Ekhirit tribe. He was a shaman and had learned his incantations from his uncle who had been a shaman. I wrote down Zamatkinov's incantations and made arrangements for a shamanist performance at the Russian Museum in Petrograd which has a very fine ethnographic division. I provided all the necessary garments, a drum and other paraphernalia. The shamanist performance took place before a small group of specialists, scholars, and students. A physician was also present who testified at the end of the shaman's trance that Zamatkinov had really lost consciousness.

The librarian at the Institute of Living Oriental Languages was Maria Kotwicz and the director of the library was Il'ya Petrovich Murzaev, who was also the director of the library of Petrograd University. He was an expert on librarianship and a very learned man who knew literature especially well and bibliography better than anyone else I knew. You could have asked him about books in any field, and he would give you several titles right off the top of his head. He was, however, an extremely filthy person, unwashed and unkempt. He never had any handkerchiefs but he blew his nose with his hand the way the Russian peasants did. Once when I met him we greeted each other by shaking hands. My right hand was so completely wet with his mucus that I had to go instantly to the washroom to wash it off.

In the summer of 1921 the institute sent me, together with the Kalmuck students, to their country where they were to vacation and I was to acquire a working knowledge of the Kalmuck language. We arrived in Astrakhan near which there were some Kalmuck settlements. I remained some time in Astrakhan in order to get everything I needed for my trip to the steppe and to make the acquaintance of the local Kalmuck administration. The Kalmuck head of the local government was Doctor Dushan. Another important person was Arshi Chapchaev, and I also remember a certain Lijiev and Liji Karvenov. They were representatives of the Kalmuck intellectuals and active in the Kalmuck government. Most of them did not know very much about administration. The one exception was a Russian named V. P. Porokh, the head of the Department of Education. Porokh had been an old teacher who knew all about schools and the routine ways of administering them.

I was issued papers which allowed us to travel to the steppe, and I went to stay among the Kalmucks living in a place called Khoshutovka near Astrakhan. I lived there in the local school because there were no other accommodations. Soon, however, I developed dysentery and malaria and had to return to Petrograd. After a long period of convalescence, I developed very bad boils on my spine so that a surgeon had to lance them. This trip weakened me very badly, and I even developed tuberculosis. Fortunately, it was stopped in its initial stage, although I still have fibrous scars on one of my lungs.

One day back in Petrograd I met my professor Lev Shternberg who asked me, "What's wrong with you? You look so pale." I told him that I had contracted tuberculosis and he immediately offered to help me. He telephoned his brother Aaron, a medical doctor, who was in charge of all tuberculosis sanatoria in the Leningrad area and I was assigned to one of them. I rested there for more than a month, had plenty of milk, eggs and other foods which ordinary people could not get, and I soon recovered. I was indebted to Professor Shternberg for a second time. First he had obtained a job for me and now he had saved me from the ravages of tuberculosis.

In February 1921 I graduated from Petrograd University and received a diploma which would be equivalent to an American M.A. The Russian system was similar to the British one. I remember that many years later when the University of London awarded a B.A. degree with honors in Turkish to my younger son Nicholas, it was recognized as equivalent to an American master's degree. My very last examination was in psychology. Professor Vitalii Stepanovich

Serebrennikov was my teacher in this subject. He was a very kind
man and a good lecturer. He used as his textbook William James's
book *Psychology* and based his own lectures on James's theories.
The examination took place in the morning between ten and twelve.

I remember the day clearly because in the afternoon as I was
returning home, I heard gun salvoes in the distance. Later I learned
that the sailors stationed in Kronshtat, the naval fortress of
Petrograd, had mutinied and demanded "Soviets without Communists." This was the beginning of the famous Kronshtat mutiny
which was very ominous for the Soviets because the rebels were
neither officers nor members of the privileged class but ordinary
sailors who had been drafted into the navy and had nothing to do
with the former ruling class. The Soviets mobilized a huge army
which marched across the frozen Gulf of Finland to try to take the
Kronshtat fortress. Artillery fire from Kronshtat broke up the ice,
and many Red Army soldiers drowned. After a savage battle
Kronshtat was taken. Some of the sailors were shot and others were
exiled, but most were pardoned. As a direct consequence of the
Kronshtat mutiny Lenin, who was still at the head of the Soviet
government at the time, proclaimed a new economic policy. Usually
referred to by its acronym NEP, this policy allowed free trade. It
also permitted the peasants, who previously were required to hand
over their entire harvest, to keep everything except a small portion
which they had to deliver to the state as a tax in kind.

Lenin's NEP also brought about an improvement, albeit
indirectly, to my family's life. In 1918 or early 1919 our furniture
and all other belongings in our apartment had been expropriated, and
several persons had been billeted in various parts of our large
apartment. In 1921 all our belongings were returned to us, and
although the house itself remained city property, we got our entire
apartment back. In addition, the population of Petrograd was
changing. On the eve of the revolution the city was bursting at the
seams with refugees and even before the war it had a population of
1.5 million. After 1918 people were leaving the city in droves, and
there was a mere half a million remaining. Those who had stayed in
our apartment either found larger quarters or left the city

altogether, and as a result my mother, sister, and I once again had all seven large rooms of our apartment at our disposal.

I had started out as an assistant at the Geographical Institute in 1919 and became concurrently a teacher of Mongolian subjects at the Institute of Living Oriental Languages in 1920. In 1921 I took on another job. The Asian Museum of the Academy of Sciences took me on as an assistant researcher because the museum's director, Sergei Fedorovich Ol'denburg, had known me and obviously expected good work from me and was confident that a good scholarly career lay before me. My job was to catalog and describe Mongolian manuscripts and xylographs, but I also was authorized to write articles or a book on any subject of my own choosing. The museum's collection of Mongolian manuscripts and xylographs was probably the largest in the world outside Mongolia, where there were many more manuscripts, but which were unnumbered and uncatalogued.[6] I happened upon a large number of manuscripts devoted to fire worship, and these I both catalogued and investigated. The result was published in an article in *Asia Major*.[7]

The Mongolian section of the Asian Museum also housed many individual collections made by scholars. One of the larger older collections was that of Schilling von Canstadt. Of the newer collections, Tsyben Zhamtsarano's and Rudnev's were the best. In 1925 a large new collection was purchased from the widow of the well-known Mongolist Aleksei Matveevich Pozdneev, former professor at St. Petersburg University and then director of the Oriental Institute in Vladivostok. The Academy of Sciences bought a large number of his Mongolian manuscripts, xylographs, books, and manuscripts of his unpublished works. When I catalogued these materials, my attention was drawn to a huge manuscript which contained the restored Mongolian text of the *Secret History of the Mongols*. The famous Sinologist Palladius had made this transcription from a Mongolian text of 1240 transliterated in Chinese and also added an interlineal translation in Russian. Palladius had given his manuscript to Pozdneev for publication, but Pozdneev published only a few excerpts, not even mentioning that Palladius had given him the entire manuscript. Pozdneev even published an article in the

Zhurnal Ministerstva Narodnogo Prosveshcheniva (Journal of the Ministry of Education) on the system of transliterating Chinese characters using Russian phonetic symbols, along with a list of Chinese characters, on the basis of Palladius. Although I remember the Latin saying *de mortuis aut nihil aut bene*, I cannot help but point out Pozdneev's behavior in this case.

I discovered very soon other incontrovertible evidence of plagiarism among Pozdneev's manuscripts, namely the first two volumes of his lectures on the history of Mongolian literature, which were published in lithographed form in the 1890s.[8] They turned out to be the doctoral dissertation of a certain Georgii Kokh (German Koch), a student of German extraction, who had developed tuberculosis and died before he could defend his dissertation. He had submitted his dissertation to Pozdneev, who kept it for a rather long time, as was customary in Russia in those days. I know of cases where doctoral candidates submitted their dissertations to professors, and the dissertations would lie around their professors' offices, sometimes as long as five or six years. In this instance, Pozdneev was shrewd enough to keep Kokh's dissertation until everyone who had ever known Kokh had graduated from the university before he published it in his own name. This flagrant case of plagiarism has never been mentioned, and I consider it my duty to bring it to the attention of historians of Mongolian Studies.

S. A. Kozin, the man who later published Palladius's manuscript with his own rather unsatisfactory commentaries and glossaries,[9] told me more about Pozdneev. Perhaps I should first say a few words about Kozin himself. He was a student of Chinese and Mongolian in the late 1890s and early 1900s, and later became the administrator *(popechitel'*, lit. guardian) of the Kalmuck region. Kozin had been Pozdneev's student and later, when Kozin was already in the Kalmuck area managing Kalmuck affairs, Pozdneev arrived one day in order to do field work among the Kalmucks and asked Kozin to assist him. Pozdneev spent a night in a rich Kalmuck's *ger* (yurt) and the next morning, before leaving, he slipped a silver statuette of a Buddha into his suitcase. The Kalmuck saw this and, without saying a word, opened the suitcase and took out his statue. This incident demonstrates that Pozdneev was by no means an honest soul. Pozdneev was a well-known and prolific scholar. I doubt that everything he ever wrote was plagiarized, because there were not enough Mongolists at that time who could have supplied him with works in such different fields as history, language, and folklore of the Mongols, but some of his publications are definitely the work of other persons.

In 1921 I acquired yet another job. I became an associate professor (*dotsent* in Russian) of Mongolian at Petrograd University. Since 1919 I had also been a salaried member of the Commission of Toponymics at the Academy of Material Culture, the former Imperial Archeological Commission. The Commission of Toponymics was headed by Professor A. F. Braun, the former director of the Imperial Philological Institute which was almost next door to Petrograd University, but it was the famous Slavicist and member of the Academy of Sciences, Professor Aleksei Aleksandrovich Shakhmatov, who offered me the latter job. He had been a member of the Commission of Toponymics and needed someone who knew Finnish, because geographical names in European Russia are to a large extent of Finnish origin, dating from the time when the Finns occupied a more southerly area than they do at present. Shakhmatov himself knew Mordvinian, a language related to Finnish, very well, had published a large collection of materials on Mordvinian folklore, and was interested in Finno-Ugric languages in general.[10] I was to investigate the river names of the Il'men' basin. The Il'men' is a lake in the Novgorod area, and many of the rivers which flow in and out of that lake and their affluents have Finnish names. I compiled a complete catalog of the names of those rivers and their geographical coordinates, but the catalog was never published.

I always seemed to have several jobs at once, but that was customary in Russia then because living expenses were extremely high and a single salary was totally inadequate. On the other hand, as a result of hundreds of thousands of intellectuals having fled from Russia, there was a serious shortage of specialists. I kept all my jobs until 1923 when the Commission of Toponymics was disbanded. The famous Shakhmatov died in 1920 or 1921, I am not sure when.

He had been living in an unheated apartment and had to haul his own
firewood on a sleigh across Petrograd. This proved too much for him
and he died of exhaustion. The commission's demise proved to be to
my advantage later when the study of such things as Finnish river
names in Russia became dangerous. This kind of investigation would
be interpreted as an attempt to hand the country over to the Finns!
I remember a geologist who had written about the Leningrad area
being part of the Fenno-Scandinavian continent, which is the correct
geological name for that region. He was severely criticized for
trying to make the Leningrad area a province of Finland and for
wanting to yield it to the Finnish Fascists!

Another event of 1921 was my first meeting with my future
wife. One day when I went to the Asian Museum to work on cataloguing Mongolian manuscripts I saw a young lady hitherto unknown
to me. Since no one introduced me to her, I just minded my own
business. But when I saw her again the next day, I realized that she
had joined the museum staff, and so I introduced myself. She replied,
"Oh, I've heard of you. I am pleased to make your acquaintance. I
am Nataliya Belolipskaya." We became good friends, she invited me
often to her apartment, or rather, to the part of an apartment which
she shared with many other people, and she told me her life story.
Both her father, a general, and her younger sister, Tat'yana, had
emigrated to Yugoslavia. Her mother had died of breast cancer.
During the first world war her father had been on the Caucasian
front where he was in charge of all captured Turkish weapons. The
family had several estates in various parts of Russia, and her father
had taught at a military school before the war and was also a
member of the Commission of History of Russia's armed forces.
When the civil war broke out, he joined Baron Vrangel's army in the
Crimea. His family was with him. Nataliya had been a nurse at a
military hospital during the war and in the ensuing civil war she
worked as nurse on a train that picked up wounded soldiers and
transported them to the nearest hospital. One day the Reds cut the
line and the train stopped somewhere in southern Russia. They did
not harm her or the wounded White army soldiers and officers, but
demanded that they also take on wounded Red army soldiers and

take them to the nearest hospital in the Red-held territory. Also on that train was a certain Kitti Drozhdzhinskaya, the daughter of the former director of a Russian high school in the Caucasus. The chief surgeon was Doctor P. I. Silin. When Nataliya found herself in Red Russia she had no choice but to go on doing work as a Red army hospital nurse.

Meanwhile, Vrangel's army had been defeated, and he and his generals fled the Crimea via Turkey to Yugoslavia. Tat'yana went with her father there, but her mother adamantly refused to leave until she had found her Nataliya. Nataliya had no place to stay, so she went to Kislovodsk in the northern Caucasus where Kitti's parents lived, and took a job as nurse in a sanatorium for mental patients. Later she wrote to her sister's godfather in Petrograd who notified her that her mother had returned to Petrograd and was living in their old apartment. Nataliya went to Petrograd and joined her mother. She also met a friend of hers, V. A. Ebermann, who was an Arabicist and had studied at the university when I was a student there. They had been friends since their childhood as they were neighbors during vacations. Ebermann recommended her as a librarian to the Asian Museum where he was working, for at that time they needed someone who knew languages, and Nataliya was excellent in German, French, and English and could catalog books as well.

When she was working as a nurse in the mental hospital in the Caucasus, she had one particularly unpleasant experience. Among the inmates was a former Cheka (Soviet secret police) commissar who had become insane after executing a Russian Orthodox priest. He had led the priest along a corridor in the basement of the Cheka jail and then ordered the priest to stop. While the priest was crossing himself, he aimed his revolver at the priest's neck and fired, but the priest did not move. He shot again and again until he had emptied the whole magazine, but the priest remained standing. The commissar emitted a loud shriek, collapsed and lost his mind. What had actually happened was that he had severed a nerve in the priest's body so that the priest had been paralyzed for a brief moment and was thus kept from falling even after death. The commissar did not, of course, realize this but instead imagined that a miracle had occurred, and that the priest might be a saint and that he, the commissar, had committed some unpardonable sin.

Nataliya's happiness at being with her mother was short-lived because her mother was already very ill from cancer. Surgery was performed by Dr. A. A. Ebermann, the father of Nataliya's friend and a well-known surgeon. He did his best, but the cancer already had progressed too far and the metastases had spread to the whole body. Nataliya's mother died in December 1921.

At that time I received from Vladimirtsov some interesting material on the old Mongolian language. He had obtained this material from Bartol'd who had been working on an Arabic manuscript composed by Ḥamd'ullāh Qazwīnī in the fourteenth century entitled *Nuzhāt al-Qulūb* (The Delight of Hearts). This work deals with the geography and cosmography of many countries. Among other things, the manuscript contains a short glossary of Mongolian words, to be exact, names of animals written phonetically in Arabic script as the author had heard those words spoken. It is more or less a phonetical transcription of spoken Mongolian of the fourteenth century. Before starting my work, I, of course, asked for Bartol'd's permission to use this material because he had not given it directly to me. He kindly consented, and I published my work later.[11] That list of animal names was the first and last research material Vladimirtsov ever gave me.

The year 1923 was important. First, I received my master's degree. My examination comittee was chaired by the dean, D. K. Petrov, professor of Spanish language and literature and a brilliant scholar in Arabic studies. The other members of the committee were Kotwicz, Vladimirtsov, Samoilovich and Ol'denburg, the latter acting for Bartol'd who was at that time in England working on some manuscripts in the British Museum. The questions did not cause any difficulties and I passed the examination easily. It is interesting to note the very friendly atmosphere of the examination, which was held in the presence of the entire faculty of History and Philology. About forty full professors and many associate professors attended. The dean opened the meeting by saying, "The first item on our agenda will be the master's examination of a certain Nikolai Poppe

80

who comes from a good family, his father having been Imperial consul-general in China and also a graduate from our university." Three years later the university was proletarianized and many professors of political subjects such as Marxism were hired. They were party members without master's or doctoral degrees, and an introduction such as Dean Petrov's became impossible. Soon a step further was taken. Degrees themselves were abolished and therefore, no one took examinations. In 1923, however, the university was still the same good old university that it had always been. As to Dean Petrov, he committed suicide in 1924. After passing my examination I worked as an associate professor at the university and the Institute of Living Oriental Languages and as a research scholar at the Asian Museum.

Later that year another important event in my life occurred. I had known Nataliya for two years but had not thought to marry her until the following event occurred. One day in December 1923 Nataliya asked me to come to her apartment because she had something important to tell me. When I arrived the next evening, she told me that a man had visited her who had secretly slipped across the border from Estonia and brought her a letter from her father. He had also enclosed one hundred American dollars—quite a fortune in those days—and asked her to join him and Tat'yana in Belgrade. Such secret border crossings were commonplace. Our professor of Japanese, S. G. Eliseev, left Russia in 1920 or early 1921 illegally. One night a motorboat was sent by some of his friends or relatives in Finland and moored at the Nikolaevskii Bridge across the Neva river. Eliseev, together with his wife and children, went to the boat as if they were going on a pleasure cruise. The only things they carried were valuables hidden in their clothes. Then the boat left, and within an hour they were in Finland having successfully eluded the Soviet coast guard. Later Eliseev went to France and taught at the University of Paris, and still later he moved to Harvard University. Another case of a successful escape was that of my future second wife. In 1920 she walked across the frozen Gulf of Finland from south to north, and once having reached Finland, she continued via Sweden to Germany where I met her during World War II.

Nataliya's news was like lightning from a clear sky. I suddenly felt that she should not leave and everything possible should be done in order to prevent this. I went home, thought the whole situation over, and wrote her a long letter in which I described the miserable life of emigrants abroad and reminded her that she had a good job at the library of the Academy of Sciences. Then I added, as the *pièce de résistance*, that I could not live without her, and I asked her to marry me. I gave her the letter the next day when both of us were returning from work. It was a Saturday. On Monday she thanked me for the letter but added that she could not give me an answer as yet because she had to think it over. One whole week passed without an answer from her, and it was almost the last day of 1923. Suddenly she invited me to her home. I asked her eagerly whether she had made her decision and she simply replied, "Yes." I asked again, "And what is the answer?" "I will stay." We became engaged, I introduced her to my mother and sister, and on Monday, May 5, 1924, we went to the city registrar's office with our witnesses. Our wedding took place in church on Sunday, May 11. Father Fedor, who would later also baptize our eldest son, officiated. After the church ceremony we celebrated at the apartment of Tat'yana's godfather, the former Senator D. F. Ognev. There we had a dinner party with wine and champagne for about twenty relatives and closest friends. Afterwards I took Nataliya to our large apartment in the house where we lived. Her belongings, which had already been moved long before, included some beautiful furniture, crystal, rugs, and paintings, and we furnished our part of the apartment quite elegantly. News of our marriage soon spread through the Asian Museum, and we held another dinner party for twelve of our friends from the museum.

Toward the end of summer we went on our honeymoon to Kislovodsk, the city which had played such an important role in Nataliya's life. It was my first trip to the Caucasus. I was impressed by the high mountains, the southern vegetation, and the beautiful scenery. For the first time I saw the Caucasians, a proud people, riding their horses, wearing very peculiar garments—long caftans and high fur caps—carrying rifles and daggers which they were at that time still allowed to carry. Later these weapons were confiscated, and only members of hunter's unions were permitted to have any kind of weapon.

We returned from our honeymoon at the end of September, to find that Leningrad, as the city had been renamed after Lenin's death in January 1924, was flooded and most downtown streets were under water for a day or two. Nataliya and I returned to work at the Asian Museum. Together with my additional salary at the Institute of Living Oriental Languages and at the university, we lived very well in the rather large apartment which we shared with my mother and unmarried sister who was still attending the university.

In April or May 1925 something unpleasant happened. Several of my articles appeared in *Asia Major*.[12] Professor V. M. Alekseev, the Sinologist, had been to Europe in 1924 and had there met Bruno Schindler and Friedrich Weller, the editors of the journal, who asked him to send articles and to suggest that his colleagues in the Soviet Union do so as well. Alekseev's invitation to contribute articles to *Asia Major* did not evoke great enthusiasm among the scholars in Leningrad, partly because very few could write in any language but Russian. I wrote my articles in 1924 and they appeared in the spring of 1925. They were my first articles to be published outside of Russia and, of course, I was very happy. Shortly thereafter we had a party and I invited Professors Alekseev and Vladimirtsov and their wives and some other scholars. Among them was Dr. F. A. Rozenberg, a specialist in Iranian languages who had published a number of works on the Sogdian language and was very well known abroad. He was also a very kind and pleasant person with excellent manners, a gentleman from tip to toe. The party went very well and everyone was in high spirits. Only Vladimirtsov sat with a morose expression on his face. When I met him again at the museum several days later, he only said, "I would like to talk to you." I went to his office where he told me that he was very surprised to see my articles in *Asia Major*, because he had intended to write on the same subjects and send them to some journals for publication. I answered that these subjects could be written about by more than one scholar because such topics could be discussed from different points of view and, in any event, my articles had not exhausted the subjects. It was a very strained conversation, and while our subsequent relations remained correct, our old friendship was never restored. I have often thought about this, but could never satisfactorily resolve why Vladimirtsov started that unpleasant conversation. Was he envious that I, a rank beginner in the field, had published several articles in a prestigious foreign journal and he had not? Did he resent my ability to write in good German while his command of foreign languages was insufficient? I still do not know for sure and I would prefer to look no further, lest I would find an unpleasant explanation for his actions.

In 1926 the first International Turcological Congress convened in Baku. I had been approached by some Turkic scholars and political leaders, who came to Leningrad together with a scholar of Estonian descent, a certain Siefeld-Simumägi. They had first asked my teacher of Turcology, Professor Samoilovich, whom he would recommend to present papers on certain subjects, and he mentioned my name. So in March I went to Baku with Samoilovich, my professor of linguistics Shcherba, my friend Anatolii Nestorovich Genko, who was a specialist in Caucasian languages, Malov, and another Turcologist by the name of K. K. Yudakhin. We went by train via Moscow. It was a pleasant journey, and the meetings in Baku were very interesting. I met many scholars and leaders of the Turks in the Soviet Union. Among the foreigners there was the famous Turkish scholar Köprülü Zade Fuad Bey, the German Theodor Menzel, the Hungarian Gyula Mészaros and others. The congress made a great impression on me because it was the first international congress I ever attended. I should mention a minor unpleasant incident which occurred in Baku. The Russian organizers of the banquet in our hotel had not taken into consideration the fact that the Turks, especially the Turks from the various Soviet Republics, being Moslems, did not eat pork. Therefore they were unable to eat the ham, sausages and other pork products of which the banquet mainly consisted.

4 Research Among the Mongols

Early in 1926 I was officially notified by the chairman of the Mongolian Commission of the Academy of Sciences that I would be sent to the Mongolian People's Republic to conduct research. This was a very happy event. I had been very anxious to travel to Mongolia ever since that commission had been established. Now my dream was about to come true. Only one circumstance somewhat lessened my happiness, and that was the thought that I would be separated for a while from our little son Valerian, named after his grandfather, who was going to spend his first summer in the country-side in Berngardovka near Leningrad.

In May 1926 Vladimirtsov, Alekseev and I went by train via Moscow to Verkhneudinsk, now called Ulan-Udè, the capital of the Buryat Autonomous Republic in Eastern Siberia. There we spent a few days and were joined by our Buryat student Balji Bambaev. Saddles had to be purchased in Verkhneudinsk because in Mongolia one could only get Mongolian saddles which were rather uncomfort-able. After buying a few saddles, we took a riverboat up the Selenga River to the Mongolian border. After thirty-six hours we arrived at Ust' Kyakhta (Mouth of the Kyakhta) and from there we went by horsedrawn coach to Troitskosavsk, a rather old and large town. Bambaev temporarily left us there, for he had to cross the border illegally. During the civil war he, like many Buryats, had fought as a Cossack officer on the anti-Communist side. His home village was in the Selenga area, and the local Buryats were Cossacks. For this reason Bambaev could not obtain a Soviet travel passport and an exit visa. When on the following day the three of us had crossed the border at the checkpoint and moved about 300 meters into the Mongolian border town Altan Bulag (Golden Spring), Bambaev was already there waiting for us. He had managed to slip across the border undetected only about 300 or 400 meters from the checkpoint. If he had been detected, the punishment would have been severe because he carried a pistol.

In Ulaanbaatar, the capital of Mongolia, there was no hotel so we were accommodated in a local school. Ulaanbaatar was a typical Chinese town. There were numerous Buddhist temples and monasteries, Chinese shops and restaurants *(kuantzu)* and only a few Russian-style houses. It was an interesting city. The former palace of the late Jebtsundamba Khutuktu (Living Buddha) who had died in 1924 had been turned into a museum and contained many interesting and valuable exhibits. There was also a stuffed elephant which, when he was still alive, had been presented to the Living Buddha by the Tsarist government. On the day of the elephant's arrival a large crowd of believers gathered and was greatly impressed when the elephant knelt in front of the Living Buddha and bowed his head. As it turned out, the elephant had been purchased from a circus where he had learned many tricks, but the believers marveled at a beast which seemingly could recognize a true saint!

Vladimirtsov and Alekseev went on to Peking where Vladimirtsov bought some Mongolian books and Alekseev did some research of his own. Afterwards they went by ship to Europe and from there back to the Soviet Union. In the meantime Bambaev and I bought some horses, found a guide who knew the country and hired several Buryat servants. We also had to buy some dry foods such as noodles, rice, macaroni, canned foods, tea, sugar and the like. We then set out in the direction of the Erdeni Dzuu monastery on the banks of the Orkhon River. First we arrived at Ching Tolgoi, a man-made mound about 100 feet high which had been a Kitan fortress. We found there the lower part of a stele in the shape of a turtle. The inscription, however, was missing, and we were told by the local Mongols that it had already been missing thirty years earlier when some "Russians" had been investigating that area. Those "Russians" were actually Radloff and his companions on their Orkhon expedition of 1891. From Ching Tolgoi we went to the well-known ruins of the Tsagaan baishing, a temple built on the left bank of the Tuula River, west of Ulaanbaatar, in the seventeenth century by Tsogtu Taiji, a prince famous in the history of Mongolia's struggle for independence. The inscription found there had been published with a German translation by Georg Huth in 1894.[1] We searched for other inscriptions and found one chiseled in a rock on behalf of Tsogtu Taiji in 1627. In 1929 I published this inscription in my report on my journey.[2] We continued our travels and arrived at Kharuukhyn Khar Balgas (The Black Ruins at the Kharuukha River) which had been a temple of the Red Hat sect many years ago. There was also a rather well-preserved *caitya*, (in Mongolian *suburgan*), a shrine with a cupola, in which often sacred books and medicinal herbs were preserved. The most interesting place we saw up to then was Khöshöö Tsaidam, where the famous Ancient Turkic Orkhon inscriptions of the eighth century are located. The inscriptions were still there but many letters were already obliterated by cattle rubbing against the stele. Birds had also done their share, filling the chiseled letters with their excrement which in the course of time became hard as cement and could not be scraped out of the letters without damage to the stone.

From there we moved on to the ruins of the ancient Uighur city of Khara Balgasun, and from there we went upstream on the Orkhon to the Erdeni Dzuu monastery which had been founded by Abatai Khan in 1586. At that time several hundred lamas were living at Erdeni Dzuu. The lamas were not overtly hostile to us but they were uncooperative and disliked our plan of photographing inscriptions and making rubbings. We were invited to see the head lama, and he asked us who we were and how we had traveled. He then asked, *inter alia*, whether we had passed through the country of the dog-headed people. These lamas struck me as utterly ignorant of the outside world. They even argued with us about whether the sun was going around the earth or vice versa and insisted that the sun circled the earth.

87

There was great splendor and magnificent art in the monastery's numerous temples, but there was also much filth. The lamas by no means observed the rule of celibacy, and near the monastery there were *ger* inhabited by women whom the lamas visited. The rate of venereal disease must have been high.

While staying near Erdeni Dzuu, I witnessed the Tsam ceremony for the first time. This event consists of masked dances and pantomime on subjects taken from the Buddhist legends, and it was interesting to see how the ordinary Mongols completely misunderstood the meaning of the ceremony. They believed Tsam to be a kind of divine service and even took blessings from the actors by touching them with the crowns of their heads, even though some of the performers actually represented a deer or some other animal which was hunted by one of the other characters.

During the Tsam performance a serious accident occurred. The rifle of one of the artists, an eighteenth-century muzzle loader, exploded and severely damaged the palm of his hand. He was bleeding profusely, and there was no physician on hand, the lama medics being of no help because they did not know anything about surgery. I therefore assumed the role of a surgeon. I could tell that the bones of the hand, in this case the metacarpus, had not been damaged. I disinfected the wound with a strong solution of potassium permanganate and stopped the bleeding by using a tourniquet. I then made numerous stitches with an ordinary needle, having no surgical needle with me, and could only hope that the man might retain the use of his fingers.

After leaving Erdeni Dzuu we photographed ancient monuments, made rubbings, and collected examples of colloquial Mongolian language and folklore. The Mongols were still very superstitious at that time. They were not afraid of being photographed or being asked questions—on the contrary, they were flattered by such attention—but they strongly resented any actions of ours which, in their opinion, might anger the "lords of the place" (Tibetan *sabdag*, Sanskrit *lokapala*), i.e., spirits dwelling in certain locations such as a particular rock. Once I tried to make a rubbing from an inscription on a stele which was lying on the ground. The side facing up bore a

Chinese inscription and it seemed easy to make a rubbing of it. When I turned the stele over, two long snakes crawled out and slithered away. My rubbing did not turn out well, and the Mongols were triumphant, saying "You see, you disturbed the lords, and this is your punishment."

I could speak Mongolian and read Tibetan, and this impressed the Mongols. In fact, by the time of this, my first trip to Mongolia, I could already speak Mongolian quite fluently. Since 1924 a young Mongol named Gombojab, who was the son of the late prince Mergen Gün, had lived in my apartment in Leningrad. He was in Leningrad to learn Russian, and while I taught him Russian I also learned to speak Mongolian—*docendo discimus*. Gombojab, who was Zhamtsarano's protégé, later went to Paris to study with Paul Pelliot, the famous Sinologist, Iranist, Mongolist, and Turcologist, and became a research scholar in his own right. In 1937, during the Great Purge, he was arrested and "liquidated." His wife Oyun Bilig, a young Buryat, and their two children, Dzoriktu and Biliktu, were exiled to the Bashkir area in the Volga region.

As for the Mongol people themselves, they were rather filthy. They never washed and those few who wore any underwear at all rarely changed it. They were lazy but also very honest. This last trait can be illustrated by the following examples. The Mongols never had any loose change. When I had to buy something, for example, a sheep to replenish my food supply, I had to pay the exact amount. Therefore I had to carry with me a wooden chest filled with Mongolian equivalents of nickels, dimes, and quarters. The Mongols were inquisitive. Each time we arrived at a place, they would ask: "What is in this box?" and "What is this?" When my guide Dagva told them it was money, they marveled and insisted on seeing it. In one of the places I visited I learned that there was an inscription on a rock somewhere about sixty miles away. I wanted to see it so I made plans to go there on horseback and return next day. "What shall I do with my box of silver coins?" I asked Dagva. He replied: "Leave it here. Nothing will happen." I did as he suggested and when Dagva and I returned the next day, everything was in perfect order. No one had taken anything.

In light of my experience I am inclined to believe this next story which was told to me by a bank clerk in Ulaanbaatar. The bank had sent silver bullion to a certain mint in the Soviet Union to have coins made. The coins came back in large sacks loaded on a truck. On the way the sacks rubbed against each other. One sack got a hole in it, and some coins spilled onto the road. The accompanying bank officer finally noticed this, and turned the truck back. He encountered a caravan and asked the headman whether he had seen money spilled on the road. "Oh, yes, we did," he answered, "it's still there." They went farther and, indeed, the money still lay on the road. Later when the money was counted only a few coins were missing. They must have rolled into the high grass by the side of the road.

The third example of Mongolian honesty took place on the steppe. I had been there for two months and had had no opportunity to send a letter or telegram to my wife in Leningrad. One day I met a Mongol who was riding on horseback to Ulaanbaatar. I asked him if he would send a telegram for me and he agreed, so I gave him money and the text of the telegram. A week later I met a Chinese on a mule-drawn cart who was also en route to Ulaanbaatar. Just to be sure I asked him to send a telegram and gave him money. Still later a Russian truck driver came along. I gave him money, a tip, and the text of my telegram. Two months later when I returned to Ulaanbaatar and was walking just across from the telegraph office, who should I meet but the Mongol. He greeted me cheerfully like an old friend and said: "Here's your money back. I didn't have time to get to the telegraph office." When I returned to Leningrad, I asked Nataliya whether she had received two telegrams in July. "No, just one," was the answer. I asked her to show me the telegram. It was the one sent by the Chinese who was apparently also an honest person. And the Russian truck driver? Let him have the benefit of the doubt: perhaps he sent the telegram but it got lost on the way.

Besides having this precious quality of honesty, the Mongols were also hospitable. Whenever we were passing a settlement, even if the *ger* were as much as a mile or more off our path, Mongols immediately came to us on horseback with large *dombo*, jug-shaped pots, filled with tea or *airig*, fermented mare's milk, for us to drink.

People everywhere told us stories, legends, and epics. They recited verses and songs so willingly that both Bambaev and I collected a large amount of folklore material. While in Erdeni Dzuu we also investigated the site of the former capital of Old Mongolia, Karakorum, which had been founded in 1220 and later, after Chingis Khan's death in 1227, became the capital of Mongolia. The site is quite near the monastery and we could see many small mounds, which indicated housing sites, and found numerous fragments of chinaware.

From Erdeni Dzuu we went to Ulaanbaatar and from there returned to Leningrad. This was my first and last expedition with Balji Bambaev. Later he graduated and returned to his native Buryatia where he got a job as a research scholar at the Learned Committee in Ulan Udè. Balji was arrested in the 1930s and jailed in Ulan Udè, but he was fortunate in having a friend among the prison laborers. One day his friend came to empty the septic tank in the section of the jail where Balji was held. He filled the receiving tank only halfway, placed Balji in it and in this manner smuggled him out of jail. His friend took the tank to a spot on the Selenga River far away from the city, where soap and a set of clean clothes awaited Balji. After a good bath, Balji Bambaev headed towards Manchuria, and he was never heard of again. It is possible that he made it to China and lived there for a long time, but he may also have perished at the time, either in Manchuria or on the way to the border.

I returned to Leningrad in late September 1926 and started preparing my materials for publication. During the summer my little son Valerian had grown and he was a friendly and good-natured child. He hardly ever cried and was in good health. Of course, he was not immune to colds and children's diseases. One day Nataliya and I went to a party and while we were gone the little fellow started running a fever. My mother was very concerned about this and called Dr. Grinberg. It was a good thing that my mother had recognized the danger and called him, because our physician found that something was also wrong with Valerian's ears. The next day we called our ear doctor Goldshtein and soon everything was all right again. Our Valerian was also an intelligent child. He was no more than a year and a half old when he uttered his first words. It was summer and the three of us were living in a rented summer cottage in Berngardovka. One day I was walking about with him perched on my arm, when he pointed in the direction of some bee hives standing behind a fence and said "bee houses." Such words are rarely spoken by children of his age, and I wonder where he had ever heard these words which are so different from the first words children ordinarily say.

My second trip to Mongolia was particularly successful and took place in 1927. I went with my colleague and friend V. A. Kazakevich, who had been a year behind me in school, and Garma Sanzheev, a Buryat who at that time was a student at the Institute of Living Oriental Languages. We left in the middle of May and traveled via Ulan Udè and Altan Bulag to Ulaanbaatar. There we separated. Kazakevich went to Dariganga, a region in the southern part of Mongolia, and Sanzheev went to the Darkhats, a Mongolian tribe inhabiting the area near Lake Khöbsögöl (Kossogol) in the northern part of the country. I remained, however, in Ulaanbaatar for about six weeks, studying Dagur, a language of special interest, because it has preserved some features of Middle Mongolian, the language of the twelfth to sixteenth centuries. In Ulaanbaatar I also found some Bargu Buryats who lived in the northwestern corner of Manchuria, speakers of Kharchin, Ordos, and the dialect spoken in Ulaan Tsab, all three in Inner, i.e., Chinese, Mongolia. I published my Dagur grammar in 1930, and the Bargu Buryat materials appeared as an article in 1931.[3]

I left Ulaanbaatar at the end of June and went on horseback to the area adjacent to the Russian border. A few days after my departure from Ulaanbaatar I fell ill with dysentery, and the local Mongols suggested I eat boiled dog testicles which, according to their witch doctors, was the best medicine. I refused to take this sort of medicine and instead took castor oil and drank strong tea, not eating solid food at all for a few days. This helped and I soon recovered. I went via Kui to the upper reaches of the Kharaa River and spent a couple of weeks in the beautiful hilly and wooded area on the Tüngeliin gol which comes down from the Khentei mountains. It is possible that this river is the one mentioned in the *Secret History of the Mongols* (1240). I collected a large number of songs and even some epics in this region. From there I went to the Amar Bayaskhalant Khiid monastery (The Monastery of Peace and Joy) on the banks of the Orkhon river and saw the relics of one of the first Jebtsundamba Khutuktus, i.e., the Living Buddhas of Mongolia. From there I went on to Chuluut where I wrote down a number of tales and a few epics. I met a shaman in Chuluut, my first and last shaman in Mongolia, and managed to write down some of his incantations. I returned to Ulaanbaatar at the beginning of September.

My stay in Ulaanbaatar proved to be highly interesting, and not only from the scholarly point of view. My friend Kazakevich had the remarkable ability to get acquainted very quickly with all kinds of people. One of these acquaintances was a certain Persander. He claimed to be of Swedish origin but was a French citizen. He was one of several adventurers then still living in Ulaanbaatar. Later they were expelled from Mongolia and jailed in the Soviet Union. It was hard to say what Persander's specialty was, but his main occupation was investigating old houses in Ulaanbaatar so as to find the exact one where Baron Ungern-Sternberg had lived during the civil war. It was rumored that in 1921, just before his capture by the Soviets, the baron had hidden his treasure under the floor of one of the houses which he had occupied, and Persander was trying to find that treasure.

In 1927 there were still many foreigners in Ulaanbaatar. I remember the Norwegian Oskar Mamen, an American by the name of Carter, a German Dr. Rot (or Roth), and many Russian merchants from Harbin, most of them of Jewish extraction. The Chinese were the most numerous of all the foreigners and, at least in my experience, also the most reliable. They were punctual. For instance, once I ordered a big book chest from a Chinese carpenter and asked him to deliver it as early as possible the next day. The man brought the chest around four o'clock in the morning when it was still pitch dark.

In the following year, 1928, I went to Buryat Mongolia. I chose to study the Alar Buryats, who lived in the western part of the then Buryat Mongolian Autonomous Republic of the Soviet Union. This region was also the homeland of Garma Sanzheev who had come to Leningrad in 1925 and had begun to study Mongolian under Vladimirtsov. Sanzheev was the first Buryat with whom I did research. He was my native informant. I wrote down a number of texts as he pronounced them and with his help I then translated them into Russian. Now in 1928, having thus acquired some knowledge of the language, I decided to go to his native place and do further study. The Alar area is thirty to forty kilometers from the Zabitui railroad station on the Trans-Siberian line, not far from Cheremkhovo, which has since become quite an industrial city. Sanzheev's village was called Taishin. In winter the Alar Buryats lived in villages of the Siberian-Russian type consisting of one or several streets fronted on both sides by log houses. Each house had several rooms and a roof made of clapboard. In summer, however, they lived in wooden *ger* in an area called Ülzeitü which is about twenty kilometers from Taishin. There I collected some epics, songs, and other folklore materials.

The Alar Buryats were semi-sedentary. They had been engaged in agriculture since the eighteenth century, but they had so many cattle that they had to pasture them far away from the fields. Therefore in summer they lived in large, mostly hexagonal wooden *ger* with floors, small openings in the walls which served as windows and large openings in the roofs through which the smoke escaped. The local Buryats were rather well-to-do. It was interesting to me that their farm hands and domestic servants were Russians. Garma's mother had died long before, and his father lived alone and was a heavy drinker. Garma had a half-brother, the son of his father's second wife. The Sanzheevs had been rich and had sold their cattle just in time so that later, when farms were collectivized they had almost no cattle at all. I lived in the *ger* of Garma's uncle Aleksei. It was a large and tidy *ger*, and I never noticed any vermin whereas

94

normally in Mongolian *ger* you inevitably were infested with lice within minutes after going inside.

For the first few days after my arrival the Buryats were mistrustful and obviously afraid that I might report on them if they said anything against the regime. They therefore tried to convince me what loyal Soviet citizens they were by telling me how happy they were and how much they owed to the Soviets for their happiness. Soon, however, they showed me old photographs in which they appeared in their best garments: the women in silk robes with golden coins sewn along the hems, and wearing precious necklaces. They said: "Formerly we used to wear beautiful garments, but we have hidden them so nobody can see them and now we try to look as poor as possible and wear only the worst garments we have." These, then, were their true feelings!

The Alar Buryats had been officially converted to Russian Orthodoxy but in actuality remained shamanist. It was strange to see them go to the Russian church, later to a Lamaist temple at a small lamasery and, finally, to a shamanistic service. Their explanation was quite logical: if one god does not help, the others might. The shamanism of the Alar Buryats contained some Buddhist and Christian elements of a later date. Once I had the opportunity to attend a *tailgan* (sacrifice) to the shamanist gods or spirits. Men came with their children, and their sisters who had married outside the clan were present as well. Wives, that is, women who had married into the clan, did not attend the ceremony. This is due to exogamy: the wives had to have come from other clans, as men could not marry women of their own clan. Therefore, wives would customarily return to their home clans to conduct their own sacrifices to their clan deities.

Several shamans were present. A mare was slaughtered and part of the meat was offered to the deities along with libations of *arsi* (the Alar form of Buryat *arkhi)*, an alcoholic beverage distilled from sour milk. The remaining meat was distributed among the participants. To my surprise, I also received a piece. This was because I was a guest of members of this clan but did not belong to any other clan. One might surmise that only members of other clans were excluded from the sacrifices, and that belonging to another clan was a more serious reason for exclusion than having no clan affiliation whatsoever.

In Buryatia, conditions in the summer of 1928 were still rather normal. Shamans were not yet persecuted, and collective farms had not yet come into existence, although rumors about them were circulating. Once I was even approached by a teacher from Golumet', a Russian village. He wanted to know why collectivization was necessary. It was by no means easy to explain the situation and at the same time avoid criticism of the current policies of the Soviet government. Fortunately his daughter, a pretty but extremely provincial girl of about eighteen, diverted the conversation in another direction, by asking me if I played the guitar.

After my return to Leningrad in August I worked on the materials collected and wrote a two-volume work entitled *Alarskii govor* (The Alar Dialect).[4] The first volume is the grammar of the dialect, the second is texts and Russian translations.

On August 25, 1928 my second son was born and we named him Nikolai (Nicholas). I had been a full professor at Leningrad University since 1925 and now, in 1928, I was also promoted to full professor at the Institute of Living Oriental Languages.

I went to Mongolia once more in May 1929. This turned out to be my last trip to Mongolia because after 1929 I could never get an exit visa. This time I only went for a short time and stayed in Ulaanbaatar where I continued my studies of Solon, Bargu, Ordos and Urat. These dialects were spoken mostly in Inner Mongolia, but many speakers also lived and worked in Ulaanbaatar. After sessions with my informants, I had time to do some sightseeing outside the city. Once I went to Bogdo Uula (Holy Mountain) and walked in a dense and beautiful forest. There were many caves with Buddhist pictures, and occasionally a wild animal appeared, for Bogdo Uula was a reservation where hunting and lumbering were prohibited. Another rule was that death sentences could not be carried out within sight of the mountain. Therefore, those who were to be shot were led into a depression behind a hill from where the mountain could not be seen, and were there executed.

I had also time to visit a few persons I knew. One of them was Dr. P. N. Shastin, a medical doctor. For a long time, Dr. Shastin had been the only European physician in Mongolia. In 1929 he was both head physician at a hospital for civilians and an army surgeon. Once I came to the Shastins for dinner, and Dr. Shastin had come home only a few minutes before and looked very tired. I asked him if he had had a very long, tiring day, and he replied that he had been examining recruits just drafted into the army. Of more than 150 men he had examined more than half showed very clear symptoms of hereditary syphillis.

I was not the only visitor in Shastin's home. Other scholars and members of research expeditions were his guests. Among the frequent visitors was a Russian botanist from the Academy of Sciences in Leningrad who turned out to know less about fauna than flora. He had heard of the very high incidence of venereal diseases in Mongolia and was extremely afraid he would catch it himself. One day when we were dining at Shastin's, I saw the botanist make a very unhappy face. He was obviously feeling ill. After dinner both of us walked home. We were staying in a house belonging to the Mongolian Learned Committee, the predecessor of the present Academy of Sciences. In earlier years walking had been dangerous because of the existence of enormous packs of ferocious stray dogs, and we still remembered the Russian soldier who had been torn to pieces by dogs. I also remembered that even as late as 1926 it was suicidal to walk alone at night. As we walked along I asked him: "What's the matter with you? You look so unhappy." He answered that he had caught venereal disease while sitting at the dining table. The proof was that he suddenly felt pain in a particular part of his body. I explained to him that this could not possibly have happened, because these diseases are not transmitted by air, and this seemed to comfort him. The irony of it, however, involved his wife who had come with him to work as a collector on the expedition. She was probably half his age (about twenty) and he, being overly concerned about his health, had obviously neglected his conjugal obligations. It was known to many that she compensated for this by having affairs with several Russian chauffeurs. I wonder what his reaction would have been if he had known about this.

After this short stay in Mongolia I returned to the Soviet side of the border, with plans to continue my summer research among the Buryats. This time I had intended to visit the island of Ol'khon in Lake Baikal. It had attracted my interest because it had a very small population of about four or five hundred people but at least fifty or sixty shamans. Unfortunately I had to return to Leningrad immediately, for a purge of the Academy of Sciences was in the offing, and I did not want to be away during such a critical event. I shall describe that event in the following chapter, but will now continue my narration about fieldwork among the Buryats.

My next opportunity to return to Buryatia came in 1930. I went to the Aga region in the easternmost part of the then Buryat Mongolian Republic bordering on Manchuria. Later this region was detached from the republic and became a mere autonomous county in the Chita region of Eastern Siberia. In June of that year I went to Ulan-Udè where I was given several assistants to work with me. One of them was the Khalkha Mongol Gombojab Mergen Gün mentioned above. At that time Gombojab was a research fellow at the Buryat Learned Committee headed by Bazar Baradiin. Bazar Baradiin was a very learned Buryat who had made a journey to Lhasa, published a book[5] and several articles in academic publications and taught Mongolian at St. Petersburg University prior to World War I.

Another assistant was Gombojab's wife, Oyun Bilig, a young Buryat. Her Russian name was Agrippina Nikolaevna Borzhonova. She had graduated from Irkutsk University, with a major in Russian, and was also a research fellow of the Learned Committee. The third companion was Bakhanov, a student at the Pedagogical Institute in Ulan-Udè. He was to learn how to do field work on dialects.

We went by train from Ulan-Udè to the railroad station Mogoitui which is located between Chita and the Manchurian border. From there we proceeded to the Russian village called Aginskoe where the famous Aga lamasery, also called the Aga Datsan, is situated. The monastery was very large at that time and housed about 300 monks. I became acquainted with some lamas and saw their very impressive printing office which contained the wooden printing blocks for about 200 xylographs. The Aga monastery also had a very fine library but later, toward the end of the thirties, it was closed and the library was actually destroyed. A film was once made in that area in which during one scene some lamas were required to form a procession coming out of the monastery, carrying volumes of the Kanjur (Sanskrit: Tripitaka), a collection of Buddhist works, on their heads. This procession of lamas walked around the monastery and here the scene ended. The books were then thrown into a ditch by the road, and the actors started on the next scene. What books were not destroyed then were later sent to paper mills for recycling. I should point out that lamas would never have done such a thing, but the movies, not only in the Soviet Union but also in Europe and the United States, are notorious for distorting the history and real life of "exotic" peoples.

After leaving the monastery we proceeded to Chiluutu, Khoito-Aga (North Aga), Urda-Aga (South Aga), and Khara Sheber. In Urda-Aga I visited Professor Gombojab Tsybikov, the well-known Mongolist whose account of his pilgrimage to Tibet was published by the Russian Geographical Society in 1919.[6] Gombojab Tsybikov is also the author of numerous works on Mongolian philology. For many years he had been professor at the Oriental Institute in Vladivostok. After the revolution he taught Mongolian at Irkutsk University, although his family stayed in Urda-Aga while he lived in a very modest apartment in Irkutsk. His one passion was cattle breeding, and he spent almost his entire salary on buying livestock. Coming from a nomad's family, he could not imagine life without a herd. He kept buying cattle and sheep until after he had retired from Irkutsk University to become a member of the Buryat Institute of Language, Literature, and History in Ulan-Ude. By then he had acquired a huge herd. When collectivization began in 1929, at first they left Tsybikov alone. In 1930, however, several months after my visit, all his cattle were taken away and he soon died of a broken heart. The Communists ignored the fact that he had not acquired his herd by exploiting the poor but by buying it with his earned salary. His widow and his foster son, who was in his early twenties at the time, were arrested and exiled to Northern Siberia where they died a short time later. This is how the life of one of the few native Buryat scholars at that time came to a close.

When I visited him, Professor Tsybikov had a comfortable and well-furnished Russian-style house. One of the rooms was actually a small Buddhist shrine which contained a model of the Buddhist Paradise, *bde-ba-can*, pronounced by the Buryats Dewaajan. On a platform of about twelve square feet were models of a palace, temples, pagodas, *caityas* and trees, all made of gilded brass and enamel, with the Buddha seated in the center surrounded by his disciples. This shrine must have cost a fortune. After Tsybikov's dispossession the collection, a real treasure, was destroyed.

From Urda-Aga I went to Khara Sheber, which means the Black or Dark Thicket. I had been told that that area was particularly interesting because the people were very backward, shamanism flourished, and folk singers could be found who knew the epics. As it turned out, I did not find anyone who knew epics, but I did collect songs, riddles, and short stories. I had also the good fortune to witness the ordaining of a young shamaness. It is too long a ritual to describe here in its entirety, so I will give only a brief account of it.

The shamaness was seated in her felt *ger* which was identical to those of the nomadic Buryats in the Aga district and quite similar to the Khalkha-Mongolian *ger* of the Mongolian People's Republic. In the center of the *ger* where ordinarily the hearth stands, a thirty-foot tall birch tree had been planted. Its branches stuck out from the *toono*, the smoke vent in the roof. About halfway up the birch was a small nest made of sheep wool containing several eggs, also made of wool. This tree was called the Mother Tree. About fifty feet away from the *ger* another birch had been planted of the same height as the Mother Tree and connected to it by a woolen string. This tree, called the Father Tree, was believed to impregnate the Mother Tree by way of the string, and the eggs in the nest were the result of this union.

The shamaness' old tutor was present in the *ger* when she began her incantations which lasted several hours without interruption. The entire ritual, called *shanar* (lit. essence, nature, character, characteristic, quality, property and animation), continued for three days and nights. At the end, the shamaness became ecstatic, fainted, and collapsed. After lying motionless for a while, she resumed her incantations but with a different voice, the voice of the spirit which had entered her body and was now speaking through her mouth. During the entire performance the shamaness abstained from food, only occasionally sipping some tea from a cup.

I had met shamans before, in Mongolia, at the *tailgan* (sacrifices) of the Alar Buryats and in the early 1920s at the Institute of Living Oriental Languages in Petrograd, but this was the most interesting performance I had seen, and I even managed to photograph some parts of it. The photos turned out quite well, but unfortunately I had to leave them behind when I escaped from Leningrad in 1941.

I also found another shaman in that area who was willing to recite incantations and invocations for me. I succeeded in writing them down and they are published in my book *Buryat-mongol'skii fol'klornyi i dialektologicheskii sbornik* (Buryat-Mongolian Folkloristic and Dialectological Collection).[7] At the end of my sojourn in Buryatia in late August I learned that the great scholar Bartol'd had died some weeks earlier. He died quite suddenly of uremic poisoning shortly after the death of his wife, a sister of V. A. Zhukovskii, mentioned earlier. His death was an enormous loss for international scholarship.

Before my trip to Buryatia in 1930, I spent the month of May in the Crimean Tatar Republic. In Simferopol' (Tatar: Ak Mesjid; English: White Mosque) there was a pedagogical institute for both Russian and Tatar students. These students were being trained by a special Tatar faculty to become teachers in Tatar schools. Nataliya accompanied me because both of us wanted to be in the Crimea in the spring when everything was in bloom. The blue sea, the cliffs, and the shore lined with cypress forests, the beautiful gardens, wild roses, wisterias, and other blooming shrubs and trees made us feel that we were in paradise. However, not everything was so idyllic. Collectivization of the farms had begun two years before, and many Tatars who had been dispossessed of their vineyards and orchards had been exiled to Siberia or northern Russia where most of them died of tuberculosis or simply froze to death. Food shortages in the Crimea were the result of this collectivization, and we were rather hungry during most of our stay.

The Crimea, especially its southern part which very much resembles Turkey, was the home of the Tatars and of the so-called South Coast Tatars. The latter are actually Turks and even speak the Turkish as it is spoken in Turkey. Village names were either pure Turkish or Tatar. I remember one village named Taushan Bazar which means the Hare Market in Tatar and another Kök Közi which means the Eye of the Sky in Turkish. The Turks and Tatars were friendly and hospitable people. They were excellent workers, and their homes were much cleaner than those of the Russians. Another prosperous ethnic group living in the Crimea were the Germans who had been settled there at the time of Catherine the Great. This ethnic diversity had deep historical roots. I could see this in the many Greek relics found in the area and in an old fortress I visited which had been built by the Genoese in the early Middle Ages. After the second world war the Crimean Tatars were exiled for having collaborated with the German invaders. The local Germans were also exiled to various places, and their whereabouts now are unknown. Today the Crimea is inhabited almost exclusively by Russians and Ukrainians.

Nataliya and I returned to the Crimea a year later, in May 1931, when the institute again invited me to teach Turkic linguistics, the comparative study of the Turkic languages, and related subjects. Many years later I met one of these former students in Germany where he had fled during World War II when the German army retreated from the Crimea. He had become a scholar and published a book on the Crimean Tatars and their struggle for liberation.[8]

After my month in the Crimea I went to Buryatia with my student, T. A. Bertagaev. Bertagaev, who later became a scholar and published several works on Mongolian languages, was a Buryat from the area west of Lake Baikal.[9] Our destination was the basin of the Selenga, a mighty river flowing from Mongolia northward into Lake Baikal. After reaching Ulan-Ude we went by steamboat to Novoselenginsk, a city on the left bank of the Selenga River. From there we proceeded to Tamcha, the administrative center of Selenga aimak which is located on the southern shore of Gusinoe Ozero (Goose Lake).[10] Tamcha is near a famous Lamaist monastery, which had already been closed by the time we visited it, and all the lamas had been exiled to various places, mostly in northern Siberia. From Tamcha we visited first the Ulaan Odo (Red Star) collective farm and later went to the Noikhan area and the Iskra (Spark) collective farm on the right bank of the Selenga where the river Khilok joins the Selenga. I collected epics, songs, riddles, proverbs, and other materials in Noikhon which many years later I translated into English.[11] This work was entitled *Tsongol Folklore* because the local Buryats speak the Tsongol dialect which is somewhere between the Buryat language and Khalkha Mongolian. The phonology is almost like Khalkha, but in other features it is like Buryat. I was quite surprised at the amount of folklore materials which could still be obtained in collective farms. I spent several weeks in the Noikhon area and when in late August 1931 I returned to Ulan-Udè, I learned that Vladimirtsov had died on August 17. I could not believe it because when I had left Leningrad he was in good health, and though he had lived a rather irregular life one would never have expected him to die so soon. The cause of his death was heart failure.

In 1931 the economic situation in Buryatia was very bad. The total collectivization of farms had been completed only a year before, and there was practically nothing to eat. The Selenga area was better off because, although butter and cheese had beeh taken from the collective farms for export abroad, it had all been returned. The products had been made in the spring, when the cows fed on wild onions and garlic, and consequently the butter and cheese were unexportable! At every place we stayed we had no trouble obtaining plenty of cheese, butter, and some bread. The Buryats justifiably blamed collectivization for all their sufferings. They called it *saldagan ezii* (the pantless old hag), meaning that collectivization was causing such widespread poverty that soon people would have no pants to wear!

In 1932 I went with two Buryat students, Lubsan Gomboin and Aleksandr Khamgashalov, and the local teacher Zandaraa Baatorov from Ulan-Ude to the Barguzin area where the Barguzin river flows into Lake Baikal from the northeast. We went by train from Ulan-Ude to Tataurovo where I found a man who owned a troika, a vehicle drawn by three horses. From there we traveled about 200 kilometers to the Barguzin area through the virgin Siberian forest on a very bad road full of ruts and loose rocks. The owner of the troika, Elisei, was good-natured and talkative, a man in his thirties, who had been one of the partisans fighting against Kolchak's army. One day when I was discussing verbs in the local dialect with my students, Elisei suddenly asked, "What is a verb? Our priest always says 'verb' during the services." What Elisei had heard was, of course, the phrase *audiamus verbum divinum* which means "let us listen to the divine word." I explained to him what a verb is, and his face brightened, "So that's what a verb is! Tell me, professor, is this also a verb?" And he mentioned a four-letter word for copulating. "Yes," I assured him, "that's also a verb. All action words are verbs." All the time we were traveling through virgin cedar forests along the shore of Lake Baikal, we could see across the lake the snow-covered mountain ridges glistening in the sunlight like white marble studded with diamonds. It was probably the most beautiful and wildest scenery I have ever seen. When we reached the village of Maksimikha, slightly more than half-way between Tataurovo and Barguzin, we stopped for the night. Early the next morning we were awakened by heart-rending wails and laments. Later we learned that the bodies of sixteen fishermen had been brought ashore from an ice floe in the middle of the lake. The men had been fishing when a sudden storm broke up the ice, and they had been tossed about the lake until they died of hunger and exposure.

We finally arrived at the mouth of the Barguzin river. It was a very stormy day, and enormous waves rolled from the lake right up the mouth of the river. We had to cross the river, which was about 500 meters wide at that point, on a raft. When we reached the middle of the river the raft pitched and rolled, vehicles and horses slid to one side, and we almost capsized. Cold and wet, we finally reached the opposite bank. We entered a house in the village there, changed clothes and warmed up with vodka and hot tea. I said to my companions, "Well, I thought for sure we would capsize, and I had my eyes on a large plank which I would have grabbed just in case." Elisei drew a switchblade from his boot, flicked it upon and brandished it in my direction. "Some other people had their eyes on it, too," he snarled and put the switchblade back into his boot. He seemed pleasant enough and witty, but in an emergency all his animal instincts would have been awakened.

In the Barguzin area my companions and I dispersed in all directions to collect interesting folklore and shamanist materials. I also found a group of Tunguses and gathered materials on their dialect and folklore. In one of the old barns I found an abandoned archive dating from the eighteenth century, and based on the tax rolls contained in it I could determine that the pedigrees the Tunguses had given me were indeed correct. In this connection, I would like to mention that the natives, both the Tunguses and Buryats, usually have very good memories and can remember all their ancestors. Thus when Zandaraa Baatorov asked people, "Whose son are you?" the answer would go back several generations. Once when an acquaintance of Zandaraa arrived at the name of an ancestor some eight or ten generations back, Zandaraa asked, "Are you of the Chono [wolf] clan?" "Yes," the man answered. It turned out that Zandaraa Baatorov had suddenly discovered one of his own relatives among the ancestors of the man interrogated.

From the Barguzin area we went by steamboat across Lake Baikal to the island of Oikhon (Russian: Ol'khon) where many shamans lived. I decided to stay about two weeks in order to find good narrators of epics and shamans. An excellent narrator was found immediately. He knew the most beautiful epics I had ever heard, but he was a fisherman and as the fishing season would last for another month, he was not able to spend time with me. Search for other narrators proved unsuccessful. It seemed none existed, or if there were any, they denied knowing any epics. An uprising of shamans had taken place less than a year before. The unfortunate shamans were arrested and deported, and as a result we had to leave Oikhon without the opportunity to record any epics. We went by rowboat to the western shore of the lake and crossed an area named

Kosaya Step' (Slanting Steppe), to a large village called Khogot, on the road from Irkutsk to Yakutsk. Khogot was the home village of my student Bertagaev, and here we met the young secretary of the local party organization who was also an excellent storyteller and knew very long epics by heart. He was, however, too busy to work with us. While we were in Khogot, a tragedy occurred. A boy who was tending pigs was found shot to death. Several pigs had also been shot and others were apparently stolen. The police came from Irkutsk, about 150 kilometers away, and set up roadblocks everywhere, and anyone transporting large numbers of pigs was stopped and searched. I do not know if the murderer or murderers were ever caught.

From Khogot we went by truck to Irkutsk and from there I returned to Leningrad in early September. It was not until 1936 that I returned to Buryatia. A linguistic conference was held in Ulan-Udè in that year. To honor the participants of that conference a dinner had been arranged by the local government and M. N. Erbanov, the regional party secretary, was present. He sat at the head of the table, with myself on his right side and across from me the commissar of the interior, Markizov. I received a Buryat national silken caftan as a gift from the government and was also presented with the national meal of honor, the *töölei* which consists of a whole sheep's head complete with a scapula and several long ribs. It was, of course, impossible for me to eat all of this, but I had the right to share it with other guests. I used this opportunity to mention to Erbanov that old customs and landmarks should somehow be preserved. For instance, I suggested at least one Lamaist monastery should be preserved as a historical and ethnographical art museum. "I disagree, professor," said Erbanov. "I'm sure you would also wish to preserve a few lamas, and I can assure you that we are keeping them in labor camps where they are being so well preserved that you need not worry about them."

This was his reply. Poor Erbanov was always and everywhere faithful to the party line, but this did not help him because in 1937, when he went to a party conference in Moscow, he was arrested and shot. That was the time of the Great Purge, but before Erbanov met his end there was an occasion soon after the conference in 1936 in Ulan-Udè, where Stalin gave a reception to honor the shock workers of Buryatia. Of course Stalin was present, and Markizov also attended since he was the foreman of that Buryat group of shock workers. Markizov's little daughter, Gelya, was with him and presented Stalin with a bouquet of beautiful flowers. Stalin took her in his arms and kissed her. This scene was photographed and reproduced in all the newspapers and displayed on posters in every school with the caption, "We Thank Our Dear Comrade Stalin For Our Happy Childhood." The photo was still on public display when Markizov and his wife were arrested. He was shot, and his wife perished in a concentration camp. Their Gelya, then four or five years old, was sent to an orphanage under another name. I wonder if she still thanked her dear comrade Stalin for her happy childhood.

My next trip to Ulan-Udè in July 1939 lasted only about ten days during which I attended a linguistic conference. I encountered hunger and deprivation. Fortunately for me, I was given a pass to the dining hall of the local party committee. When I first arrived there, the manager told me, "I will also give you your bread ration, if you don't mind." Surprised, I asked, "But why? Can't I get it elsewhere?" "Oh, no," he informed me, "you won't find any bread in the city." He gave me one kilogram of bread which consisted of a loaf and a single slice. I took it very reluctantly, and on my way back to the hotel I heard someone running after me. It was a young woman who begged me, "Citizen, please give me that slice of bread you're carrying. My children have not eaten for two days. There's absolutely nothing to eat in the whole city." I gave her not only the slice but the entire ration. I was astonished when she fell on her knees and thanked me profusely. I thought of the expression, "The word 'man' sounds proud." Would Gor'kii still have said it under these conditions?

In summer 1940 I was again in Ulan-Udè to help organize a *dekada* of Buryat arts. This *dekada* was to be performed for the government in Moscow, and it was thought that Stalin himself might attend. I was invited to check the historical and ethnographic accuracy of every aspect of the stage plays, including costumes and weapons. The *dekada* took place in the late fall of 1940 in Moscow, but Stalin did not attend, and stars and other decorations were so few that most participants were greatly disappointed.

My last trip to Buryatia was in May of 1941. At that time a conference was held to discuss the publication of the Geser epic which had been declared the Buryats' national epic. In 1940 the Kalmucks had organized a celebration for the 500th anniversary of their Jangar epics. It is interesting that the Kalmucks had approached Stalin and asked him for permission to organize the celebration. He was agreeable, but he changed the wording. Instead of "Jangar, the Kalmuck national epic," he decreed that it read "Jangar, the epic of the Kalmuck people." Actually the Jangar epic only appeared after 1771 when a large number of Kalmucks fled from Russia to Mongolia. Jangar contains numerous Buddhist elements whereas in 1440 most Oirats, to which group the Kalmucks belonged, were not Buddhist but still shamanist. The Buryats, however, wanted a national epic of their own and Geser, which is ultimately of Tibetan origin, was proclaimed their national epic.

Soon after my return to Leningrad the Soviet Union was engulfed in World War II. Before I proceed to that period, however, I must mention some events in the years 1930 to 1941 which had a great influence, mostly adverse, on my life and my work.

5 The Purge of the Academy of Sciences

As I mentioned in the previous chapter, when I returned from Ulaanbaatar to Ulan-Udè in August of 1929, I learned that a purge of the Academy of Sciences was imminent. I decided to cut short my research and return directly to Leningrad. My trip, however, proved to be more difficult than anticipated. Chinese troops under the command of Chang Tso-lin, the warlord of Manchuria, had attacked the Soviet-owned Chinese Eastern Railroad which had been built across Manchuria by Russian engineers during Tsarist times. As a consequence of the war in Manchuria, train schedules on the Trans-Siberian railroad were seriously disrupted, and I had to wait many hours for a train. When it finally arrived in Ulan-Udè, it was already thirty-six hours behind schedule and it was not the express train for which I had waited, but a very slow train. It took me along the southern Trans-Siberian route through Chelyabinsk, and eleven days later I finally reached Leningrad. Under normal conditions, the same trip would have taken only five or six days. I learned from the newspapers that fighting between the Red Army and the Chinese warlord troops had been heavy and that the Soviet Union had decided to sell the Chinese Eastern Railroad to the Chinese central government. In 1929 the Soviet Union was not ready for a serious confrontation with its eastern neighbor and therefore sold the railroad at a very low price. The Russian railroad employees were mostly refugees from revolutionary days and they were promised identical jobs in the Soviet Union. In 1937, however, most of them were accused of spying for Japan and other "imperialist" nations and thrown into concentration camps.

Very soon after my arrival in Leningrad the purge began. It was still summer and many scholars were either on vacation or expeditions. The permanent secretary of the Academy of Sciences, Sergei Fedorovich Ol'denburg, was in France discussing cooperation between scholars of the French and Soviet academies. Many scholars were worried that the purge might begin without the actual head of the academy present. My former professor and immediate superior at the Asian Museum, Professor Vladimirtsov, was in the countryside not far from Leningrad. Nataliya and I went to see him in order to discuss the situation and to see what he thought about it all. At Vladimirtsov's cottage we also met Fedor Aleksandrovich Rozenberg, nominally the deputy director, but actually the real director of the Asian Museum because Ol'denburg was too busy as secretary of the academy to spend much time at the museum. We discussed the situation, and both Rozenberg and Vladimirtsov expressed the hope that those in charge of the purge would not really dare to do too much damage to the academy, even in Ol'denburg's absence. They were greatly mistaken because purges had already begun in many other scholarly institutions as well as in offices and factories, and what we read in the newspapers did not give us much confidence that our purge would be any less bloodthirsty. Even eminent, and in some cases irreplaceable, specialists were fired or exiled. Being by nature mistrustful and rather inclined to pessimism, I viewed the situation as grave. The events of the next few weeks proved me right.

A few days after our visit with Vladimirtsov the purge began. All scholars and employees were suspended from work and were required to gather every morning in the academy's large meeting hall at exactly ten o'clock. This became the routine for about two weeks. The committee conducting the purge consisted of four men. Its chairman was a certain Figatner, an employee of the Commissariat of Workers' and Peasants' Inspection which supervised the work of the government. The other members were the GPU (secret police) official Sadovskii, the director of the Hermitage

Illus. 15.   The Academy of Sciences of the Soviet Union

Illus. 16.   The Meeting Hall of the Academy of Sciences

Museum Kiparisov who was either Communist or pro-Communist, and the director of the Institute of Living Oriental Languages P. I. Vorob'ev. I knew Vorob'ev because I was professor at his institute. He was a Communist but rather reasonable and less dangerous than the other members of the purge committee. I doubted that he would denounce anyone to the secret police even if he learned anything compromising. Serious matters would have been reported, but I felt Vorob'ev was too decent to report on someone just because that person was the son of a former official, or because that person had married the daughter of a former army officer. I also hoped that he would use his influence to dissuade the other members from taking too drastic action, but it turned out that I was mistaken. He was evidently in no position to oppose them for after all, as a Communist he, too, was subject to party discipline.

I had never witnessed such disgusting scenes as those which occurred during our purge. The individuals being interrogated tried to please the members of the purge committee. Sometimes they were servile and acted in a very degrading manner. I remember an employee in the administrative office of the Academy of Sciences, who had been a member of the Tsarist police and during Tsarist times had published some anti-Semitic brochures in which he advo- cated pogroms. He now tried to exonerate himself by inventing all kinds of excuses. He was humble and almost ready to kiss the boots of the members of the purge committee. In spite of this he was, of course, fired from his position and arrested. What happened to him afterwards I do not know. I must say that none of us felt any pity for him. In fact, we found him doubly revolting, first because of his shameful anti-Semitic activities in the past and now because of the undignified manner in which he tried to exonerate himself. I think that he might have fared a bit better had he answered the questions put to him in a more forthright manner. At least he would have made a better impression on us. By contrast, Nataliya, who was librarian at the Institute of Oriental Studies, chose quite a different attitude. When her name was called, she stood up and was asked, "Is it true that you are the daughter of a Tsarist general?" "Yes, I am," she answered. The next question was, "What can you add to this?"

"Nothing," she replied, "why should I?" There were no further questions. She was told to sit down and later, when the names of the purged ones were read from a list, she was not among them. I think that everyone should have behaved the way she did.

Many of those purged aroused pity and sympathy. For instance, there was a scholar by the name of Tsarevskii who worked in the Institute of Zoology. He was a priest in a church during his spare time, conducting Holy Communion, baptizing children, and performing other church duties without pay. His activities had not brought harm to anyone; on the contrary, many dying people got consolation and the last sacrament from him and certainly felt better than if they had died without the presence of a priest. It was unbelievable how the members of the purge committee ridiculed him. Even some of the academy's own employees made fun of him and treated him in the most disgusting manner. One of them, a certain Il'inskii of the Antireligious Museum, asked him, "Say, Holy Father, is it true that you believe in this nonsense?" Another would cite some unimportant passage from the Old Testament, such as Noah's Ark, and ask, "Do you, as a zoologist, really believe that there were only so few species of animals in the world that seven pairs of each could be crammed into an ark?" Of course the poor man did not respond to these mocking questions. It was quite obvious that the victim of this mockery suffered deeply not so much for himself but because of the revolting blasphemies which would disgust even a cultured atheist. It is everybody's right to object to religion but no one has the right to hurt the religious feelings of others. Tsarevskii was purged and arrested. Then he disappeared.

Many great scholars suffered the same fate. The well-known zoologist and corresponding member of the Academy of Sciences Byalynitskii-Birulya was also fired, arrested, and disappeared. The same fate befell the geologist P. V. Vittenburg, the head of the Yakut Commission of the Academy of Sciences, who had for many years conducted geological research in the Yakut Republic which led to the discovery of enormous amounts of oil, diamonds, gold, and various minerals. Even harmless old ladies who had been working at menial tasks in the library were not spared. A certain Mrs.

Gundelach, of German extraction, was fired and later disappeared because she had been the tutoress in an institute for daughters of the nobility. The director of the library, F. A. Martinson, was questioned and actually examined in Marxist-Leninist literature. As the director of a scholarly library, why should he have been versed in journalistic articles on Leninist problems? He was also arrested and disappeared.

Another scholar who suffered a tragic fate was a Dr. Skriba—novich who had been active in the German community of St. Petersburg under the Tsars. He had given popular lectures on various subjects in history and literature and wrote articles in newspapers. His tragedy was that immediately after the revolution he had emigrated to Latvia and had lived in Riga for several years. In 1925 or 1926 he decided to return to the Soviet Union where he got a job at the library of the academy from which he was now purged. One of the things that incriminated him was that he had returned to the Soviet Union, obviously having been sent by his foreign masters as a spy. Without any hard evidence, he was arrested and disappeared. The archeologist Lemeshevskii, who was a well-known scholar at the Museum of Ethnography and Anthropology, should also be remembered. In order not to fall victim to the GPU, he had illegally procured a Portuguese passport. It did not save him, however, as he was fired and arrested as a foreigner secretly living in the Soviet Union.

Our acting director of the Institute of Oriental Studies, as the Asian Museum had been renamed in 1925, F. A. Rozenberg, or Uncle Teddy, as many of us called him, was not exactly fired, but it was strongly suggested that he retire. He did and lived in his apartment for about another year or two with nothing to do. He evidently could not stand such a life and died of what I would call *taedium vitae*. In other words, he was fed up with life. A well-known anthropologist and ethnographer, A. M. Mervart, and his wife, both research scholars at the Museum of Ethnography and Anthropology, were also arrested. They had spent the war years in India and in 1925 they returned to the academy. In 1927 they received exit permits for a trip to visit their parents in the Netherlands. Two

114

years after their return they were arrested. I wondered why they had not remained in Holland. I was already at that time firmly resolved never to return from abroad, if I should ever be so lucky as to get an exit permit for myself and my family. To conclude the list of those purged and arrested there was the secretary of the Institute of Oriental Studies, M. M. Girs, who had served under the Tsar as a diplomat in Persia.

One morning the purge committee announced that a conspiracy had been uncovered in the academy. A large number of incriminating documents had been found in the archives. These documents had been obtained from the headquarters of the Constitutional Democratic Party which had ceased to exist shortly after the revolution, since most of its members had fled from Leningrad to destinations abroad or elsewhere in Russia. In fact there was absolutely no conspiracy because the documents had been officially sent by a Soviet agency to the academy. Nevertheless, as punishment for this "plot" the permanent secretary, Ol'denburg, was relieved of his duties and retained only his membership in the Academy of Sciences. The job of permanent secretary was given to a certain V. P. Volgin who had been an associate professor at Moscow University and whose sole "scholarly" work had been a history of the socialist movements in the world. The famous scholars S. F. Platonov, the greatest authority on the history of Russia, especially the history of the early seventeenth-century "Time of Troubles," E. V. Tarle, historian of Western Europe, and N. P. Likhachev, whose specialty was paleography and ancient Russian literary works, were all immediately arrested and exiled. Both Platonov and Likhachev died in concentration camps. Tarle survived and was later freed because he had always been rather anti-German and as a historian he ascribed the guilt for World War I solely to Germany. At the time of the purge the British and French were regarded as the greatest enemies of the Soviet Union, but Germany, being rather weak during its Weimar Republic days, was seen as less vicious. Therefore it was politically unacceptable that Germany should be made the scapegoat of the war. When Hitler came to power, of course, the situation changed drastically, and Tarle was released. He again became a

115

member of the Academy of Sciences where his anti-German attitude was then remembered and he became a kind of court historian of the Soviet Union, winning the Stalin Prize three times.

New members of the Academy of Sciences were elected very soon after the purge to replace those arrested and liquidated. Among them was the notorious Trofim Denisovich Lysenko who claimed to have developed new strains of vegetables by using Marxist methods. What he actually did was plant potatoes in flower pots in his room. With special fertilizers the potatoes grew to the size of cabbages which he then passed off as a new kind of potato. He was an outspoken enemy of true geneticists, such as the great N. I. Vavilov who fell victim to Lysenko's intrigues, was arrested and died in a concentration camp.

The Academy of Sciences had always been a research body, but now it had to train so-called aspirants, candidates for a kind of master's degree, who spent a couple of years taking courses as well as doing actual work under the guidance of a specialist. I later received some of these aspirants, and they were rather poorly qualified. We scholars also had to attend Marxist-Leninist courses. The kind of nonsense we were told by our instructors was unbelievable. For example, in December 1936 the so-called Stalin constitution was promulgated. One of our lecturers announced that the Soviet Union was now a multi-national state. He then proceeded with an attempt at a definition. "A multi-national state," he intoned, "is not the same as a patchwork of various nationalities who have nothing to do with one another, like the former Austro-Hungarian monarchy. It contained the Czechs, Slovaks, Hungarians, Rumanians, Greeks, and many other nationalities. Since they had nothing in common, the state fell apart." Of course, neither Rumania nor Greece had ever belonged to Austro-Hungary, but such elementary facts were quite beyond the ken of our learned instructors.

New work methods, like those used in factories, were now introduced in the Academy of Sciences. One such method was called socialist competition. This meant that everyone was urged to over-fulfill his quota. Instead of writing one article, two articles, instead of one book, two books, and so on. Likewise, instead of finishing an article in one or two years, we were requested to write it in six months. I am not going to comment on this because everyone reading these lines knows that such methods have nothing to do with scholarly work. One can never know when one will make a discovery or how long an experiment may take. A solution may be found in a few days, but it is just as likely that years are required. For example, can a deadline be set for the solution of the cancer problem? These production techniques were rather like an undignified, senseless, and ridiculous game. The Academy of Sciences was still strong, however, because it had kept a number of excellent scholars and therefore good results were achieved—no thanks to the party and the Soviet government—even though it was obligatory to mention it each time one made a discovery. Rather, good work was done in spite of them.

Another new method introduced after the purge was team work. The institute's Mongolian department which I headed after Vladimirtsov's death, was ordered to compile a complete Mongolian-Russian dictionary. My closest aide in this project was K. M. Cheremisov who later published several dictionaries of his own.[1] Also part of our team were G. N. Rumyantsev and B. I. Pankratov, as well as G. D. Sanzheev who was living in Moscow. The material was collected in the following manner. Each member of the team received several Mongolian books which he was to read, underlining each word which was to be included in the dictionary, and marking the context in which the word occurred with vertical lines. Later the book was given to a student who wrote the word concerned in the upper right-hand corner and the passage in which it occurred on a card. These cards were then returned to the team members who translated the word and its passage. Then master cards were made up, listing all the meanings of a word taken from the individual cards. Finally the information was typed on sheets of paper and edited by me. The dictionary was ready for publication in 1940, but it was never published because the Mongols abandoned their old script in 1941 and adopted the Cyrillic alphabet. This manuscript of more than 2,000 typed pages is still gathering dust in the Academy of Sciences.

After the purge, work at the Academy of Sciences became

difficult because of constant interference by the party cell. The director of the Institute of Oriental Studies became a mere figure-head, and the actual head of the institute was the secretary who was a member of the Communist Party. A vice-director in charge of finance and supplies was appointed, and on his second day he demanded to see the library. Our library contained about one million books as well as large numbers of manuscripts in Arabic, Persian, Mongolian, and other languages. When he saw the huge rows of stacks, he asked, "Have all of these books been read?" "Oh, no, not all of them," was the answer. The new deputy director then decreed, "In that case no more books will be acquisitioned until all of these have been read." Fortunately this official did not last long. Even the party members must have realized that he was unsuitable for work in an academic institution, and he was replaced by a more educated person.

Because of the party's interference, some important work had to be discontinued. My Mongolian department was putting together an anthology of old Mongolian literary works. There were didactic works, including wise sayings and maxims attributed to Chingis Khan, epics, and excerpts from translations of Chinese novels such as *San Kuo Chih*. This collection was denounced to the party cell by my aspirant Artemov, and the party ordered our work to be destroyed since it was "incongruous with our times." Two hundred pages, about half of the book, had already been printed. They were sent to the paper mills.

Censorship also became a serious problem. In the 1930s I was working on the *Muqaddimat al-Adab*, an Arabic-Persian-Chaghatai Turkic-Mongolian dictionary of the fourteenth century. The censors found fault with almost every word. Thus the phrase "the tree was hung with fruit" aroused the censor's suspicion: "Could you not specify *who* hung fruit on the tree?" I replied, "Certainly not he whom you suspect would have hung it. The tree itself produced the fruit." "Then say so," he ordered. I had to explain to him that in a dictionary words must be translated precisely. He also insisted on eliminating all anatomical terms such as posterior and womb, but I agreed only to replace them with Latin equivalents.

The work was finally published in 1938-39, but not quite as I had planned it. In addition to the changes caused by censorship, I had to change the word "Chagatai" in the title to "Turkic" because Samoilovich, who had helped me much with the Turkic part, objected to the term "Chagatai" and insisted on using "literary language of Central Asia." Ironically, I also had to omit Samoilovich's name from my list of acknowledgments because in the meantime he had been arrested and disappeared in the summer of 1938. Likewise, I had to drop all mention of F. A. Rozenberg, specialist in Iranian and particularly Sogdian, who had helped me with Persian words. He had been forced to retire and became a kind of "unperson." I also had to omit all mention of Fitrat and Gāzī 'Alī Yunusov, two Uzbek scholars who had been instrumental in procuring a copy of the dictionary. Both were arrested and shot during the liquidation of the Uzbek intellectuals in 1937.

At that time of the academy's purge the well-known Marxist historian Mikhail Nikolaevich Pokrovskii was arrested for having ascribed too much importance to mercantile capitalism.[3] Any mention of trade, trading, or trade relations was forbidden, and so I had to delete in the preface to the dictionary just mentioned the sentence: "Trade relations and other contacts with Mongols in the thirteenth and fourteenth centuries resulted in the compilation of glossaries and dictionaries." Another taboo was any discussion of the genetic relationship of the Mongolian languages because the party was afraid that awareness of this relationship might foster nationalistic ideas and bring about Pan-Mongolism. Consequently, in my comparative linguistic study which forms a part of my book dealing with that dictionary and which had already been set and printed[4] I had to eliminate all references to Buryat, Kalmuck, and Khalkha and replace "Buryat" with "North Mongolian" and "Kalmuck" with "West Mongolian." It was a simple change, but it meant resetting and reprinting eighty-eight pages.

While I watched these censors carrying on in this fashion, I thought, "How weak they must think the regime is if linguistic relationships are deemed politically dangerous. And how ignorant and primitive they are!"

Vladimirtsov was elected full member of the Academy of Sciences in 1929. Actually he was to be elected the year before, but a difficulty had arisen. The Sinologist Alekseev was Vladimirtsov's senior, and it was impossible for Vladimirtsov to bypass Alekseev. Thus in 1929 when two vacancies opened up, both men were elected. For the first time, Communist party leaders were also to be elected as full members, but their candidates, including N. I. Bukharin and A. M. Deborin, were voted down, and this created an enormous scandal. The party called for new elections and warned the academy that the party leaders must be elected or else. For the first time in its long and distinguished history, the academy was to acquire full members whose qualifications were far below those of full members in Tsarist times. Looking at the new members, one could only say, *sic transit gloria mundi.*

One of the most unpleasant consequences of the communist penetration into the Academy of Sciences was the frequent harassment of scholars whose works were at odds with the current political line. One such scholar was the geographer and historian G. E. Grum-Grzhimailo, well known for his travels in and works on Mongolia. I knew him well and we were on friendly terms, although I disagreed with his historical theories which Bartol'd had already rejected in highly critical reviews before the revolution. The forum for such attacks after the Soviet purge of the academy was the so-called meeting of criticism and self-criticism. The aspirants, i.e. graduate students working toward degrees roughly equivalent to M.A. and Ph.D. degrees, arranged such meetings. In Grum's case, it was Berlin, Artemov and Ulivanov, all communists attached to the Mongolian section of which I was the head. Also attending Grum's "trial" were members and aspirants of the related sections, such as China, Japan, and Turkey. Most of them were communist as well. The harangues against poor old Grum-Grzhimailo were mean, cruel and very unjust. As the head of the Mongolian section, I chaired that meeting and tried to make it less harmful to the "defendant." Fortunately, nothing untoward resulted from the meeting. Grum-Grzhimailo was never arrested, and he died from natural causes at his home a few years later.

The most disgusting accusation concerned Grum's book on Northwestern Mongolia and the Uriangkhai region which had been written before the revolution. In that book, Grum argued that it would be unreasonable to grant independence to the Uriangkhai region, also known as Tuva, which was populated by a mere 70,000 primitive tribesmen. It would be much more sensible, argued Grum in his book, to incorporate that region into a modern, civilized nation. Unfortunately for Grum, in 1926 the Soviets decided to bestow upon the Tuvan region a semblance of independence, and for eighteen years that region existed by the name of the Tannu Tuva People's Republic. Therefore, at the time of Grum's "trial," his pre-revolutionary views ran counter to Soviet policy. In 1944, however, when world attention was focused elsewhere, the Soviets annexed Tuva and converted it into the Tuvan autonomous republic, an integral part of the Soviet Union. One is indeed justified to ask, "What was Grum-Grzhimailo's crime when the Soviet Union eventually did precisely what he had advocated before the revolution?" If the charges of imperialism hurled against Grum at that meeting were justified, they should have also been applied against the Soviet Union in 1944.

Before concluding this chapter, let me add that many famous scholars such as Platonov and Tarle were put in concentration camps to make room for those party newcomers. The irony of fate had it, however, that Bukharin and many others who had been added to the academy in 1929 were themselves shot or imprisoned during the Great Purge of 1937-38 when the revolution, like Chronos of yore, began to devour its children.

6 Life in the Thirties

The 1930s were a time of shortages of every kind and years of political terror such as were never witnessed before. In 1930 the sixteenth congress of the Communist Party called for an intensive program of industrialization and the socialist revamping of the economy which was to include the total collectivization of farms. Hearing rumors about the impending loss of their farms, thousands of farmers slaughtered their cattle and destroyed their grain so that when collectivization actually did begin, there were many empty cattle sheds and empty grain bins. Starvation soon swept the country. In 1930 the streets of Leningrad and of many other cities were swamped with beggars. Old men and women, and young women with infants in their arms stood or sat at street corners, imploring all passers-by, "For Jesus' sake, give us some alms." Most beggars had come from the Ukraine where some four million people died of starvation in 1930-31.

Ration cards were issued, even though all stores in Leningrad were empty. It was virtually impossible to obtain meat, butter, milk, and many other essentials, and only bread was given on coupons. At that time Anastas Mikoyan was appointed the commissar of food supplies, and people joked, "Since Mikoyan has become the food commissar, all foods beginning with the letter M have disappeared."[1] Soon special stores were opened for high officials, members of the secret police, scholars and important specialists.

Special passes were issued to those who were eligible to buy there, and I received such a pass, too. In these "closed stores," *(zakrytyi raspredelitel')* that is, closed to everyone except a relative handful, we could buy such things as shoes, clothes, food, and cigarettes at fairly low prices, but even in these stores some items were not always available. Black markets flourished. When I needed a suit I went to my former tailor, who was working in a government-owned tailor shop, to ask him if I could buy some cloth. He told me to come to his home because he could not discuss the matter there in the store. I went to his home and he showed me some excellent woolen material. He told me that he was working as a cutter in a men's suit factory. He had to cut twenty suits out of one bolt of material, but he managed to cut in such a way that twenty-one suits came out. "And this," he said, "is the twenty-first suit." My new suit certainly turned out to be expensive, but if I had not bought it from my old tailor I would never have been able to get any suit at all.

In this connection I should like to say that the black market at that time was full of stolen goods. In fact, it turned out at the very beginning of the 1930s that one could buy only stolen goods. It was impossible to buy fire logs, the only heating material available for homes. The janitor of our apartment house often came to us and asked if we needed some fire logs. He could get them because a barge with fire logs had moored at the end of our street. Its cargo was destined for some government offices. "At night," the janitor said," my boys can bring you any number of cubic meters you wish. It will cost you only fifty rubles a cubic meter, and I can saw the logs for you for twenty rubles per meter."

Not only thievery but also graft flourished, but first I should mention that in 1931 we moved from the house which had belonged to my grandparents to a smaller apartment at 37 Lermontovskii Prospekt. New regulations permitted only nine square meters per person, plus another nine square meters for a living room, and one additional room of twenty square meters for scholars and writers working at home. There were four of us in our family and we had a maid, thus we were allowed a total of seventy-four square meters. As extra space in our old apartment was to be given to persons without accommodations, we decided to move to a smaller apartment. My mother who had been living with us moved in with my sister whose apartment was in the district of Petrogradskaya Storona near the zoo.

To continue the discussion of graft, I must mention that the manager of our apartment house, whom I knew only by his first name and who, incidentally, was later killed in the war against Finland, came every month to collect the rent. Once he came and asked us to pay for several months in advance because he needed the money for remodeling. I gave him the money, but then he also asked me to lend him some money because he had to buy something for his family and he was short of cash. I gave him fifty rubles which he never returned. He thanked me and added, "I've always said that you are a good citizen and a nice person. The other day I was summoned to the "Big House" (the popular name for the GPU headquarters) where they told me that your father had been with the Oriental Parliament and that I should keep an eye on you and report everything concerning you. But I said that you are absolutely all right and that I can vouch for you." He was obviously telling the truth about the GPU who must have told him about my father's work in the Oriental Department of the Ministry of Foreign Affairs. He only confused "Department" with "Parliament." We soon had additional evidence that the secret police was interested in us. One day when my wife and I returned home from work, we found our maid crying and no dinner prepared. In the evening of that same day she announced that she was going to quit. When my wife asked her whether she quit because her wages were too low, she answered that it was not that but that she had been summoned to the secret police and told to report on what we talked about and who visited us. My wife told her to stay and to tell them everything because we had nothing to hide. She stayed, and we never asked her how often she had to report to the secret police.

These two incidents were disturbing because I had already made my acquaintance with the secret police. Early one morning in 1927 the bell rang, and our maid answered the door, then knocked on our bedroom door and said in an agitated voice, "They've come for you!" I dressed perfunctorily and went out. There were two men who told me politely, "Please don't worry. You will come back. You need not take any belongings with you. We only want to talk to you." Still, I was frightened. We went by car to the secret police building and there I was led into a room where a senior official sat. He, too, was very polite and said, "You were consul-general in China, weren't you?" I answered, "No, I was not. I was born in 1897 and at that time my father was consular secretary. When he died in 1913 I was a teenager. I could not possibly have been a consul-general because I was too young." I saw that I had frustrated their scheme. They whispered to each other and then the one behind the desk asked, "But are you a loyal citizen of the Soviet Union?" I said, "I certainly am. I'm doing my best. I have published some important scholarly works, so I think that I am also a useful citizen." "Well," he said, "you know all kinds of languages. Suppose we intercept a letter in a language we don't know. Would you translate it for us?" I said, "In the case of letters in languages I know I certainly would." "Good, that's all. Please sign this paper with your promise not to talk to anyone about this, and here is your pass. You may go home." I went home to my wife who had been terrified all the time I was gone, and she was greatly relieved to see me back.

Thievery and corruption were everywhere in the 1930s. Once I badly needed some iron sheets to have the leaky roof above our apartment repaired. I went to the buildings department of the Academy of Sciences and talked to a roofer who promised to do the job and even offered to bring along some iron sheets. The Academy of Sciences had recently been reroofed, and some of the discarded sheets were still usable. He cut out the good parts and repaired the entire roof of our apartment house. As a precautionary measure, I had also asked for and received from the buildings department a certificate declaring the iron sheets reusable surplus and permitting me to remove them from the academy grounds. About three months later I was suddenly summoned to the crime division of the police precinct station. I wondered what this was all about and found out very soon. They asked me politely where I had obtained the iron sheets, and I told them. I also gave them the name of the manager

126

of the buildings department. The police telephoned him and, satisfied with his answer, let me return home. I had been summoned because no iron sheets could be purchased legally so they assumed that mine must have been stolen.

Corruption was also rampant. In order to buy tickets on a train to Moscow or other destinations, one had to line up by six o'clock the evening before departure. By morning thousands of people would have gathered in front of the ticket office to vie for the twenty-five tickets which were to be sold each day. Where did the other tickets go? Some were reserved for intermediate stations between Leningrad and the final destination of each train, but most of them were sold illegally at exorbitant prices. Some friends of mine told me of an elderly woman whose son was a redcap at the Moscow train station in Leningrad. He knew the clerk in the ticket office and for a bribe of 50% of the ticket price, which he shared with the clerk, he could obtain tickets. When my family and I went on our vacation to the Caucasus, I always bought our tickets through that redcap. Another experience involved painters. Paint could be obtained either in a state-owned store or, more easily, on the black market. If one also needed a painter, one could readily find several of them loitering around stores selling paint and wallpaper. I hired a man to paint for us who was employed by a state-owned construction firm. He agreed to come around ten in the evening and paint all night long. When I asked him whether this moonlighting was not too strenuous for him since he had to return to his regular job the next morning, he laughed and said, "You see, citizen, right now we are supposed to be painting some of the new government offices, but I don't get tired because we just pretend to work. After all, they pay us only 300 rubles a month, so why should we knock ourselves out? You can't live on lousy wages like that. But I'm charging you 300 rubles for a single night's work, and I'll do a first-rate job for you." The same attitude could be encountered among furniture movers and workers in many other trades. They derived social status from employment in state-owned enterprises for which they actually did little or no work at all, but most of their income came from private citizens for whom they did excellent work.

One had to stand in line to buy anything, and people soon fell into the habit of joining as many lines as possble. One first joined up at the end of a line and then asked the person in front of him, "By the way, what are they selling today?" One waited to buy regardless of what was being sold, for if a particular item was not needed at one time, it would surely come in handy later. "Later" meant the item would, in all probability, no longer be available in stores. What preciously little was on sale in stores was invariably of poor quality and often mismatched. For example, it was quite common to find boxes with two left shoes or two right shoes. There were also lines in restaurants and what we would call in the United States cafeterias. It often happened that while you would still be eating your meal, several people would be lined up behind your chair waiting for you to leave. Many of them did not have enough money to buy their food, and they would whisper into your ear, "Citizen, would you please leave something on your plate for me?"

Because of severe shortages, real tragedies occurred. For example, it was almost impossible to get medicine. Once a woman's small son became ill with diphtheria, and a physician prescribed vaccine but warned that it was hard to get. He said he would return in two hours and she should have the ampules by then. She went immediately to a pharmacy but they did not have the vaccine. She went to other pharmacies, but none of them had the vaccine either. Finally, the woman found a pharmacy which had the vaccine. With great relief, she asked how much it would cost. The price was sixty kopecks, but when she tried to pay the pharmacist said, "This is a Torgsin pharmacy. We accept only foreign currency." Torgsin was an abbreviation of *Torgovlya s inostrantsami* (Trade with foreigners), and stores with this designation sold goods for dollars and other foreign currencies as well as gold and diamonds. When the woman heard this, she became hysterical. Fortunately for her, there was another customer, a foreigner who very kindly paid for the woman's vaccine with a few American cents. The woman kissed his hands and feet; she was deliriously happy because her child would now be saved.

The miserable living conditions gave rise to a kind of gallow's humor among the people. All kinds of jokes made the rounds, and one of them indicated just how little faith people had in official propaganda. The Soviets had often prophesied the coming of world revolution. Two American businessmen visiting Moscow saw a man perched on a high tower and asked him, "What are you doing up there?" "I am looking for the coming of the world revolution," he said. "As soon as it appears on the horizon I have to report to the authorities." The businessmen went to their hotel, held a consultation, and decided to hire the man to look for the end of the Great Depression which was then plaguing much of the world. Perhaps, they felt, this man could see the end coming and bring hope to the despairing Americans. The next day they asked the man, "Would you like to come to the United States and stand on top of the Empire State Building and look for the coming of the end of the depression?" "I'll have to think it over," he replied, "I'll give you an answer tomorrow." The next day the man answered, "I am not going. Your depression will be over in a couple of years, but my work here is a lifetime job."

The year 1936 brought sadness to my family because in February Nataliya became ill with a disease that much later would be diagnosed as multiple sclerosis. That summer she did not take the children to Kislovodsk in the Caucasus as usual. Instead, they spent the summer with our faithful former maid Anis'ya who had married and was now living in Ligovo on the outskirts of Leningrad. Nataliya went to a sanatorium to recover from her illness, while I had to go to Buryatia to attend the linguistic conference I described in Chapter 4. In December 1936 my younger son Nicholas became ill with scarlet fever, and my wife soon contracted this disease, as well. They were both sent to the hospital. No sooner did Nicholas return home then he became ill with the measles which he had evidently caught in the hospital. This time he almost died. After Nicholas had finally recovered, it was my turn to get scarlet fever, and the last of all to get it was my elder son Valerian.

In 1933 the United States became the first country in the world to recognize the Soviet regime. This act certainly encouraged Stalin to prepare for his "Great Purge," but first he needed a plausible pretext. He soon found it. The very next year S. M. Kirov, the popular first secretary of the Communist party committee for the Leningrad region, was murdered, allegedly on Stalin's orders, by a certain Nikolaev because, as rumors had it, Stalin had become increasingly jealous of Kirov's popularity. Nikolaev's trial was held in secret. It lasted only one day, and in the evening of the same day he was shot. This procedure was most peculiar because all other political trials were long drawn-out affairs, with the defendents eventually confessing their real or alleged crimes. Still more peculiar was the fact that a short time later the chief of the Leningrad regional NKVD, the same man who had presided over Nikolaev's trial, was also executed. This chief of the Leningrad NKVD bore the name of Medved' ("Bear") and his accuser was the head of the national NKVD in Moscow, called Yagoda ("Berry"). This episode gave rise to the following joke. Question: "What is the difference between a forest and the NKVD?" Answer: "In a forest the bear eats berries, but in the NKVD the berry eats the bear."

Soon after Kirov's murder, identification cards were issued to most of the urban population of the Soviet Union. Those who had in advance been sentenced to expulsion from the cities (priests, unemployed old women, many pensioners, and those who had held important positions under the Tsar) were denied a card and were forced to move to the countryside, sometimes to remote locations. One such unlucky person was my father-in-law's old friend and godfather of my sister-in-law, the former Senator D. F. Ognev, at whose apartment my new bride and I had celebrated our wedding in 1924. He had to leave Leningrad and died two or three years later.

Kirov's murder was the justification of the Great Purge which began in 1936. In early 1937, while I was still in the hospital with scarlet fever, the Great Purge was under way and quickly spread to my corner of the world of scholarship. The learned Buryat lamas and physicians Tomirgonov and Tserenov, both living in Leningrad, were arrested. The next victim was the well-known Khambo Lama, i.e., the head of the Lamaist clergy in Buryatia, Agvan Dorzhiev, who was arrested in spite of the fact that he was the diplomatic representative of the Dalai Lama and over eighty years old. I knew Agvan Dorzhiev well. He was a very learned and amiable man, a great scholar and a very influential person in the Buddhist world. My family and I used to visit him during our summer vacations in Kislovodsk where he, too, used to spend his holidays. He was sent to the Aleksandrovskaya jail near Ulan-Udè, the capital of Buryatia, where he died in 1940.

At the same time, arrests also began in the Academy of Sciences. My junior colleague A. I. Vostrikov, a Tibetanist and Sanskritist, and a student of Shcherbatskoi, was arrested. He was the son of a priest, and in order to remove any suspicion that he himself was a believer, he had joined the League of Militant Atheists. However, he committed a grave mistake for when he invited some members of that league to his home he had forgotten to remove his icons from the wall. His visitors saw the icons and made quite an issue of them. At a general meeting, attended by both members and non-members of the league, Vostrikov was accused of duplicity, attempting to mislead the league, and of being a hidden enemy. The absurdity of these accusations disgusted A. G. Shprintsin, a Sinologist, to the point where, with tongue in cheek, he confessed to having a Buddha statuette sit on the mantelpiece at his apartment. With mock contrition he admitted how wrong he had been in harboring such dangerous opiate of the masses and with a final flourish he offered the statuette as a gift for the Anti-Religious Propaganda Museum.

Vostrikov and I had been co-authors of a publication on the annals of the Barguzin Buryats, and I felt very uneasy about his fate. For a while he was left alone, but soon he was arrested and disappeared forever. Solzhenitsyn mentions him in his *Gulag Archipelago* as one of its inmates.[2]

One day in spring 1937 my aide Kazakevich and I received an order to prepare ourselves for a journey to Mongolia from the president of the Academy of Sciences, V. L. Komarov, a famous botanist and head of the Mongolian Commission. The Mongolian government, through the Foreign Service, had asked the academy to send scholars to conduct field work. Neither of us was enthusiastic about the journey, foreseeing nothing but trouble, but after an interview with Komarov we accepted this assignment with great reluctance. Several weeks later we were summoned to Komarov who told us that exit permits had been denied to both of us, and then he added, "We thought both of you to be loyal citizens of the Soviet Union and chose you as prospective members of the expedition." This was certainly a remark unworthy of the president of the academy. He had no right to talk to us in that manner, completely disregarding the fact that Kazakevich was a senior research scholar and I had been a corresponding member of the academy since 1932. Did he not know that the Soviet Union was experiencing political terror of a kind never before seen in the world? Both Kazakevich and I were greatly worried, expecting momentarily to be arrested and exiled to a concentration camp.

Luckily, nothing untoward happened to us, and when summer came my family and I went to Anapa, a small town on the shores of the Black Sea, because the physicians had recommended that all of us spend some time there to recuperate from the diseases that had plagued us during the previous winter (Illus. 17). While I was in Anapa I received a letter from my secretary, T. A. Burdukova. She wrote that both Kazakevich and Zhamtsarano had been arrested. Zhamtsarano had been exiled from Mongolia to Leningrad in 1932, soon after the anti-Communist revolt in that country. Some members of the Mongolian government had already been arrested in 1932, but Zhamtsarano had merely been sent to Leningrad where he went to work in my Mongolian department of the Institute of Oriental Studies of the Academy of Sciences. I created ideal conditions for him. He could choose his own research topics and come and go as he pleased. While in Leningrad he wrote several important works, including *Mongol'skie letopisi XVII veka* (The Mongolian Chronicles of the Seventeenth Century) which many years later was translated into English by Rudolf Loewenthal.[3] So Zhamtsarano was finished. He died in jail in his native Buryatia some time between 1940 and 1945. Very soon his friend, Bazar Baradiin, the director of the Institute of Language, Literature and History in Ulan-Udè, who had also left his native country and had been teaching Mongolian at Leningrad University, was also arrested.

As for Kazakevich, he had always feared arrest, and being

Illus. 17. The Author and his Family at Anapa in 1937.

particularly cautious, he thought to protect himself from suspicion by becoming very active in the trade union of "Workers of People's Education" to which all scholars had to belong. He served the interests of the community by finding scarce publications, theater tickets and the like, and by editing the weekly wall newspaper. His tragic fate was the result of a mistake he made. In 1932 he applied for a travel grant for research in Germany and France. He arrived in Berlin a few days before Hitler's seizure of power on January 30, 1933 and worked at the Völkermuseum (Ethnographic Museum) where he often met with Professor F. D. Lessing, later professor at the University of California at Berkeley. In Paris he worked with Paul

Pelliot but also visited his former schoolmate, the physician Bohnstedt who had emigrated from Russia soon after the revolution. When Kazakevich was preparing for his trip to Germany, I asked Sergei Ol'denburg, at that time the director of our institute, why a junior researcher was given a travel grant and I, a senior researcher, was not, Ol'denburg replied, "If you knew what kind of task Kazakevich has been given you would have refused to accept that grant." I never learned what kind of work Kazahevich had to do besides research. It might have been of a political nature. Of course, I would have never accepted any suggestions to do something other than scholarly work. Now, several years later, it became clear that I had been lucky not to have received that grant because Kazakevich, as it become known through the jail grapevine, was accused of having been instrumental in Hitler's rise to power (!) and of visiting emigrants in Paris. Kazakevich died in a concentration camp around 1943. His books and papers, like those of Zhamtsarano, were taken by the NKVD, and his wife, Zoya Vasil'evna, was exiled to Kazakhstan.

After my return to Leningrad from Anapa to resume my activities at the academy the purges continued. Besides Kazakevich and Zhamtsarano, my department also lost the Buryat aspirants Bolodon and Gomboin to the NKVD. Other departments of the Institute of Oriental Studies, universities, and other learned bodies were in the same position.

A meeting was convened at the institute to condemn the arrested "enemies of the people" and to formulate a new research plan. After the arrested had been condemned by a unanimous demand for "death to the traitors," the plan was discussed. One item in question was whether the text of the old Indian treatise on economics, *Arthaśāstra* should be published. M. I. Tubyanskii, a student of Shcherbatskoi, rose to remark that it was unnecessary to do this work because a good translation had already been published in Rome by the well-known scholar Giuseppe Tucci. Tubyanskii was immediately attacked for trying to prevent Soviet scholars from doing work that a Fascist had already done. After all, his detractors maintained, a Fascist cannot do a good translation. Tubyanskii objected saying, "Fascism has nothing to do with translations. A Fascist still can make an excellent translation." This statement was, of course, very foolhardy on his part and proved to be his undoing. As a Buddhologist he was already regarded as a person engaged in hostile activities. The study of Buddhism was regarded as incompatible with Marxist-Leninist ideology. This attitude toward Buddhism has never changed, and even in the 1970s the well-known Buryat Buddhologist Dandaron was arrested and subsequently perished in a concentration camp.

During the remainder of 1937 and early 1938 more members of the Institute of Oriental Studies of the Academy of Sciences were arrested, never to be seen again. These included the secretaries of the institute, D. P. Zhukov, G. V. Shitov, N. G. Talanov, and the director of the library, P. E. Skachkov; the Sinologists Shprintsin, Shchutskii,[4] B. A. Vasil'ev, Papayan and Kokin, the latter two being the authors of a book on the history of ancient China.[5] The fate of most of these victims is unknown. We do know, however, that Papayan was tortured to death. A so-called Spanish helmet was placed on his head and his head was slowly crushed until his brain was squeezed out.

Other victims of the Great Purge included my friend A. N. Genko, a specialist in Caucasian languages, and the well-known Japanologist N. A. Nevskii. Nevskii had returned from Japan in the 1930s. He had lived there since the beginning of World War I, as the war and the ensuing revolution and civil war had prevented him from returning home earlier. When in the early 1930s Shchutskii went to Japan and told Nevskii how good working conditions were in the Soviet Union, Nevskii decided to return with his Japanese wife and their little daughter Nelli. They moved into an apartment in the same house where another Japanologist, N. I. Konrad, lived. It was at 17 Tserkovnaya on the Petrogradskaya Storona. One night in early 1937 Nevskii and his wife were arrested, and the next morning Konrad's wife, N. I. Fel'dman, passing by Nevskii's apartment, noticed that the door was ajar and heard whimpering inside. She entered the Nevskiis' apartment and found little Nelli all by herself. The Konrads took her in and later adopted her. Konrad himself was also arrested but later released. In all, about forty out of a total of ninety members, or almost half, of the Institute of Oriental Studies were arrested. About the same percentage was also arrested in the other institutes. Even full members of the Academy of Sciences, including V. M. Perets, E. F. Karskii, and A. N. Samoilovich were arrested. Karskii had already been arrested when the Finnish scholars J. J. Mikkola and V. J. Mansikka came to Leningrad to visit him. As I spoke Finnish I was ordered to take care of these visitors although they were Slavicists and spoke perfect Russian, but I could not tell them the truth about Karskii. Instead I had to lie to them saying Karskii was on a trip and was not expected back in the near future.[6]

Police terror sometimes took grotesque forms. In the Buryat republic the brother of the commissar of education, Khabaev, was arrested and questioned every night about who had recruited him into an alleged spy organization. In order to terminate these interrogations which deprived him of his sleep, he "confessed" that his recruiters had been Artos, Portos and Aramis, the three musketeers in Alexandre Dumas's famous novel. The secret police discovered the true identity of these characters a couple of years later, during a period of relative calm, and released Khabaev's brother.

Another case was that of a Buryat teacher who feared arrest on political grounds and being sent to a concentration camp. He discussed this matter with his wife, and they persuaded her sister, who was underage, to accuse him of raping her. She did, and he was sentenced to three years in an ordinary jail and thus saved from slave labor. Before Stalin rose to power, rape had been punished severely, especially if it affected minors. Thus when six or seven rowdies raped a fourteen-year old girl in Chubarov Pereulok Street in Leningrad, all of them were shot. Now in the 1930s, rape, like theft of private property (but not of state property!) was punished with only a few years in jail.

I heard another story about a group of engineers. Once in Siberia I shared a train compartment with a man who had been one of several engineers who had been arrested and ordered to confess their "crimes." After having been grilled every night for more than

136

a month, they decided to confess that they had blown up a railroad bridge across a certain river. Two years later they were summoned to the commandant of the concentration camp who rebuked them for having lied. "We did not lie!" they retorted. "Yes, you did," the commandant insisted. "There is no such river in the entire Soviet Union and there is no such bridge." They had invented the entire story simply to put an end to interminable interrogations.

Finally, I would like to tell the following story that one of my colleagues in the Academy of Sciences told me when both of us were already in Germany during the war. He had been arrested and accused of having become a member of a German spy ring. He denied this charge, of course, but finally, after weeks of seemingly endless questioning, he announced that he would make a confession. His interrogator turned friendly at once, offered him pen and paper, and my colleague "confessed" that he had joined a British spy ring headed by a certain Mr. Lockhart. "You should have seen his face fall when he read this!" my colleague told me. "He had been utterly frustrated." "But why?" I asked. "Because," came the reply, "as the interrogator told me, 'Everything went so well. We were talking about German espionage, and then you come up with this nonsense about British spies. We don't have such a case in our files.'" My friend was released after a few months.

Times were so terrible that Nataliya could not sleep at night. She would sit up by the window and watch the traffic in the street, and whenever a car stopped by our house she became terrified. The cars of the secret police, nicknamed "black ravens," usually came around five in the morning. Many years later I saw Zuckmayer's stage play, "The Devil's General," in which the general remarked about Nazi Germany that "in other countries when the bell rings at five, people know it's the milkman." In the Soviet Union it was certainly not the milkman because milkmen no longer existed.

Speaking of arrests and deportations, I should point out that sometimes it was good to be out of town when a wave of arrests was rising. Valerian's godfather, the engineer P. P. Mokievskii, was surveying the line of a future railroad somewhere in the Far North when the police came after him in Leningrad. They searched his

apartment and left empty-handed. They did nothing to his wife nor
to his father, P. G. Mokievskii. The latter, however, was so worried
that he died of a heart attack. When several months later Engineer
Mokievskii returned to Leningrad, the arrest wave had run its course
and he was safe. However, he found his job with the railroads much
too dangerous because he could easily be accused of sabotage and
subversion, so he quit and became an engineer with the electric
streetcar construction office. Mokievskii died of starvation in
besieged Leningrad in 1942.

In 1937 I had my second brush with the secret police. I had to
appear along with the Estonian scholar Kurre, a Communist but a
very decent and pleasant man, as a witness in the case of the Finno-
Ugricist D. V. Bubrikh. Bubrikh had been arrested about a year
earlier after having been denounced as a Finnish nationalist. At that
time, the communist government of the Karelian autonomous
republic had been accused of subversive activities and many of its
members were executed. Among those who perished were E.
Gylling, K. Manner, and many other leaders of the Finnish
Communist Party. At the NKVD headquarters we were received by
Comrades Strogii and Serdityi. As was the case with all NKVD
officials, their names, which mean "Severe" and "Angry," were cover
names. They questioned us about Bubrikh. The charges against him
were utter nonsense because Bubrikh was not a Finnish nationalist;
on the contrary, in all his works Bubrikh always toed the official
party line. For instance, when there was a move to introduce
Finnish as the literary language of Karelia, Bubrikh stoutly
championed the Karelian language instead. Kurre and I explained
this to the NKVD and to our great surprise Bubrikh was freed soon
thereafter. It should be added, however, that they did not free
Bubrikh because of our testimony. They had already decided to free
him, but being overly cautious, they needed some justification. If
their superiors should later accuse them of having freed an "enemy
of the people" they could say that they had acted on the basis of
Kurre's and my expert testimony. My friend A. N. Genko was also
freed at that time.

In 1938 the Institute of Living Oriental Languages (not to be confused with the Institute of Oriental Studies of the Academy of Sciences) was closed, perhaps because all its directors had been arrested and disappeared. After Kotwicz had returned to Poland, P. I. Vorob'ev became the director. Although Vorob'ev had been a very cautious man and had been in the Soviets' favor for a long time, he too, was later arrested. His story is very interesting. In 1929 Stalin wanted to become the leader of the party, but the Leningrad organization was headed by the very influential Grigorii Zinov'ev. Vorob'ev happened to be in Moscow at the time where he met a friend, an old party member by the name of Bolotnikov, who told him, "Things are not as simple as you think. The Leningrad organization may be in favor of Zinov'ev, but Stalin who is already an important person in the Communist party and the de facto ruler of the Soviet Union will certainly win out over him. Be careful when you return to Leningrad and don't vote for Zinov'ev." Vorob'ev returned to Leningrad and during the election at the regional party committee, he voted against Zinov'ev. He was immediately expelled from the party, but the very next day it became known that Stalin had become the secretary general. Of course Vorob'ev was instantly reinstated, and all those who had expelled him were severely punished. Now, however, Vorob'ev had fallen in disfavor and was arrested. He was succeeded as the director of the Institute of Living Oriental Languages by the Buryat M. I. Amagaev. Amagaev had been a member of the Comintern who in the late 1920s was sent to Mongolia to carry out the Comintern's leftist policies. These turned out to be disastrous. Mongolia was not yet ready for collectivization and the closure of all Buddhist monasteries, yet these "improvements" were enforced through sheer police terror. When in 1932 an uprising broke out, a new political course was adopted for Mongolia and Amagaev was made the scapegoat. Accused of being a leftist, he was demoted and exiled to Leningrad where he became the director of the institute. After his arrest, his position was given to a certain Frantsevich, then to another former Comintern member by the name of Shami, and finally to a certain Denisov who was director when the institute was closed altogether in 1938.

Of these various directors I knew Amagaev the best because,

being a Buryat, he often talked to me in Mongolian and obviously liked and trusted me. He once made the very interesting comment that in Mongolia there was actually no socialism or even any system which could be considered preparatory to socialism. "What Mongolia has is state capitalism," he said, adding, "actually the same that we have here in the Soviet Union." That was, of course, a very strong admission from a party member and a former Comintern member. Amagaev had been well trained by the party, but his general education was rather poor. I remember him once discussing certain program changes he wanted to make when he lamented, "Unfortunately my proposals did not meet with renaissance among the professors." He mistakenly used "renaissance" instead of "resonance."

In 1938 I became ill with colitis and had to be hospitalized. This was the result of several bouts of the dysentery which I had initially contracted in Mongolia and Buryatia. That year also marked the end of the Great Purge. Ezhov, the chief of the NKVD, was arrested and executed, and he was replaced by Beria. The mass arrests were replaced by a permanent, creeping form of police terror, like an acute illness which gradually becomes a chronic condition.

The 1930s were years of almost total isolation for scholars working in the Soviet Union. We were afraid of having any contact with other countries. In the 1920s I could publish my articles in *Asia Major*, *Ungarische Jahrbücher*, *Kőrösi Csoma Archivum* and other foreign journals, and I corresponded with G. J. Ramstedt, Willi Bang-Kaup, Kai Donner and other scholars. Late in 1933 I received a letter from Bang who asked me to send him my curriculum vitae and list of publications because he intended to propose me for corresponding membership in the Berlin Academy of Sciences. This was a flattering proposal but also dangerous for me. I remembered that V. N. Beneshevich, a well-known Byzantine scholar, had been elected as a corresponding member of the Bavarian Academy of Sciences, and that this produced a storm in the academy in Leningrad. A meeting was convened in which Beneshevich was accused of having contacts with a Nazi Academy of Sciences which had obviously elected him as a reward for services rendered to Nazism.

Beneshevich was arrested and never seen again. I also remembered the case of the academician S. A. Zhebelev, a great scholar in ancient Greek history. In 1928 he contributed to an article to the *Seminarium Kondakovianum*, the organ of Russian emigré scholars living in Prague.[7] Accusations were hurled at Zhebelev and the book was branded as "Scandalium Kondakovianum." Somehow Zhebelev survived that stormy meeting.

Returning to Bang's suggestion, I must say that I was afraid to send him my curriculum vitae and simply procrastinated. The case was soon solved, for in 1934 Bang died of acute appendicitis. I was very sorry because we had become good friends, but his death released me from my dilemma. Is it not macabre to owe the solution of a difficult problem to the death of a dear friend?

Meanwhile the nation lived in a state of political frenzy. Trotskii had been expelled from the country. Zinov'ev, Bukharin, Pyatakov and other old Bolsheviks had been executed. The secret police, the NKDV, was suspicious of everybody and sometimes its actions were simply grotesque. One day my sons returned from school and told us that their copybooks had been taken away because the picture on their covers was counterrevolutionary. As a matter of fact, the picture merely illustrated the text of Pushkin's introduction to his poem "Ruslan and Lyudmila," specifically the following lines which are given here in Walter Arndt's translation:

> An oak tree greening by the ocean,
> A golden chain about it wound,
> Whereon a learned cat in motion
> Both day and night will walk around.
> On walking right, he sings a ditty,
> On walking left, he tells a lay.
> A magic place; there winds his way
> The woodsprite; there's a mermaid sitting
> In branches....[8]

The picture showed the oak tree, the cat, the mermaid, and when one turned the picture around, one could see, with a certain

141

amount of imagination, a face in the roots of the oak tree. The
NKVD or the school board had decided that the face was that of
Trotskii! Consequently, all copybooks had to be collected and, in
spite of an acute shortage of school supplies, sent to the
papermills. There was, of course, no face in the roots, and only the
unhealthy fantasy of paranoiacs in their fear of their own people
could see what was not there.

The above mentioned picture and the verses it illustrates
evoked a parody which was then circulating in the schools. I give my
own translation of that parody:

> The oak was felled and is no more,
> They took the chain to Torgsin store,
> They minced the cat; meatballs were made,
> They gave no passport to the maid,
> And woodsprite is in Solovki.

Torgsin, as noted earlier, was the name of stores selling goods for
gold or foreign currency, and Solovki is the name of a thirteenth-
century monastery on an island in the White Sea that had been
turned into a notorious concentration camp.

Such was the political climate in the thirties. As for food
supplies and other commodities, the situation was usually rather
difficult, although some improvement became noticeable toward the
end of the decade. As mentioned earlier, I had access to a closed
store since 1932 when I became a corresponding member of the
Academy of Sciences (Illus. 18). I also had the privilege of eating in
the dining room reserved for members of the Academy. It was very
elegant having individual tables covered with impeccable white
tablecloths, pretty Tatar girls as waitresses, and excellent food.
The service was very good. At the same time, the dining hall for
lower ranking scholars and employees was filthy, food was poor, and
service was atrocious. Orwell had not yet written his *Animal Farm*,
but my colleagues and I already knew that some animals were more
equal than others.

АКАДЕМИЯ НАУК
Союза Советских Социалистических
Республик

ЧЛЕН-КОРРЕСПОНДЕНТ
АКАДЕМИИ НАУК СССР

НИКОЛАЙ НИКОЛАЕВИЧ
ПОППЕ

Президент
Академии Наук СССР

Избран 29 марта 1932 года

Illus. 18. The Author's Academy Pass

One noticeable improvement in the food supply was a sudden and continued supply of oranges in 1936 whereas before there had been none at all. A school teacher once asked her students whether they had ever eaten an orange. None had. This became known to the authorities who dismissed her for asking useless and provocative questions, and she was deported to Siberia. But in 1936 oranges became plentiful because in the Spanish civil war the Soviet Union supported the Popular Front with weapons, food, instructors and regular army troops posing as volunteers. The ships carrying men and supplies to Spain took on oranges as ballast for their return trips.

Nineteen thirty-nine was an eventful year. In March or April I had the opportunity to prove the usefulness of Mongolian Studies to the Soviet government. One day I was asked to come to the office of the secretary of the Institute of Oriental Studies where I was introduced to a major-general named Bogdanov. He was the chief of the Soviet border commission whose task it was to delineate the frontier between Mongolia and Manchukuo. The two countries and their patrons, the Soviet Union and Japan, had been involved in a border dispute which gradually escalated to armed clashes, the battle at Khalkhiin Gol being the most serious of them. In order to stop hostilities and prevent further incidents, the frontiers were to be delineated with the greatest precision. General Bogdanov had come to ask for old Mongolian and Chinese maps on which the border was marked clearly. We showed him several Mongolian maps of Eastern Mongolia which he studied intently. Although he could not read Mongolian, he had expert knowledge of the topography. Time after time he pointed to rivers, lakes, and monasteries marked on the map and called out their names, and each time I confirmed that he was correct. When he left, General Bogdanov took several maps along to use in meetings with Japanese and Manchukuo officials. I also lent him the atlas of China which the Jesuits had compiled in the seventeenth century. The general thanked us profusely, told us that the Japanese and Manchukuo claims were absolutely baseless, and promised to return the maps as soon as possible.

General Bogdanov was the second high-ranking military officer who made a good impression on me. In 1936 fortifications were being built along the border between Siberia and Manchuria. This prompted Kazakevich and me to write to Marshal K. Blyukher, the commander-in-chief of the Far Eastern military district, asking that all stone statues and other relics often found in the steppe be mapped. He promised us that he would do so, but unfortunately he could not keep his promise because a short time later he was arrested and shot. His wife, Zoya Aleksandrovna, and a lady friend of hers, Zoya Sergeevna, the divorced wife of the Japanologist G. O. Monzeler, who lived with her and who was a Sinologist, were arrested and sent to concentration camps where they probably perished.

In the summer of 1939 I went to a sanatorium in Essentuki in the northern Caucasus which had mineral water said to cure all kinds of diseases of the digestive organs. My family stayed in Kislovodsk that summer, which was only about thirty kilometers away, and I visited them frequently. One day in August we heard the news that a pact had been concluded between the Soviet Union and Nazi Germany. This was followed by the German invasion of Poland on September 1, and a short time later the Soviet Union attacked the Poles from the rear. The second world war had begun. Poland was defeated, and history repeated itself. Just as at the end of the eighteenth century, during the time of Catherine the Great, Poland was divided between Germany and Russia. When we returned to Leningrad, I contracted a very severe case of angina and was treated with antibiotics. September had already arrived, but there was absolutely no heating fuel to be found anywhere in the city. As soon as I had recovered, I went to a lumber yard and bought two hundred logs, from four to five meters long and about twenty centimeters in diameter. I had them cut into firewood and used them as fuel all winter. It was actually a pity to use such good timber as firewood but nothing else was available.

The winter of 1939 came early and it was very cold. One day I was summoned to the Leningrad military district headquarters where I was shown a book written in Finnish which I recognized immediately as being a triangulation of Finland. The officers asked me if I could translate it for them. Of course I could translate it because I spoke Finnish fluently, but I did not want to have anything to do with it, so I told them that I did not know Finnish. It turned out that I had made a wise decision because shortly thereafter we heard rumors of Soviet troops massing along the Finnish border, and we read in the newspapers that the Soviet Union was negotiating with Finland. The Soviets wanted to obtain the Karelian isthmus and some other parts of Finland in exchange for a territory twice as large, but the Finnish government adamantly refused the offer because they were being asked to give up a densely populated and industrialized area in exchange for virgin forest and swamps.

At the end of November 1939 I went to Moscow to deliver a paper on the Mongolian epics at a meeting of the Division of Language and Literature of the Academy of Sciences. In the evening after the meeting everybody saw in *Pravda* the headline, "A Clown as Prime Minister of a Nation." It was an article about Finland and its prime minister Cajander. All participants in the meeting at the

Academy looked at each other silently. That same evening I took the express, the Red Arrow, back to Leningrad. It was December 1, and the temperature was minus fifty degrees Centigrade. The newspapers carried the news that Finland had attacked the Soviet Union, and the following day it was announced that a revolution had broken out in Finland and a new government friendly to the Soviet Union had been formed, headed by the Finnish member of the Comintern, Otto Kuusinen. The official announcement added that a Finnish revolutionary army had been formed to fight alongside the Soviet army against the fascist-bourgeois Finnish government. Of course, all this was utterly untrue, because it was absolutely incredible that a small country like Finland could attack the Soviet Union.

A couple of days later, we learned by word of mouth that a unit of the Red Army had fired several grenades in the direction of another Soviet military unit while simultaneously a Soviet border patrol invaded Finnish territory and killed several Finnish soldiers at a border post. At the same time, I came upon direct evidence that the official announcement was untrue. When I boarded a streetcar, I saw a soldier in an unusual uniform. Everybody looked at him with great astonishment and I asked him, "Who are you?" He said, "I am a soldier of the Finnish Liberation Army allied with the Soviet army." Then I asked him in Finnish, "Where is your home town?" and he answered in Russian that he did not understand. I repeated my question in Russian and he replied, "I am from Ryazan'." Ryazan' is near Moscow, far from the Finnish border, with a wholly Russian population. Two women were riding in the same streetcar, and one of them said to the other, "I remember those uniforms; we were sewing them in our factory last year." It was clear, then, that preparations for an attack on Finland had been in the works for at least one year.

The Russians fared poorly on the Finnish front, suffering tremendous losses. Both Professor M. V. Shtein and the research scholar Solodukho of the Institute of Oriental Studies each had a son who was killed in action. V. I. Belyaev, an Arabicist and former student of I. Yu. Krachkovskii, was severely wounded in one of his legs and limped for the rest of his life. One of my students worked in a field hospital in Leningrad that was set up in a school. I asked him what the name of his hospital was and he told me that it was the 240th Field Hospital. Then I asked him how many wounded they had at any given time. He said about 250. Assuming that there were 240 military hospitals and that each hospital averaged 250 wounded soldiers, the total would have been about 60,000. This is an unbelievably high number, if one takes into consideration that the total Finnish army had no more than 40,000 men during peacetime. Besides, 240 was certainly not the total number of field hospitals. In summer 1940 there were no sanatoria or rest homes open to civilians. All of them had been converted to military use. The entire Caucasus and Crimea were full of soldiers who were wounded or whose arms and legs had frozen and required amputation.

The Soviets had 600,000 men on the Finnish front, of whom 150,000 were said to have been killed and another 300,000 severely wounded and crippled for life. In other words, the Soviets suffered altogether 450,000 casualties fighting against a country with a population of only about four million people. In the end the Soviet Union won but it was a Pyrrhic victory; never had such a small piece of land as the Karelian Isthmus been conquered at such high cost in human lives. Many years later some Finnish friends told me what it was like on the front. The so-called Mannerheim Line consisted of bunkers, about 200 to 300 meters apart, with six or seven soldiers in each of them. Each bunker's field of fire overlapped with those of the two neighboring bunkers, so that wherever the Russians attacked, they would be caught in a crossfire. Thus pinned down against the frozen ground, tens of thousands of Soviet soldiers froze to death, and those few who dared get up were killed by Finnish gunfire.

Although the Soviet press and radio confined themselves to laconic reports that stubborn fighting was going on or no significant changes had occurred, I was well informed about the true situation at the front. The library of the Institute of Oriental Studies subscribed, *inter alia*, to the French-language *Journal de Téhéran* which every day brought the latest news from Swiss sources. The Soviet censors minutely examined all European and American papers but evidently never thought that a paper published in Iran would publish full details of the war against Finland.

The Finns had to cede several parts of their country to the Soviet Union and pay large reparations, but they managed to preserve their freedom and independence. I very much pitied the Red Army soldiers who were killed and wounded, because they had nothing to do with starting the war against Finland; but I must confess that I also admired the Finns' successful resistance and their quality of *sisu* which roughly means "guts." Their victories at Salla and Alakurtti filled me with joy.

We spent the summer of 1940 in Berngardovka near Leningrad where friends of ours had a cottage. The summer was passing uneventfully when the "phony war" or, as the French called it, "la drôle de la guèrre," suddenly and unexpectedly became a real war. The Germans landed in Norway and then defeated France. After the British army had been chased off the continent, Great Britain was supposed to become Germany's next victim. With Germany's attention thus diverted away from its eastern frontiers, the Soviet Union seized this opportunity to pressure the governments of Estonia, Latvia, and Lithuania into letting the Red Army enter their countries, ostensibly to protect them against Nazi Germany. As soon as the Soviet army entered the Baltic states, however, Soviet soldiers in civilian disguise and local fellow travelers appeared on the streets with red banners and posters proclaiming, "We demand that our country become part of the Soviet Union!" In response to this "popular" demand, the Soviet Union then swallowed up all three countries. During the same summer while I was traveling across Siberia to Buryatia, long trains of so-called Stolypin (i.e. prison) cars were hauling the first groups of an estimated total of 20,000 Estonians, 30,000 Latvians, and 30,000 Lithuanians to concentrations camps in Siberia. I obtained these figures from Estonian, Latvian, and Lithuanian refugee organizations in Germany in 1945-46. Judging by the number of trains, crammed full of deportees, which I had seen on my way through Siberia, these figures appear credible.

These events formed the background of my life at that time and greatly influenced my scholarly work which, despite all kinds of ideological obstructions, proceeded satisfactorily. There was, however, some danger that scholarly work might become impossible altogether.

What could save us scholars? And what could liberate everyone, scholar, worker and peasant, from police terror? Many Soviet citizens thought a war might preserve them from annihilation. In war, to be sure, a total of perhaps three to four million soldiers would die, but this was the number of people who died in our concentration camps every year. These were the thoughts of many people in the Soviet Union at that time. Were they correct? Yes and no. On the one hand, my family and I were saved by the war, for we managed to leave the Soviet Union only because the territory where we happened to be in 1942 was occupied by the Germans. From a wider perspective, however, the war brought the world only losses and no gains at all. I should add, though, that such thoughts at this time were shared by many people, including myself. On my travels in Siberia I often had contact with Russian peasants who would say to me, "If only war came! We would then know how to act!" Later, when war broke out, hundreds of thousands of soldiers surrendered and offered to collaborate with the enemy. The Germans, however, with incredible stupidity spurned this offer of cooperation and treated the Soviet prisoners of war with cruelty, often letting them starve to death.

The second half of 1940 and the first three months of 1941 brought changes for the better. Quite unexpectedly one could now buy many things which had previously been unavailable. This included not only foodstuffs but also clothes. At the end of May 1941 I returned from Buryatia to Leningrad. People there were ill at ease and were talking secretly of an imminent war. Suddenly at the beginning of June TASS announced that the capitalist press was disseminating rumors about German troop concentrations along the Soviet frontier. It went on to denounce these rumors as utterly false and as another attempt by the capitalist press to undermine Soviet-German amity which was, of course, stronger than ever. This TASS announcement fooled everyone. Instead of preparing for the worst, we decided that my wife and children would again try to spend their summer vacation in Kislovodsk in the Caucasus. I obtained train tickets for them through the redcap I mentioned earlier, and on June 16 my family left for the Caucasus.

I had to stay behind in Leningrad for another two weeks because some students were to defend their candidate dissertations, and I planned to join my family around July 1. One of my own students, a certain Korol', who wrote on the Mongolian historical work *Bolor Toli* (Crystal Mirror) was to defend his work. Among the other persons to pass their candidate examinations was Vera Tsintsius, now a well-known scholar. She had returned from jail shortly before so that she was still in a terribly poor mental condition. She could not say two words without crying. Her dissertation, however, was so brilliant that Professor L. V. Shcherba, the general linguist, and I decided to tell her that she should present it for her doctoral degree and submit something else for the candidate examination. She agreed and submitted a description of a Tungus dialect, defending it brilliantly.

When Nataliya left with our children for the Caucasus, she gave me tickets for a guest performance of the Moscow Theater in Leningrad. At the time she bought the tickets, she had not yet known exactly when we would leave for the Caucasus. Since I would otherwise be alone she suggested that I invite one of her lady friends to go along to the theater. As it turned out, her friend could not make it and so I took my secretary Taisiya Alekseevna Burdukova instead. On June 21 the two of us went to the theater and returned to our respective homes rather late. During the night I heard airplanes flying above our apartment house and I was annoyed, thinking that it was another one of those air force holidays. The next morning, Sunday, June 22, when I got up everything was quiet, but I heard on the radio, "Comrade Molotov will make a very important announcement." Shortly thereafter, the announcement came, "War has begun. The Germans have crossed the border and Kiev, Sevastopol and Minsk have been bombarded by the German air force."

The war took Stalin and his government by surprise. They obviously had believed a totalitarian country would not attack another totalitarian country just because they shared many features.

When Stalin first learned about the German attack, he closeted himself in his study and remained incommunicado for three full days, all the while pacing across the room like a wounded tiger. The generals, not daring to undertake anything without his orders, waited.

After the partitioning of Poland in 1939, Stalin had ordered the defense line along the old border dismantled and moved westward to the new border. When the Germans attacked the Soviet Union, the transfer of guns, steel bunkers and other equipment from the old to the new defense line had still not been completed.

In addition, many Soviet soldiers were unwilling to fight, and a large portion of the civilian population even welcomed the Germans. All of these facts allowed the Germans to sweep into the Soviet Union virtually unopposed. Stalin had once boasted on the occasion of a military parade in Moscow before the war that "we shall answer the enemy's blow with a threefold blow and beat him, with little bloodshed on our side, on his own territory." As is well known, before the Germans were ultimately crushed, they managed to reach the Caucasus and the Volga River, almost 2,000 miles from the German frontier.

7 War Comes to Russia

World War II had started in September 1939. Now, almost two years later, it had spread to the Soviet Union. The war, which many people in the Soviet Union had hoped for, had suddenly come. But I could not really be happy because I could imagine how many people would be lost, how many would be killed, how many cultural treasures would be destroyed, and how many people would become homeless. And, supposing the Germans would win, would it be possible to do scholarly work under their rule? Here in the Soviet Union I had been a professor since 1925 and a member of one of the most famous learned organizations in the world, the Academy of Sciences, since 1932. But somehow I had a feeling that Germany would lose the war. The Soviets were reckless and would not hesitate to sacrifice ten or twenty million people in the war in order to win the final victory. For the first time I had a nightmarish vision of the Soviets not only conquering Germany but also half of Europe and making these countries Communist. The forebodings of mine came later true: Poland, Czechoslovakia, Hungary, Bulgaria, Rumania, Albania and the eastern part of Germany became Soviet satellites.

The next day, Monday, June 23 I went to the Academy where I met the Sinologist Alekseev. He said, "Is it not terrible? What shall we do? The Germans might actually conquer us. The Soviets are preferable if for no other reason than we already know how to deal with them. But do we know the Germans? Will we be able to continue our work under them?"

Alekseev's fears seemed to be justified in the beginning. The Germans advanced very fast. In about ten days they had already swept into the Baltic states of Lithuania, Latvia and Estonia. I remember also my conversation with V. V. Struve, the well-known Egyptologist and director of the Institute of Oriental Studies, at the beginning of July. "The Soviets," he said, "are certainly far from ideal, but I am sure that the Germans will lose the war. Since I never bet on a loser, I think that we should go on cooperating faithfully with the Soviets to the very end." I agreed with his analysis but, in the innermost recesses of my mind, I saw a different plan of action. I preferred to join the Germans temporarily by retreating with them into Germany, in order to emigrate to Great Britain or the United States. But at that time I did not have the faintest idea if and how this could be accomplished.

The situation in Leningrad was growing worse day by day. It became clear that the Germans would soon reach the city, and I wanted to get out if for no other reason than to join my family who were on vacation in the Caucasus and had nothing but summer clothes with them. As the war was likely to be a long one, they also needed winter clothes which could not be bought in the Caucasus but only in large cities. I also had two other important reasons for wanting to leave Leningrad. The first was that more arrests were made immediately following the German invasion. Anyone who had ever been arrested or who had been merely summoned by the secret police was arrested again. A. V. Burdukov was among this group and, as I learned later, he died in jail of starvation because prisoners were not fed in besieged Leningrad. The same fate also befell a junior researcher at the Institute of Oriental Studies named Volin and thousands of others. Since I had also been summoned by the secret police in 1927, I feared that I might also be arrested. My other reason for wanting to leave Leningrad was that I had twice been called to appear before the draft board. The first time they simply registered me and did not ask any questions, but the second time they asked me if I knew Finnish or Rumanian. I could not speak Rumanian but I knew Finnish very well. Nevertheless, because I did not want to become a translator or interpreter in the army, especially not against Finland which I liked very much, I told the draft board that I did not know either language. They let me go, but the question kept nagging me whether they would let me go again a third time. It was quite possible that my translations for the Finns visiting the Academy of Sciences would be remembered and I would finally be drafted into the army as an interpreter.

My chance for escape came soon. Right after the German invasion the Academy of Sciences was being prepared for evacuation, and its scholars were to be sent to cities according to their specialties. I was assigned to the Kalmuck Republic, which was a stroke of luck for me; first, because the Kalmuck research institute had repeatedly invited me to do research there, and second, because Elista, the capital of the Kalmuck Republic, was fairly close to the Caucasus where my family was staying. It was possible that I might be able to spend the war together with my family. At that time the thought did not cross my mind that the Germans might conquer Elista. Although it had become clear that Stalin's boastful words that not an inch of Soviet territory would ever be yielded to the enemy were empty phrases, I still could not accept the idea that the Germans would occupy most of the European part of the Soviet Union and reach the banks of the Volga.

Getting to Elista proved to be a major undertaking because all railroad lines to the Kalmuck Republic and to the Caucasus led through Moscow, and Moscow had been declared a closed city. No outsiders were permitted to enter or pass through Moscow, so I had to look for other ways to go south. One was by ship, and this was the route I chose. I left Leningrad on July 18, 1941 taking with me two suitcases and two large bundles of clothes, topcoats, blankets, and other things for my wife and children because it was absolutely impossible to buy anything outside of Leningrad. I found a man with a cart who was willing to transport my belongings to a pier on the Neva river. There a small river boat took me to Shlissel'burg where the Neva flows out of Lake Ladoga. There I took another steamer through a canal along the southern shore of Lake Ladoga to a place called Sviritsa, where the Svir' River, coming from Lake Onega, enters Lake Ladoga. After almost two weeks I finally reached Rybinsk on the Volga where I had to wait three days for the next steamer to take me down the river. It was impossible to find any accommodations in Rybinsk, so I went to the local museum, showed my credentials, told them that I was a scholar with no place to stay, and asked whether I could stay overnight in the museum. I was permitted to sleep on a couch in a small empty room. In the apartment for the museum porter there lived a young woman with her small child whose husband had just been drafted. That evening she invited me for tea, but she apologized that she would have only hot water because neither tea nor sugar had been available for more than two years. I took along some tea, sugar, candy, and cookies which surprised the young woman. "Where did you get these?" she asked. "I brought them from Leningrad." "Oh," she said, "here in Rybinsk we've had absolutely nothing at all."

From Rybinsk I rode on a large steamer to Astrakhan where I had to cross the Volga, which is very wide at that point, to Kanukovo, formerly called Kalmytskii Bazar (Khal'mag Bazaar). Kanukov had been a revolutionary, and the town was renamed in his honor. There I slept on a wooden cot in a school, for lack of any other accommodations, and waited for a bus which a few days later took me to Elista. As soon as I had put down my suitcases and bags, I took a train from Divnoe, some ninety kilometers from Elista, to Kislovodsk, arriving there on August 21. In peacetime, Kislovodsk could be reached from Leningrad in three days, but this trip took one month and three days. On August 25, my younger son Nicholas' birthday, all four of us, together with our dog, left for Elista where we arrived a few days later.

At the Pedagogical Institute I taught courses in Mongolian philology and the history and syntax of the Russian language to the senior students who were being trained to become teachers in Kalmuck schools. There was also a research institute under the directorship of I. K. Ilishkin, a Communist Kalmuck, who was a decent and honest man. Later, one of the teachers at the Pedagogical

Institute was a certain Lipin who was Jewish. He had left besieged Leningrad, where he had almost starved to death, with his wife, his sister-in-law, his young son and another young boy who was the son of his brother who remained in Leningrad. Late one night in December the train carrying them arrived in Astrakhan. It was rainy and cold and, with the street lights turned off and all windows curtained, the city was pitch dark. Lipin and his family were strangers in the city and had no idea where to find shelter. They could not stay at the railroad station because it closed between midnight and seven in the morning. They went to the police station, but the police told them, "We are not a hotel and we don't give out hotel information to strangers. Get out of here!" They spent the whole night outside in the rain. Lipin's small son caught a severe cold, then pneumonia, and died.

Another instructor at the institute was an air force officer named Gosudarev, a very pleasant and friendly man, who taught the military subjects currently mandatory for all students in the Soviet Union. When the director of the institute and the party committee demanded that all teachers turn over two months' salary for the purchase of government bonds, Gosudarev objected that the teachers could not possibly afford to donate that much money because they were already living on a starvation diet. The physics teacher, a certain Braga, overheard his remarks and denounced him, and Gosudarev was arrested and disappeared.

We lived in the dormitory of the Pedagogical Institute, along with other instructors and students. Our room was on the upper floor of the two-story dormitory and had three iron beds, a couch, four chairs, a table, a wardrobe and a cupboard. The winter 1941-42 was very severe. The snow in the steppe was three feet deep, and the temperature plummeted to forty degrees below freezing. Our room was very large but had only a small cast iron stove. It normally used coal or wood, but neither being available, we tried our best with coal dust and dried reeds. The stove smoked a lot but warmed our room to only around 57 degrees Fahrenheit or about 9 degrees Centigrade. One day we learned that Selvin, the institute's deputy director for finance and economic affairs, had been seen pushing a wheelbarrow filled with excellent coal in the direction of his house. We soon discovered that the basement of the institute was full of this high-grade coal, but it was for the exclusive use of officials and administrators who lived in good apartments in special buildings with central heating which actually worked. They also received coupons for clothes and other merchandise which were unavailable to the rest of us. With reference to Orwell's *Animal Farm*, I can testify that I have seen many animals being more equal than others, and that in Elista I belonged to those who were less equal.

Food was scarce, and our only warm food was a thick millet gruel which we obtained at the dining hall of the Pedagogical Institute. I received 800 grams of black bread per day and each member of my family 500 grams. I also received one kilogram of sugar a month and the others only half a kilogram each. With great difficulty I managed to get a pass for the dining hall of the party committee which served good food. Since only employees could be served there, I gave my millet soup and bread to my wife and children.

In addition to all these privations, the omnipresent NKVD was also active in Elista. Soon after my arrival in the fall of 1941, the deportation of all persons of German origin began. The entire population of the Volga German Republic, some 600,000 persons, was exiled to Soviet Central Asia, and many died en route. A certain Marika Ruppen, who was a student at the institute, was also deported by the NKVD, and her father, an army officer, was discharged and arrested. I was also summoned to the NKVD to have all our identification cards inspected. Fortunately we were listed as being of Russian origin. When the cards were first issued back in 1937, the interrogating official in Leningrad had only required verbal answers to various questions. My principle had always been never to make myself conspicuous, because the first rule of survival in the Soviet Union was never to draw attention to oneself. So to the question of ethnic origin, I had answered "Russian." The chief of the local NKVD, by the name of Sobachkin, thought this peculiar and asked, "But your name is not Russian." I quickly responded, "My great-grandfather was from Czechoslovakia," and this satisfied him.

Our children went to school. Valerian was placed in the ninth grade, the next to last grade of a typical ten-year high school, and Nicholas was in the sixth grade. Both of them were the best students in their classes because they had come from Leningrad where the schools were much better than those in the Kalmuck Republic. Toward the end of November all students in the upper grades of high schools and at the Pedagogical Institute were mobilized and sent to Kotel'nikovo near the Don River in order to build anti-tank ditches. Valerian was sent there, too. His living conditions were very difficult and he had to work outside in very cold weather. He returned at the end of January 1942, tired and exhausted and with a very severe cold. In addition, he had also lost the watch which he had received for his birthday on April 19, 1941. While spending a night in one of the peasant houses near Kotel'nikovo, he had taken his wristwatch off in order to wash up, and when he returned five minutes later, it had been stolen. A few days after his return, he became severely ill with pneumonia and had to be hospitalized. His young and strong body overcame the disease, and by the end of March he had recovered and returned to school. His teachers were very fond of him and tutored him privately so that he could catch up, and at the end of the school year he moved up to the tenth and last grade of his high school.

In spring 1942 I received a job offer from the Pedagogical Institute of the Karachai area, which was located in the city of Mikoyan Shakhar. I decided to go there because we were all fond of the Caucasus, and Mikoyan Shahar was not far from our beloved Kislovodsk. Toward the end of July 1942 we went by truck from Elista to the Divnoe railroad station, where we boarded a train bound for Cherkessk. From Cherkessk another fifty kilometers by truck took us to Mikoyan Shakhar. Here we obtained a well-furnished three-room apartment not far from the Pedagogical Institute with a kitchen, bath and central heating. The Pedagogical Institute made a very pleasant impression and its director, G. G. Leonov, was an amiable man.

Life in Mikoyan Shakhar was peaceful, but the situation at

the front was catastrophic. The Germans had already taken Rostov-on-the-Don on July 25 and were coming closer. At the beginning of August the local government announced the draft of age groups and Valerian was among them. Fortunately the conscription proceeded alphabetically, with one or two letters being called up each day. We calculated that my son's turn would come about on the tenth day. I was desperate because I feared that if he were drafted we would never see him again. Losses had been tremendous, and they were bound to be still greater once the Soviets started their counter-offensive. A few days after the call-up began, I was walking in the street when I noticed that all draft posters and announcements had been taken down. I asked someone and he told me in a whisper that the Karachai and other mountaineers had refused to hand their sons over to the draft board and therefore the whole draft had been canceled. I was overjoyed. On August 8, the order came for the entire population to evacuate Mikoyan Shakhar and to go by foot about 300 kilometers to Kizlyar near the Caspian Sea. Nothing came of the order as the only people who actually left were civilian and military officials as well as party members. Before they left I went to the military commandant and asked him to take me and my family with him. He replied, "You are not a party member, Professor. Nothing will happen to you. We will return soon and everything will be all right. Anyway, we have only a few cars and too many people, so we could not take you with us even if we wanted to." As we were to find out soon, his refusal was a blessing in disguise. The local mountaineers ambushed the commandant and his entire convoy. Everybody was killed, and the bodies were later found in the forest not far from Mikoyan Shakhar.

As soon as I had found out I had to remain with my family in the city, I went to the food distribution office and asked them to give us some flour and other foodstuffs which would at least keep us alive until the Soviets returned. They replied, "We have nothing." However, as soon as the Soviets left the city, the local population started plundering the stores and warehouses, carrying off large barrels of butter, sacks of flour, and sugar. So the Soviets' last official word to us had turned out to be yet another lie. I stood by helplessly. To join the looters would have been much too dangerous as several people had already been badly stabbed. Not only stores were plundered but also the party committee building and the library. The looters burned the Communist propaganda library, called the "Red Corner." Several statues of Lenin and Stalin were toppled and smashed to bits. Both sides of the street were littered with typewriters, infant scales from the maternity ward, and many other things. The looters had abandoned these items when they discovered they were too heavy and quite useless to them.

There were several Jews living in the city and one of them was a student at the Pedagogical Institute. I met him in the street one day before the Germans moved in and asked him, "Why don't you leave the city?" He replied, "But, Professor, why should I? The Germans are a civilized people, the people of Lessing and Goethe. It is all Soviet propaganda about them." "No, my friend," I said, "unfortunately this is no propaganda. You see, I am of German extraction and I am not a party member, so nothing will happen to me. But you are in great danger if you stay." He did not believe me and about two weeks later, soon after the Germans had occupied the city, neighbors denounced him to the Gestapo. He was arrested along with his family and several other families. They were all gassed in a panel truck constructed in such a manner that the exhaust gas went into the interior of the truck.

The crimes committed by the Gestapo units in German-occupied areas were cruel and inhuman. But how could the Germans find out who was a Jew? The population in many areas of the Soviet Union is dark-eyed and has a darkish complexion. It is extremely difficult to tell a Jew from a non-Jew. But the Germans had no trouble finding Jews: the local population reported on their Jewish neighbors.

Anti-Semitism has always been strong in Russia and, later, in the Soviet Union. Under the Tsars pogroms were commonplace. After the revolution, anti-Semitism became even stronger because in the first few years after the revolution many Bolshevik officials were Jews. The people equated Jews with communists and regarded the Soviet government as a Jewish government. Nasty anecdotes about Jews in general and Jewish commissars in particular circulated. I remember in 1920 a government agency in charge of food supplies in Petrograd with the acronym PEPO which stood for *Petrogradskoe edinoe potrebitel'skoe obshchestvo* (Petrograd United Consumers' Organization). It was instantly reinterpreted as *Petrogradskie evrei prodovol'stviem obespecheny* (Petrograd Jews are Provided with Food).

Calm returned the day after the looting. Everything that could be stolen had been stolen. The streets were virtually deserted, and an eerie calm settled over the entire city. Suddenly I saw a huge dust cloud in the distance. It was caused by a cavalry unit approaching the city which, to my great amazement, consisted of Caucasian natives who had deserted to the Germans. "Who are you?" some people asked. They replied, "We are the Führer's auxiliary troops." They were soon followed by a Russian regiment who announced that they were "the Führer's Cossacks." People were eagerly pumping them for news when suddenly we heard in the distance a loud rattling noise. The first German unit was approaching on personnel carriers designed to traverse any kind of terrain. It was the 49th Corps of the German army. The soldiers were disciplined, friendly and helpful. Order was restored in the town immediately, and it gradually dawned on us that we were no longer Stalin's subjects. A new life lay before us.

8 On the German Side

On the second day of the German occupation a public meeting was held in the town square in which a German officer, Major Vital, announced that the very first task of the population was to form a new local government. The German interpreter translated the word "to form" incorrectly. Since German *bilden*, "to form," can also mean "to educate," he announced that the first task was to educate the self-administration. People started to ask each other, "Whom are we supposed to educate? We don't have anyone!" and Vital snapped, "What's going on here?" I spoke up, "Major, the interpreter made a mistake," whereupon the officer asked me to render the order in proper Russian. First a Russian was elected mayor, and then the Karachais elected their own nationality committee. They elected Kazi Bairamukov, who had been hiding in the mountains since the uprising in 1930, as president of the committee. His deputy was Aliev, a well-educated Karachai teacher who also spoke Russian very well. The committee also included a certain Karakotov and Totorkulov. Totorkulov had studied in Istanbul and spoke excellent Turkish. The chief of police of the Karachai area was Laipanov. He was related to the area's party committee secretary who had fled with the other party officials, before the Germans arrived. I asked a Karachai student at the Pedagogical Institute, by the name of Ali, what he thought of the elections. He replied, "The Germans are certainly preferable to the Soviets, but what we Karachai would like best of all is to get back our Ak Padishah (White

Tsar)." The student was alluding to the fact that in Tsarist times the Karachais were exempt from taxation and the military draft.

After the meeting a small celebration was held. I was invited to the officers' table, and they asked who I was and why I spoke German so fluently. After I introduced myself, one of the officers said, "My ancestors also lived in St. Petersburg. Have you ever heard the name Koenig?" "Yes," I answered, "if you mean the 'Sugar Koenig,' he was my great-great-grandfather." "He was my great-great-grandfather, too!" the officer exclaimed. Thus I met in the Caucasus my remote relative, Captain Walter Koenig, whom I was to meet again in Germany after the war. Later I was asked several times to act as interpreter between the Russian mayor and the German commandant, Lieutenant Ott, a general's son and a very nice young man. He was later killed in action and succeeded in Mikoyan Shakhar by Captain Ratgeber.

I also became acquainted with Captain Schuster, the chief of the C-1 (intelligence) section of the 49th Corps, who invited me to his office. There I also met Major Hromatka, who was very much interested in the passes leading across the mountains into Transcaucasia. In order to get to Schuster and Hromatka, I simply walked into corps headquarters without a pass and through several rooms where maps were lying around unguarded. The Germans considered anyone who declared himself an enemy of the Soviets to be their friend. It would have been quite easy for any "friend" to steal a map or plant a time bomb. The Soviets had undoubtedly left many undercover agents behind. G. G. Leonov, the director of the Pedagogical Institute in Mikoyan Shakhar, and his deputy had told me before leaving that they were going to join the local partisans. I am certain that they often entered Mikoyan Shakhar in disguise.

The Germans greatly impressed the Karachais when they distributed copies of the Koran in Arabic. The books were only about six by four centimeters in size so that it was necessary to hand out a magnifying glass with each copy. This was a clever ploy to win support among the Karachais, Kabardinians and other Muslims in the Caucasus, but whatever good will this gesture generated was lost soon after the German SD (*Sicherheitsdienst*, security service), a branch of the notorious SS, began to exterminate the Jews. Mikoyan Shakhar had very few Jews, but there were many in Pyatigorsk and Kislovodsk who had recently been evacuated from western Russia. The Germans lost no time in divesting them of all their property and redistributing it among the non-Jewish population. Greed encouraged the local riffraff to denounce Jews, and without this avid collaboration, the Germans would have had a difficult time identifying Jews in the Caucasus because nearly everybody there was dark-eyed and had a dark complexion.

One day an SS officer arrived who wanted to inspect the children's sanatorium in Teberda, a health resort for tuberculosis patients. I was asked to accompany him as his interpreter. As soon as we arrived at the sanatorium, the manager rushed up to us and said in Russian, "We also have some Jewish children here." I translated this statement as "We have children of various nationalities here." "Oh, I'm not interested in that," the officer replied, "just find out if the hospital needs any medical supplies, so I can have them delivered." I translated this for the manager but, in order to cover myself, I added that the problem of nationality would be discussed later. This incident proves that, with a bit of adroit manipulation an interpreter can influence the fate of many people. I ran a risk, of course, by not knowing whether the director of the sanatorium understood enough German to detect my alterations.

After the SS officer and I returned to Mikoyan Shakhar, he suggested that I move to Kislovodsk because a German agency was there to provide accommodations, food, and other help for people of German descent. I accepted his offer and moved with my family to Kislovodsk where we got two rooms in an apartment and bought food in a special store reserved for ethnic Germans. I also learned that a primary school had been organized by my old schoolmate, Professor A. G. Sorgenfrey, and his wife Renate, née Steininger, a teacher of German at Leningrad University. We enrolled Nicholas in that school while Valerian worked part-time as an interpreter. Although he had not graduated from high school, he could not attend any school in Kislovodsk because the Germans allowed only elementary schools to remain open.

In November I was called to Nal'chik in the Kabardinian region where a problem arose with the so-called Mountain Jews. These people were Jewish by religion but ethnically Iranian. The German occupiers were of two opinions. The SS, true to form, wanted to annihilate the Mountain Jews. The army officers, however, were opposed to this plan and called on me as kind of expert witness in their dispute with the SS. In Nal'chik I met Professor Deeters, a professor of Bonn University and a well-known specialist in Caucasian languages, and Captain Theodor Oberländer, the commandant of Nal'chik, who was very sympathetic to the Mountain Jews and opposed to the gassing of all Jews. Oberländer was a former minister in the Weimar government and after the war the refugee minister in the Adenauer government and then professor at Bonn University. I wrote a memorandum about the Mountain Jews in which I pointed out that Tsarist laws had not treated them as Jews but as Caucasian mountaineers. Furthermore, their real name was Tat, and scholarly literature had indicated that the Tat were people of Iranian origin who spoke an Iranian language. I also suggested that the Tat leaders invite the Germans to a party with wine, song and dances. All spectators including the SS Obersturmbannführer (Major) Pesterer, enjoyed themselves immensely and agreed to a man that the Tat were not Jews. Pesterer himself said, "We're not interested in their funny religion. If they want to be Jewish in religion, we don't care. It's the racial Jews we're against." I was happy that I was able to help save the Tat people from annihilation. Otherwise, the Tat might have gone the way of the Krimchak in the Crimea. The Krimchak were also of Jewish religion, but racially Turkic, and were exterminated by the Germans.

A second but much more tragic event occurred during my stay in Nal'chik. One day a man went to the local German military headquarters and introduced himself as a former NKVD chauffeur. He reported that for several weeks before the Germans conquered Nal'chik, every night he had transported people from the local NKVD jail to a certain place outside the city, and each time he drove his empty truck back to Nal'chik. He took the Germans to the place that was his nocturnal destination, where a probe about three feet

166

into the ground revealed some corpses. The Germans then ordered a full-scale excavation and mobilized many men from the local population. A pit was revealed, about 150 feet long by 50 feet wide, in which hundreds of corpses were stacked like cordwood. Many people recognized their friends and relatives among those corpses which were not too badly decomposed. The Germans arranged a solemn mass funeral at which a Russian Orthodox priest and a Muslim mullah officiated, and a German military band played funeral marches. The nationality committee of the Kabardinians, headed by an intellectual by the name of Beshtokov, attended the services. This, then, was another Katyn, that infamous place where the Soviets had murdered thousands of Polish prisoners of war. The discoveries at Katyn and Nal'chik proved that the Soviets murdered their prisoners en masse whenever the enemy came too close.

This is not an assumption but a fact. A student at the University of Washington told me that her parents had been arrested and confined in the jail at Khar'kov. Shortly before the Germans reached the city, NKVD (secret police) officers doused the entire jail with gasoline, and all inmates were burnt alive. She was a little girl at that time who was taken in by some friends. Later, her friends fled with her to Germany and ultimately emigrated to the United States.

I stayed on in Nal'chik through December, and my wife and younger son joined me. Valerian had to stay in Kislovodsk to work as an interpreter. Food in Nal'chik was more plentiful, and we had a Christmas feast for the first time in many years: a fried goose, some cakes made of flour, and even a bottle of wine. The military situation, however, was not at all peaceful, and there was a rumor that the Germans were about to evacuate. Indeed, the German retreat was officially announced on January 1, 1943.

I decided to leave with the Germans for three basic reasons. I remembered the annual tedium of filling out questionnaires asking, among many other questions, whether I had ever been on the territory occupied by the White Army. I was now on German-held territory, and it would have been extraordinarily risky to state this on a questionnaire after the Soviets reoccupied the area. Besides, the local population collaborated with the Germans, and my few stints as interpreter *in the interest of the local people* could be called collaboration. Finally, if we followed the retreating Germans we would have a God-sent opportunity to leave the Soviet Union and migrate to a country where people enjoyed freedom, such as the United States or Great Britain.

Nataliya, Nicholas and I, together with our dog Johnny, left Nal'chik by truck and headed north. There was not enough time to get Valerian to come with us. Another translator, one who had worked for the local German civilian administration, was on the same truck, as well as a woman with her son. This woman had been a typist in the local NKVD, and when the Germans came she gave them all carbon copies which, contrary to regulations, she had saved. With the aid of these carbon copies the Germans were able to discover many Soviet agents and execute them. We went by truck to the Mineral'nye Vody (English: Mineral Waters) railroad station. From there all the ethnic Germans as well as Russian and Caucasian refugees were to be transported farther west by train. An uninterrupted stream of refugees was moving along each side of the highway all the way from Nal'chik to Pyatigorsk, a distance of about 120 kilometers. Assuming an interval of about two meters between marchers in each of the two columns, I would guess that about 120,000 people were fleeing from the Soviets. A grim scene of thousands of German guns, tanks, and even personnel carriers bogged down in the swamp-like ground on both sides of the road provided the backdrop for this terrible evacuation.

We waited for a train in Mineral'nye Vody for two days, and all that time we were constantly bombarded by Soviet planes. The Germans then decided to truck all of us to Kursavka where another attempt would be made to put us on a train. A large band of partisans was rumored to be operating near Kursavka, but we finally managed to leave in a boxcar. Our dog was not permitted into the car, but a very nice polite young officer by the name of Kefinger took care of him in another car. Unfortunately Johnny was a very disobedient dog, and during one of our stops at a station, while the officer was walking him without a leash, the dog ran away. When we reached Nevinnomysskaya we had to wait a long time while once again Soviet planes bombarded us. Some bombs fell so close that the sides and roof of our boxcar were peppered with sand and pebbles. Finally the train resumed its journey, first to Kavkazskaya, now called Kropotkin, and then, after much delay, to Rostov. The moment we crossed the Don River the Germans blew up the bridge behind them, for the Soviets were closing in fast. If our train had been slightly delayed we could never have crossed the Don, and we would have fallen into the hands of the Soviet army.

After a few more days we reached the Ukraine. There were many Italian and Rumanian soldiers in that region; the Rumanians even looked rather picturesque in their tall fur caps. Finally, on February 1 we arrived in Khortitsa on the Dnepr River. We had already spent one month jammed together with thirty to forty other passengers in a boxcar. With only straw to lie on and no opportunity to wash, we had all become infested with lice. The air inside the car was atrocious, what with constant coughing and sneezing and children crying day and night. In addition, we were terribly hungry because we had only been able to stop at a few stations, and food had been virtually unattainable. The only other passenger in our boxcar whom I remember was an ethnic German with the strange name of Zehzahn. One day a brown-shirted SA *(Sturmabteilung)* storm trooper boarded our train and examined everyone's identification cards. When Zehzahn showed him his card, the storm trooper yelled, "You Communist swine!" and slapped him. Zehzahn retorted that he had never been a Communist, but he was dragged off the train, and I never learned what happened to him.

In Khortitsa we were sent to the city bathhouse where we washed and deloused ourselves and changed our clothes. Two days later, on February 3, we continued on to Nikopol', farther on the Dnepr River. There, Nicholas, Nataliya and I were assigned to a room and were given a few sacks of sunflower seed shells to burn in our stove. We stayed until March 23 when we, along with many other refugees, were put on a train and shipped westward to Lemberg, now called L'vov.

An organization in charge of ethnic German refugees accommodated us in an excellent hotel where several other scholars were also staying. After examining my credentials, the organization decided that I should proceed immediately to Berlin where specialists on Soviet nationalities were badly needed. I was assigned to the Wannsee Institute, located in the Wannsee suburb of Berlin. I went alone to Berlin, arriving there in about thirty-six hours. After a night's rest I took the elevated train to Wannsee where I met the director, Professor Achmeteli, who was an Armenian and a member of the Nazi party (NSDAP). I also met Dr. Wagner, an ethnic German from Russia, who was the secretary, and Dr. Emil Augsburg, a graduate of Marburg University in Slavic languages and literatures. All three men spoke very good Russian. One research scholar, Dr. A. P. Svechin, was Russian but a German citizen.

The institute's task was to study various aspects of the Soviet economy, politics and science and make reports to the German government. It probably had one of the best Russian-language libraries outside the Soviet Union. The institute was an intelligence organization that collated materials from openly published sources but did not engage in covert activities. Germany had at that time several such institutes, including one each for East Asia, America, and the Soviet Union proper (as opposed to its minority peoples, who were studied at Wannsee), the latter located in Breslau, now called Wrocław. All of these institutes were supervised by the so-called Stiftung für Länderkunde (Geography Foundation), headed by an SS officer by the name of Krallert. The foundation, in turn, reported to the Amt VI (Intelligence) of the SS (State Security), headed by Count Schellenberg. Although Amt VI was part of the *Sicherheitshauptamt* (Chief Security Office) headed by Kaltenbrunner, it was sufficiently far removed from the Gestapo and other branches so that after the war it was not labeled as a criminal organization. My task consisted of compiling a large work on Siberia to include such aspects as history, ethnography, culture, and natural resources. This work was never finished.

I had to return to L'vov immediately to take Nataliya and Nicholas back to Berlin. For the first month in Berlin we lived as

170

the institute's guests at the Hotel Roxy on the Kurfürstendamm, which was still operating at the same location when I later visited Berlin in 1957. Afterwards we moved into two large rooms in an apartment at 58 Uhlandstrasse. This apartment belonged to a woman who spoke Russian rather well even though she had emigrated from Russia when she was a child. She was also rather critical of conditions in Germany and expected Germany to be defeated. She had many acquaintances among intellectuals and once invited me to give a lecture to a group of them in her sitting room. She also wanted me to meet Goebbels, Hitler's propaganda minister, and explain to him the tragic situation in which Germany had placed itself but that, of course, proved to be impossible. Even high-ranking German officials failed to get an audience with him. Needless to say, I was not keen on meeting Goebbels because he would have hardly appreciated my firm opinion that Germany had already lost the war.

Around June 1, 1943, we had a joyous reunion with my elder son Valerian who, as I explained earlier, had been working as an interpreter in Kislovodsk when we left Nal'chik. A boy of only seventeen, he had traveled by himself through the Kuban area in war-ravaged Russia all the way to Germany. He had somehow obtained our Berlin address and located us without any difficulty. That term Nicholas entered a Russian-German school whose principal was a certain Dr. Besseller, and Valerian enrolled at Berlin University in special preparatory courses for students who had not yet graduated from high school. These courses had been organized for the many refugees who had come to Germany and wanted to continue their education, but had not received their high school diplomas.

In Berlin I met some relatives who had emigrated from Russia right after the revolution. Among them was Willi Diederichs, my mother's cousin, whom I mentioned in Chapter 3, and my great-aunt Mathilde Boetz, my maternal grandmother's sister, whom I will mention again later. Without her help we might not have survived in Germany.

I also met Professor Erich Haenisch, the well-known Sinologist and Mongolist, whom I had first met in 1927 or 1928 in

Leningrad when he spent a few days there on his return from China. In April 1943 I visited him at his home in the Zehlendorf district. He welcomed me as if it had been only a few days since our last meeting and ushered me into his study where, without further ado, he pointed to a large portrait of Emperor Wilhelm II and said, "I remain faithful to my emperor. I don't recognize the present rulers of my country." This was very courageous of him because I could have reported him to the Gestapo but, being a gentleman from tip to toe, he obviously assumed that I could be trusted.

He soon invited me to Berlin University to lecture on Mongolian and Turkic languages, such as Tatar, and comparative Altaic linguistics. I had an excellent group of students. One of them was the son of the well-known historian Heinrich Treitschke. Another student was Professor Haenisch's son, Wolf, who later became a professor of Japanese at Marburg University. Arash Bormanshinov, a Kalmuck, later emigrated to the United States where he obtained his Ph.D. degree and became a professor first at Princeton University and later at the University of Maryland. Another Kalmuck in the class was S. O. Stepanov who was later also to go to the United States where he is still working. Finally there was the Ukrainian Mikhail Brynjovskii who died soon after his arrival in the United States.

In August 1943 we moved into our own apartment. It had three rooms, a bath and kitchen, and was on the third floor of a house on Flensburger Strasse, just opposite the Borsig Bridge. The previous tenant had died, and with the help of some acquaintances I managed to get the apartment. Some furniture came with the apartment. I bought additional pieces from the deceased tenant's relatives, and we had already bought other household items on ration coupons. We were amazed that after four full years of war we could still buy all of these furnishings in Berlin, whereas in Leningrad such items had been unavailable even in peacetime. We were lucky to get the apartment when we did because soon thereafter the apartment house on Uhlandstrasse was severely damaged in an air raid.

The well-known Turcologist Annemarie von Gabain, a student of my deceased friend Willi Bang, arranged an appointment for

Nataliya at the Charité Hospital in Berlin, where for the first time in many years her illness was correctly diagnosed as multiple sclerosis. Again through von Gabain's good offices, Nataliya was sent to a rest home free of charge and I was to accompany her. We spent the month of October in a rest home called Eichhof, located in Lauterbach, Hesse. It was very beautiful there and absolutely quiet. This was in sharp contrast to Berlin where we had air raids almost every day. Sometimes bombers flew over Lauterbach, but they always dropped their bombs on nearby Kassel, badly damaging that city.

Back in Berlin, the first three weeks of November were relatively quiet even though we still had our daily air raids. On the evening of November 21, 1943 there was an alarm and, as usual, I led Nataliya, who by then was greatly handicapped and could hardly move on her own, to the air raid shelter. I also took two suitcases with our most valuable belongings. Valerian had gone to see a play and Nicholas' school had been evacuated two months earlier to Niederwürschnitz in the Erzggebirge (Ore Mountains) near Chemnitz. Consequently, only Nataliya and I were at home that evening. Suddenly we heard a terrible explosion. I looked through a crack in the door of the air-raid shelter and saw that the house was on fire. We all scrambled out through an emergency exit. I ran back to the shelter to get our suitcases, and we fled across the Borsig Bridge to the other bank of the Spree River where we found a bench to sit down and rest. We were surrounded by flames. It was almost impossible to breathe and acrid smoke stung our eyes.

This was a new type of warfare. Many districts of large cities and even entire towns were bombarded which did not contain any military or industrial installations but which were purely residential. The same tactic was used in Vietnam where civilians suffered from air raids much more than combatants. It is highly questionable whether such air raids had any strategic significance. In Vietnam, at least, they did not help the United States to win the war.

After about two hours I walked back over to the heap of smoldering rubble that had once been our apartment house. There I met Valerian who had returned from the theater. The two of us

walked to the bench where Nataliya was sitting to wait for day-
break. In the morning Valerian went to stay in a friend's house until
he could find other accommodations. While I was out looking for
food I quite unexpectedly met Nicholas who had just returned to
spend a few days' vacation with us. Sadly I had to tell him to return
to Niederwürschnitz, for we no longer had a place to stay.

Nataliya and I and others who had become homeless in the air
raids were taken to Cottbus in Silesia where we were put up in an
emergency shelter and given food. While spending several nights
there on wooden benches and bunkbeds in a large common dormitory
for men and women, I tried to determine where we should go from
there. The Wannsee Institute had already been evacuated from
Berlin. They originally intended to move it to Passau, Bavaria, but
this plan fell through. Instead it was evacuated to Plankenwart
Castle near St. Oswald, not far from Graz, Austria. Since we did
not have any place to stay in Berlin, Nataliya and I decided to rejoin
the Wannsee Institute in Austria. Valerian found a room for himself
and was to remain in Berlin to continue his preparatory courses at
the university.

Plankenwart Castle had been built in the thirteenth century
and had remained almost unchanged for half a millenium. Professor
Achmeteli picked us up in Graz and took us there by car. It was
very cold inside and the institute's library had not yet been
reassembled. Books were lying about the floor in large piles. We
were assigned a well-lit room with several windows in one of the
castle towers. The room had a stove with beautiful pot-shaped tiles,
hence called *Topföfen* (pot stoves) in German, and there was plenty
of coal for heating. Food, however, was a problem. We had no
kitchen, only an electric hotplate which was good for heating up
coffee, tea, or soup. The nearest stores and restaurants were
several kilometers away from the castle in the village of St.
Oswald. It was easy for me to walk to the village, but Nataliya
could not accompany me, especially since the snow was almost knee
deep. I took meals from the restaurant back to the castle where we
warmed them up on our hotplate. Nataliya subsisted this way from
early December 1943 to the middle of March 1944. Once during our

stay Valerian joined us for a brief time because he had been bombed out yet another time in Berlin. He returned, however, thinking he might possibly find a room in the Berlin suburbs, from where he could commute to the university.

It became quite clear that we could not stay with the Wannsee Institute at Plankenwart Castle any longer. I went to Berlin to see the director of the East Asia Institute, Professor Walter Donat, whom I had met a few months before in Berlin. Donat was a Japanologist and a member of both the NSDAP and the SS. He was, however, a very pleasant and decent man. Later, in fact, when the Third Reich was about to collapse, he told me that he would give all employees of the institute money to tide us over until we found other jobs. Donat also demonstrated his decency on another occasion. When one of his secretaries was denounced to the Gestapo for listening to American and British broadcasts, Donat had gone to the Gestapo and vouched for the girl's loyalty. Donat readily accepted me and settled the problem of my transfer from the Wannsee Institute to his East Asia Institute. This institute was located first in the Oranienburger Strasse, but after this site was destroyed in an air raid it was transferred to Dahlem, and finally to Marienbad in the Sudeten, a region of Czechoslovakia which the Germans had annexed in 1939 shortly before they occupied the entire country.

As a member of the East Asia Institute, I was commissioned to write two reports, one on Mongolia and another on the mentality of the Mongols. I do not know exactly why the Germans regarded the Mongols' shamanist and Buddhist beliefs as important. In my opinion, these beliefs were of no importance to Germany's war effort. I also wrote a book on the Mongolian People's Republic, which was to have been published in Berlin by Walter de Gruyter. I had even received the galley proofs, but Germany collapsed before the book could be printed. After the war, when I had an interview with a British officer by the name of Gottlieb, a native of South Africa, I lent him my galley proofs of that book, but he never returned it. I heard later he committed suicide. In addition to my work at the East Asia Institute, I wrote an article on the language of the Mongolian square script and the *Yüan-ch'ao pi-shih*, i.e., the

Secret History of the Mongols, a work written in 1240, which was published in 1944.[1] In addition it was then that I wrote my Khalkha-Mongolian grammar which was eventually published by Steiner in 1951. Valerian also worked at the institute as a part-time errand boy.

As soon as I was settled at the East Asia Institute and had obtained two rooms in a house in the Marienfelde district of Berlin which belonged to an elderly lady, I returned to Plankenwart to take Nataliya to Berlin. Nataliya, Valerian, and I lived in Marienfelde for only a month, until we could no longer endure the almost nightly air raids on the nearby Daimler factory. We then stayed briefly with Professor Jáschke, a Turcologist, who lived near Berlin, and after that we found two rooms in Zehlendorf-West, a suburb of Berlin. It turned out that we did not stay there very long either. It was soon clear that Nataliya could not stay in Berlin because of the daily air raids, and so I took her to Niederwürschnitz where Nicholas' school was located. Nataliya was given board and room in an inn. Nicholas visited his mother often, but his school was soon evacuated again to Bad Luhatschowitz (in Czech Lázně Luhačovice) in Moravia. I never quite understood why his school was transferred that far east because the Soviet army was just about to enter Hungary. In the summer of 1944, a few days after the Allied landings in Normandy on June 6, I visited Nicholas there. Bad Luhatschowitz was a beautiful spa in a breathtaking natural setting.

Valerian and I soon became homeless again when the house in Zehlendorf-West was destroyed in an air raid. Valerian moved to a place in Hohenneuendorf, near Berlin, from which he commuted daily to the university, and I moved into a room in the house of an elderly lady on Lagarde Strasse, not far from our previous apartment. The air raids became more dangerous with each passing week. In March 1944 I remember that during a visit with Valerian who was staying with some friends an air raid occurred. As we were sitting in the basement shelter, we suddenly felt a strong gust of wind and heard the whistling of a bomb followed by a terrible explosion. The bomb had struck the sidewalk next to our shelter. The ceiling came crashing down, mortar fell from the walls, and we heard the sound of water. The bomb had broken a water main, and the basement was flooding so rapidly that we had to scramble to get out into the open in time. Valerian and I spent the rest of that night with my friend, the geologist Professor A. F. Lebedev, whom I had first met in Kislovodsk and who now lived near me in Berlin. The next morning Valerian returned to Hohenneuendorf. I knew I also had to make plans to leave Berlin, especially as the East Asia Institute had just been evacuated to Marienbad (in Czech Mariánské Lázně) in the Sudeten. First, however, I managed, with the help of the Turcologist Annemarie von Gabain who had connections, to move Nataliya from Niederwürschnitz to the rest home Sophienhöhe in the Rhön Mountains of Thuringia where she was well taken care of. When I returned to Berlin, I could no longer sleep at nights because of constant air raids. I therefore often spent the nights with some Kalmuck friends in Frankfurt/Oder and returned in the morning to Berlin by train.

Speaking of the Kalmucks, there were thousands of them in Germany. The German army even included a Kalmuck cavalry corps of several thousand soldiers. I do not remember the name of their commander. The German liaison officer was Baron von Kutschenbach and the chief-of-staff was Mukoven (in Kalmuck Mūköwün) Khaglyshev, who had been a student at the Leningrad Institute of Living Oriental Languages and later had worked in the publishing house and newspaper office in Elista. I think that I was right in regarding Khaglyshev as anti-Communist, but he was denounced as a Soviet agent and shot. Most of the cavalry corps perished in battles against the Soviets. When I arrived in Berlin in April 1943, I read in a newspaper about the Kalmuck nationality committee. I went to its headquarters and got acquainted with the president, Shamba N. Balinov, an intellectual who had left Russia soon after the revolution. The committee also included D. I. Remilev, the priest Mönkin, and the Kalmuck prince Tundutov. Balinov gave me the address of my uncle's widow (the wife of Vasilii Poppe), and I visited her. I had not seen her since 1917 when she still worked as a secretary in my uncle's law office. In 1943 her son was a soldier in the German army.

177

After the East Asia Institute had moved to Marienbad, I remained a few extra weeks alone in Berlin. One day I visited my friend, Professor D. V. Grishin, who had been a professor of Russian literature at the Elista Pedagogical Institute in 1941–42 and who was now living in Berlin. Grishin told me that in August 1942, a month after I left Elista, the Germans had marched in. The deputy director of the institute who had also been professor of mathematics, was immediately elected city mayor. Another professor, who taught Russian, also became an official, and one of the women on the teaching staff, who was a writer, worked with her husband in the office of a newspaper published by the Germans. In other words, most of my former colleagues in Elista had changed over to the German side and later came to Germany. At Grishin's apartment I also met a Russian in civilian clothes whom Grishin introduced as General D. E. Zakutnyi. He had been captured by the Germans and was now working in the propaganda office of the army of General A. A. Vlasov whose name I had heard before.

Zakutnyi was an interesting conversationalist who told me how he had been taken prisoner in Kiev. He condemned the Soviets not only on political grounds—he was strongly anti-Communist—but also for their total mismanagement of military affairs and interference with the commanders' lines of command, thus bearing the responsibility for some defeats. Zakutnyi placed most of the blame on Stalin's obsolete strategy of holding onto territory at all costs. Stalin did not realize that World War II was the first major mobile war. There were no fixed and well-defined front lines, and the army's main task should have been to maintain its combat strength. Instead, Stalin ordered the Red Army to rigidly defend every square foot of territory, and he even coined a new term, *stoyat' na smert'* (stand to the death). His strategy caused enormous losses. Entire divisions, corps, and sometimes even armies were engulfed by rapidly advancing German troops and then were either annihilated or taken prisoner. It was not until Marshal Georgii K. Zhukov took over in December 1941 that Stalin's ruinous strategy was replaced by a highly flexible and ultimately successful mobile strategy.

The day after my visit with Grishin, on July 20, 1944, I left

Berlin for Marienbad to rejoin the East Asia Institute. I got up early and went to the Anhalter railroad station. I soon noticed that something unusual must have happened because Gestapo officials frequently boarded our train and checked identity cards. At one station down the line a German entered my compartment and asked me whether I had heard about an attempt on Hitler's life. I had not heard nor read anything, so he told me what had happened.

I arrived in Marienbad rather late in the evening and went to the Hotel Westend where the research scholars and employees of the East Asia Institute were housed. There, much to my surprise, I also met Mrs. Augsburg, Mrs. Wagner and other wives of my former colleagues of the Wannsee Institute which was still in Plankenwart Castle in Austria. A few days later I went via Schweinfurt and Mellrichstadt to Sophienhöhe to take Nataliya to Marienbad where the two of us were to live by ourselves, as Valerian was studying in Berlin and Nicholas was still with his school in Bad Luhatschowitz. Both sons visited us in Marienbad. Nicholas came first. We celebrated his sixteenth birthday on August 25 and all three of us went to the theater. Later Valerian came from Berlin.

During that time I received a letter from my friend, the Japanese scholar Shichirō Murayama (Illus. 19), whom I met for the first time in early 1944 when I lived on Lagarde Strasse in Berlin. He was a doctor of philology who had studied Georgian, was greatly interested in Altaic languages, and had read some of my works. He invited me to his apartment near Halensee station in Berlin. Murayama lived there with the secretary of the Japanese embassy, Dr. Sugiura. Both men were very hospitable and I visited them several times, and twice we spent many hours together in an air-raid shelter. Donat knew Murayama but did not want him to know the real purpose of the East Asia Institute. I think that the Japanese knew perfectly well what kind of an institute it was. Anyway, several months later I received a letter from Murayama informing me that he urgently needed to see me. He arrived in Marienbad some time in late fall 1944. He presented me with a small bag of rice, probably about ten pounds, and some other foodstuffs as well as about 250 Swiss francs. Murayama surprised me by openly talking

Illus. 19. Shichirō Murayama, March 1950

about the imminent collapse of Germany. He also told me that the Japanese embassy would soon be evacuated to Bad Gastein in Austria. In case the Americans would advance into Austria, Sugiura and Murayama planned to move closer to the Swiss border and, at the last moment, slip into Switzerland. I later learned that Sugiura had made it across the border, but Murayama stayed in Bad Gastein and was taken prisoner by the Americans.

Soon after Murayama left, Nicholas returned to Bad Luhatschowitz, but from there his entire school was sent to Bratislava, the capital of Slovakia, to build ditches and other anti-tank

defenses. The military situation in the east had steadily deteriorated, so when Nicholas visited us again after his stint in Bratislava, I
did not let him go back to school. He was sixteen years old and
could be easily drafted into some auxiliary anti-aircraft or bazooka
unit. I had heard that many boys even younger than Nicholas had
already been mobilized. He stayed with us, and we did not register
him as a resident with the police, which was, of course, risky, but I
was determined not to sacrifice him. After the war I learned that
the only son of my former schoolmate and brother of my second
wife, had been drafted at the age of fourteen and killed on the front,
so it was very wise that I did not let Nicholas return to school.

We managed to save Nicholas from danger, but disaster
struck in December when Valerian was drafted. This was a heavy
blow to us and caused Nataliya and me much worry. Valerian was
sent to Denmark for basic training and was then assigned to a
battalion of railroad guards. Most of his buddies, being from
Lorraine, hated Germany greatly and told Valerian repeatedly that
the moment they arrived at the front they would cross over to the
Allies. Valerian later told us about conditions in his battalion and
the cruelty with which some soldiers were treated. For instance,
their sergeant sought to "cure" a soldier with a weak bladder by
wrapping him into a wet sheet and making him sleep in an unheated
room. Of course the soldier became so ill that he had to be discharged from military service. At the end of March 1945 Valerian
sent a letter informing us that his unit was about to be sent to the
front. That was his last letter before leaving, and we were
extremely worried because we did not know which front he was
being sent to. Only after he returned from a prisoner-of-war camp
did we learn the full story. His battalion had been assigned to a
Panzergrenadier (tank-supported infantry) regiment destined for the
eastern front, but the Soviet army had already cut the railroad lines
to eastern Germany. Consequently, Valerian's unit was sent to the
western front which at that time was somewhere near Kassel. No
sooner had they disembarked from the troop train at Marienhöhe,
near Kassel, than they heard artillery fire in the distance. Their
commanding officer ordered them to cross a bridge, but at that very

moment an American tank appeared on the bridge, fired a round which tore the officer to pieces, and the entire battalion surrendered. The unit's entire combat service lasted less than one hour.

Valerian and his unit were interned near Compiègne in France where they were put to work in the forests. They were fed poorly and were constantly hungry, but the black truck drivers who transported them between the camp and their work site were very friendly. Each time they passed a potato field the drivers would stop their trucks and tell the prisoners by sign language to collect some potatoes for themselves. The French women working in the fields were, of course, furious and shouted horrible insults at them, but the black soldiers found the scene most amusing. In October all the soldiers in Valerian's battalion were released from the prisoner-of-war camp. This was due to the simple fact that the soldiers from Lorraine were now considered French citizens and Valerian, whose home address was listed as Marienbad, was regarded as a Czech.

I had several experiences in Marienbad which made a lasting impression on me. I witnessed two air raids in two consecutive nights against the city of Dresden. Each time it took more than one hour for the air armadas to fly over Marienbad, and shortly thereafter we heard explosions and saw the sky turn dark red with fire, even though Dresden was about 150 kilometers away. A beautiful city was destroyed, and with it hundreds of thousands of people, mostly civilian refugees. On another occasion Nataliya and I were walking to a restaurant when we passed a huge crowd of people who turned out to be Jewish women being herded by SS guards from the concentration camp in Teresienstadt to some unknown destination. One of the guards yelled at me, "Honor the flag!" meaning that I should have saluted the swastika banner. "I'm very sorry," I said, "but as you can see, I'm escorting a handicapped person." It was a frightening and revolting sight. Nataliya almost fainted when she heard whips and saw a Jewish woman fall to the ground. These were some of the most terrible aspects of everyday life in Germany.

Seeing those hapless Jewish women driven by their SS torturers to their "final destination," I was wondering how far human bestiality could go. Then another thought crossed my mind. Perhaps many of these women could have escaped their martyrdom if Great Britain and the United States had permitted those shiploads of Jewish refugees to land before the war. Instead they had sent them back. I have never been able to understand this action, especially in view of hundreds of thousands of Cubans, Vietnamese and other people so warmheartedly welcomed to the United States in later times. Why the change? Were not the Jews in a greater predicament? Or did the British use the same excuse as when they had refused to let in the Tsar's family: "His Majesty's Government do not think this is the appropriate time for...."?

In Marienbad I also became acquainted with General Vlasov whose headquarters was in nearly Karlsbad, now called Karlovy Vary. He still kept up a civilian administration, intended to serve as the basis for a future non-Communist government of Russia, in a hotel on Adolf-Hitler Strasse in Marienbad. I was very skeptical of the Vlasov movement's chances of ever ruling Russia. Germany was near defeat, and I had learned from my colleagues in the Wannsee Institute and from Donat, the director of the East Asia Institute, about the decisions reached at the Yalta Conference. Although those decisions were being kept secret, German intelligence had obtained photographic copies of the Yalta agreement from the Albanian butler at the British embassy in Turkey. Therefore, although I became acquainted with some people in Vlasov's military and civilian headquarters, I stood aloof from and did not participate in any of their activities.

I did, however, have a rather long conversation with Vlasov, and he struck me as a man of action and a born leader. He was over six feet tall, very intelligent, and seemed very alert. He envisioned the Russia of the future as being a federation similar to Switzerland and the United States. He wished to realize the ideal Soviet Union envisaged by the Constitution in which each republic was guaranteed full cultural autonomy and the right of secession. Private property would be guaranteed to everyone. He hoped for full religious freedom and the separation of church and state. As Vlasov regarded himself only as a military leader and had no intention of becoming the political head of his visionary non-Communist Russia, he expected political power to be handed over to the deputies of a constituent assembly who would, in turn, choose the future government of the entire federation. Similar assemblies were to elect the governments of each constituent state. Vlasov was also prepared to right the wrongs inflicted on other nations, like Finland and Poland, by returning territories previously annexed by the Soviets. Such facilities as industrial plants, factories, dams, electric power stations, and railroads built by the Soviets were to remain government property, but those confiscated from private owners after the revolution were to be returned to their legal owners or to their heirs. Any improvements or additions to these facilities which the Soviets had made, however, were to remain state property, and the original owners were to be fairly compensated for pre-revolutionary buildings and machinery. "Of course," Vlasov said with an air of resignation, "the first thing we have to do is defeat the Soviet Union." He knew that the time for implementing his vision had long since passed. In addition to Vlasov I met his generals F. I. Trukhin, G. N. Zhilenkov, V. F. Malyshkin, and V. I. Mal'tsev. Zhilenkov was the chief of Vlasov's political department. As the former secretary of the Moscow city committee of the Communist party, he was the right man for the job. Trukhin was, if I am not mistaken, Vlasov's quartermaster, and Mal'tsev was the chief of the air force.

After Germany's surrender, the Allies extradited all of them to the Soviets. Churchill and particularly Eden played an ugly role when they forcibly extradited about 40,000 Cossacks, even though some of them had left the Soviet Union before 1939, and their extradition was contrary to the Yalta agreement. When they were received by the Soviets, all of these hapless victims were tried and executed, some by hanging and others by firing squad. Churchill and Eden were anxious to please the Soviets because they wanted British prisoners of war repatriated who were in camps in eastern Germany, then occupied by the Soviet army. The British also hoped to extract concessions from the Soviets. The Soviets, however, never made any concessions, and their stock reply to any request or suggestion was "Nyet."

9 In Post-War Germany

By May 1945 the Americans had penetrated deep into Germany and were expected to reach the Sudeten any day. Hitler had committed suicide on April 30, and Germany's collapse was completed with its unconditional surrender on May 9. Sunday, May 6, was the Russian Orthodox Easter, and Nataliya wanted us to go to church. When we were halfway between the hotel and the church, we saw several American tanks and infantrymen approaching. They ordered everyone to return home, and the next day they evicted all of us from the Hotel Westend. With nowhere else to go, we went into the forest where we found a deserted cabin and spent the night there. On Tuesday I managed to get a room for Nataliya, Nicholas and myself in the Waldmühle (Forest Mill) inn where we went, along with the few meager belongings we had been permitted to take out of the hotel. Soon, however, it was rumored that the Americans were going to hand Marienbad and the entire Sudeten over to the Soviets. For this reason, those of us who were refugees from the Soviet Union immediately decided to flee farther west into Germany which was only about twenty-five kilometers from Marienbad.

Nataliya was by this time unable to walk, so there was nothing I could do but to leave her in the care of some Czech friends who, as victims of German aggression, were not afraid of the Russians. With knapsacks on our backs, Nicholas and I hiked in the direction of Bavaria. We crossed the frontier late at night near the village of Mähring, and from there we walked through Tirschenreuth and Bayreuth all the way to Staffelstein near Bamberg. I knew that my former schoolmate, Professor A. G. Sorgenfrey, whom I had last seen in the Caucasus and who in the meantime had worked in a German library in Ratibor, Silesia, was now living with his family in Staffelstein. We found a room in a private home there and had a much needed rest. Our rest did not last long, however, because after a few days all the former employees of the library in Ratibor were arrested. This was because the library had been part of the *Ostministerium* (Ministry for Eastern Affairs) which had been responsible for the civilian administration of occupied areas in Poland, the Soviet Union, and the former Baltic republics. The day after these arrests I was summoned by the American Army CIC (Counter-Intelligence Corps). An officer, who spoke Russian rather poorly but could make himself understood, wanted to know whether I had any connection with those arrested. I denied it, saying I was simply trying to escape from an area which would soon be occupied by the Soviets. He let me go but made me promise not to leave Staffelstein. As soon as I returned to our room, however, Nicholas and I packed our few belongings in our knapsacks and fled. We could not use the streets because they were being patrolled by American soldiers who were checking identity cards against a list of people who were not allowed to leave the city. We went to the backyard and climbed over the fence into the garden of the neighboring house which was near the edge of the forest. Having reached the forest, we walked parallel to the highway for about four kilometers, and then we left the forest and emerged onto the open road where we continued our walk. I did not have any compunctions about deceiving the CIC officer. I regarded him as a potential enemy since he might actually have arrested me later and even extradited me to the Soviets. In my opinion, an enemy, even a potential one, should be deceived, if necessary.

We arrived in Bamberg, a city which, at least in those parts which we walked through, seemed to have escaped any damage from air raids. From there we traveled in an empty boxcar through Aschaffenburg and Hanau to Frankfurt where we switched to a

186

passenger train almost up to Kassel. In Kassel I found a truck driver whom I bribed with about fifty precious grams of coffee to drive us to Herford in Westphalia.

Our destination was the large Böckel estate near Herford (Illus. 20). My maternal great aunt, Mathilde Boetz, lived there.

Illus. 20. The Manor in Böckel

She was the only person we knew in West Germany and whose address we had. If she had not lived there, we probably would not have gone to Böckel. Nicholas and I and some other people stayed in a detached building on the estate. The estate belonged to another, more remote relative, Hertha Koenig, the great-granddaughter of my maternal ancestor Johann Georg Koenig and niece of the zoologist Alexander Koenig. She was a very talented woman and an excellent writer and poetess who personally knew many other German poets, including Rainer Maria Rilke, who used to come to Böckel.[1] She was, however, a bit strange, being extremely shy and tending to avoid human contact whenever possible. I remember her passing through one of the rooms at her estate, a huge mansion of about twenty rooms where only a handful of people lived, and muttering to no one in particular, "This is terrible, all these people!" I wonder what Hertha Koenig would have said about a Soviet communal apartment of eight rooms, housing twice that number of families! At least, she should have seen the film "Ninochka" starring Greta Garbo.

Nicholas and I stayed in Böckel for a month before we made a long trip back to the Sudeten to find Nataliya. This time we went by train via Marktredwitz to Tirschenreuth. From there we walked to Mähring, where Nicholas found a man who was willing to take him across the border in exchange for some real coffee. Nicholas went with him and returned after two days, bringing some of our belongings, including our family album which we had been unable to take with us when we first left Czechoslovakia. He had seen his mother, given her my letter and address, and told her about our life in Böckel. He informed me that, along with all other sick persons who were not Czechs, she would soon be taken to Berlin. As a matter of fact, she was no longer living in the Waldmühle, as she had been placed in one of the hospitals in Marienbad which was later moved to Berlin.

Nicholas and I returned to Böckel. Summer passed, and when fall came Nicholas entered the boys' high school in Bünde, six kilometers from Böckel. On October 28, 1945, while both of us were sitting in our room—I remember I was helping Nicholas with his Latin homework—Hertha Koenig suddenly came rushing into our room shouting, "Come quickly! Something wonderful has happened!" We followed her into the kitchen, and whom did we see but Valerian, standing there in his shabby uniform, looking haggard and hungry but otherwise in good health. How often I had thought about him, and how many terrible thoughts had come into my head. But, there he was—alive!

188

Soon after that more good news came in the form of a letter from Nataliya. She was now in a Lutheran home for sick and handicapped persons in Wuhlheide, a suburb of Berlin. I immediately wrote back to her and also to Willi Diederichs in Berlin, asking him to visit her to help her in any way he could. At the same time Hertha Koenig swung into action. She knew Pastor Friedrich von Bodelschwingh, the son of the founder of well-known Bethel Nursing Home near Bielefeld. It was common knowledge that under Hitler when all handicapped people were to be killed, Bodelschwingh declared that the Nazis would have to kill him first before they carried off any of his patients. The Nazis left him alone because of his worldwide reputation. Since Hertha Koenig had donated large sums of money to his nursing home, she sent me to Bethel with a letter of introduction. I went there and talked to one of Pastor Bodelschwingh's aides who promised to try to bring my wife from Wuhlheide. That was not an easy task because Wuhlheide was in the eastern zone of Germany. Even so, in those days and as late as 1947 communications with the eastern zone of Germany were less difficult than they have been in recent years. The following summer one of Bodelschwingh's nurses escorted my wife from Wuhlheide to Bethel and from there to Böckel.

On December 31, 1945 I received more good news from my friend, Professor K. H. Menges, who was teaching at Columbia University. I had previously written to him through his parents who lived in Frankfurt. At that time one could not send letters outside Germany, but Menges' parents had connections with Americans and they were in a position to mail my letter. In that letter I had asked Professor Menges to find out if it would be possible for me to get a job at one of the American universities. He answered that he had talked to somebody about this, and yes, something could be done for me.

Menges, an ardent Socialist, had come to Leningrad in 1927, before Stalin had taken power, and liked many aspects of life in the Soviet Union. By contrast, conditions in Germany under the Weimar Republic were rather bad, and the Nazi movement was rapidly gaining strength. Menges believed in ideal socialism which was the opposite of the Nazi system. With such convictions, Menges could not remain in Germany, so he left and finally went to the United States where he became a professor at Columbia University. By that time, the Stalin era with all its atrocities had descended on the Soviet Union, and Menges became an outspoken anti-communist. He was especially hostile to Stalin's brand of communism which he considered quite different from that of Marx and Engels.

In early 1946 I decided that waiting for an invitation took too long, and that a faster way to emigrate might be by going through an UNRRA (United Nations Relief and Rehabilitation Agency) refugee camp. In March Valerian went to Munich to enroll in an UNRRA university, Nicholas went to Stuttgart to attend the senior year in high school, and I went to an UNRRA camp in Hamburg where there were many Estonian refugees, some of whom I knew. After Estonia had been annexed by the Soviets, many thousands of Estonians had fled to Sweden and later to Germany. I told my Estonian friends everything that had happened to me and my family and asked them whether I could get admitted into a camp for Estonian refugees. The president of the Estonian committee, a well-known astronomer, Professor Öpik, who later taught at Dublin University, signed a certificate which admitted me to another camp for Estonians and Latvians located in Melle, not far from Böckel. After Nataliya had been brought from Berlin to West Germany, I was able to place her in that camp as well. I did not have any language difficulty there because Estonian is close to Finnish, which I spoke well. The Estonians even told me that I spoke like a native of the Viru district in Estonia.

While living in that camp, I became a teacher of English for Estonian children. Everything was quite normal and satisfactory for us until one day a relative of mine, Georg Schlieps, who lived with his family in Böckel came to visit us. He was accompanied by a British woman in military uniform who suggested that I leave the camp because the Soviets were looking for me and it was unsafe for me to remain there. I told her that I had no place to go, so she promised to try to find a solution. When she returned a few days later, she took me to Böckel where I found a British officer waiting for us.

I always had a premonition that the Soviets would someday come looking for me. Once when I visited an Estonian organization in Lübeck I was shown an Estonian newspaper published in Sweden in which there was an article about me. It said that, according to the Soviet press, I had participated in the Kalmuck revolt in the fall of 1942 and in fact had been responsible for the Kalmucks changing over to the German side. Because of this article, I tried to live as inconspicuously as possible and I saw to it that I received no letters directly. My letters to America were mailed by Professor Menges' father in Frankfurt, and those to England were sent by Pastor Hans Haenisch, Professor Erich Haenisch's brother, who lived in Lemgo, near Böckel. Every six to seven weeks I would pick up my mail at these two locations.

The British officer introduced himself as Captain Smith. Of course this was not his real name; all members of the British CIC were either Smith or Jackson. He told me that it was impossible for me to remain in Böckel because the Soviet commandant of Berlin, General Tyul'panov, had applied to his British counterpart for my extradition. Smith asked me what my plans might be. I told him that not long ago I had received a letter from Professor Gustav Haloun, the Sinologist who had escaped from Nazi Germany and was now teaching at Cambridge University, telling me that the university intended to invite me there to teach. I had not actually asked Haloun for the job, but the invitation was the result of a memorandum drawn up by him and signed by Sir Gibb and several other prominent British scholars. Haloun learned about me through the well-known writer on Mongolia, Owen Lattimore of Johns Hopkins University, whom I had asked to help me to find a job in the United States. Lattimore wrote me a rather unpleasant letter saying that because of my activities in wartime Germany I had no chance of ever going to the United States.

A short time later I also received a letter from Dr. Ethel John Lindgren, an anthropologist at Cambridge University. I think that somehow she had learned from Lattimore of my interest in a job in America and then told Haloun about me. Dr. Lindgren also warned me not to write to certain people in Great Britain and the

United States because she knew them to be sympathizers of the Soviet Union. Nothing ever came of that invitation to Cambridge because, as I learned later from the British CIC officers, the Attlee Labor government refused to grant me a visa. Of course I should have considered this before, because it was well known that even under Churchill's government, at the initiative of Anthony Eden, all refugees, Cossacks and soldiers associated with the Vlasov army, had been extradited to the Soviets. At that time the Allies were still ignorant about the true situation in the Soviet Union and believed that the Soviets were their allies, and that, therefore, everyone who was anti-Soviet must have been a Nazi or, at least, a Nazi collaborator. It took some time—much too long—before they realized that there had been not only Nazis and their sympathizers in Germany, but also refugees who had merely managed to escape from Soviet domination and were not the least bit sympathetic to the Nazis. At the time of my talk with Captain Smith, however, the invitation to Cambridge still seemed almost certain.

Captain Smith took Nataliya and me to his house in Lage, some twenty or thirty kilometers from Böckel, where we spent several months together. We were very well treated for we were given our own room and excellent food and I soon recovered from my worries. Of course all this time I was still hoping for the invitation to Cambridge to come through. A few weeks after we moved, Nataliya was transferred to a nursing home where they again confirmed the diagnosis of her illness as multiple sclerosis. I remained alone in Captain Smith's home in Lage. From time to time my boys visited me, having been warned, however, that they must not reveal my whereabouts to anyone. When Captain Smith went on furlough to his farm in Northern Ireland, I was transferred to a center for German specialists in Alswede near Lübbecke as, obviously, I could not stay alone at his house. Most of the other specialists had been smuggled out from the Eastern zone. I remember one man and his wife who were Baltic Germans and who had been smuggled out of Leipzig disguised as members of the British occupation force. There were also some very famous scholars, including the atomic physicist Otto Hahn, who were later sent to Wimbledon near London. The

Americans had a similar center, with Wernher von Braun being one of its stars.

At the beginning of 1947 I was informed by a British officer that his government would not issue an immigration visa to me. Instead he would take me to Frankfurt where the Americans were interested in seeing me. There I met a Mr. Carmel Offie who was political adviser to General Lucius Clay. I also met an American congressman whose name was never given to me. He asked me what I thought about Chiang Kai-shek's chances for success, and I told him that the Chinese Communists would certainly take all of mainland China. At the end of our interview the congressman and Offie both told me that I would be transferred to the United States. When I was taken to Offie's office a second time in 1948 that same congressman was there again, and he remarked that the situation in China had indeed deteriorated, just as I had predicted. At that time Chiang Kai-shek was about to leave mainland China and transfer his government to Taiwan. Later I learned that Offie had worked at the American embassy in Moscow before and during the war when William C. Bullitt was ambassador and my friend, Professor William Ballis, was naval attaché. Menges told Ballis, who at that time was a professor at the University of Washington in Seattle, that I was looking for a job at an American university. Ballis, in turn, relayed the information to Professor George E. Taylor, chairman of the Far Eastern and Russian Institute. Since neither Taylor nor Ballis knew me personally, they could only go by what Menges had told them. During all this time—the years 1947, 1948, and parts of 1949— Nataliya remained in nursing homes, first in Windelsbleiche near Senne and later in Lippstadt.

The summer of 1947 was extremely hot and dry. I was very miserable in Lage where the heat in my room gave me frequent and violent headaches. One day a British officer visited me and introduced himself as Mr. Morris. I later learned his true name, but I will refer to him only as Mr. Morris. He was of Polish origin and we gradually became friends. In fact, we still corresponded even after I left Germany, and I visited him in London in 1956. He told me he had come to take me away. When I asked exactly where he was taking me, he only said, "Wait and see." That was typical of British secretiveness and of their proclivity to act in a Sherlock Holmesian manner. Very soon I noticed that we were heading east and I began to get very uncomfortable. I remembered that only a short time earlier the British had extradited many people to the Soviets, and at that moment I did not know what to expect. We went through Braunschweig and finally arrived at Wolfenbüttel which was about thirty kilometers from the Soviet zone. There I spent all of July and part of August in the house of the local CIC. Since the city had not suffered severely from the bombings it was still a very interesting place. Wolfenbüttel is the town where Wilhelm Busch, the famous author and illustrator of humorous tales about Max and Moritz, had lived. In August I was taken to another CIC house in Brake near Lemgo where I was informed that my sons would soon be able to go to England. First the British CIC asked its American counterparts to bring my sons to Lemgo. Valerian came from Munich and Nicholas arrived from Stuttgart-Zuffenhausen to where his school had been evacuated. We lived together for one month until September 1947 when they were taken by car to Hoek van Holland, and from there they sailed to England. They finally ended up in a hostel in Wellington in Shropshire where they lived and worked for quite a while. I was happy that the boys had made it safely to England.

It was very interesting, living in the British CIC house in Brake. Various people were brought there for interrogation in a room which was located directly under mine. Although I could not distinguish words, I was always able to tell by the intonation whether Russian, Estonian, Polish, or some other language was being spoken. Once an officer of the Soviet occupation force was brought in. He was Jewish and had a young German woman with him whom he wanted to marry. Since the Soviets did not permit their officers to fraternize with Germans, he had sought asylum with the British. I had been told not to reveal my identity to the Soviet officer and his girl friend—I had been introduced to them as Mr. Winter—and to converse with them only in German. One day, however, one of the British officers returned from a party rather tipsy and asked me in

Russian, "How goes it?" The next morning when I saw the Soviet officer, he asked me in Russian exactly the same question, "How goes it?" and he added, "You are probably Mr. Winter just as I am Mr. Summer." After that we spoke only in Russian, but we still did not introduce ourselves to each other.

In November or early December 1947 I decided to pay a visit to my relatives in Böckel. I went by train from Lemgo to Bieren and from there I walked about one and a half kilometers to Böckel. When I arrived, my relatives received me with great alarm. "Go back immediately," they advised me, "the Russians were just here and wanted to take you away." As a matter of fact, four men had come a few days before. They included a Soviet officer, a Soviet soldier, the mayor of Muckum (a village near Böckel) and a German policeman. The Soviet officer behaved very politely and said he wanted to see me in order to convey greetings from my sister back in Leningrad. He also wanted to persuade me to return to the Soviet Union where I could work much more successfully at the Academy of Sciences than anywhere abroad. He was very surprised to learn that I was not there. Fortunately, no one in Böckel knew where I was staying at that time. My relatives living there only told him— probably in order to misinform—that some American officers had taken me to an unknown destination. The Soviet officer had to go back empty-handed. Many years later, when Valerian made several business trips to the Soviet Union and met my sister, he learned that she had absolutely no knowledge about the officer's visit to Böckel and that she had never tried to send greetings to me. In other words, what the Soviet officer said was nothing but a clumsy lie.

In 1948 West Germany started its first post-war government and carried out a monetary reform. A new currency was introduced overnight, and stores soon offered all kinds of food and merchandise. The political situation in Germany also changed drastically. The Berlin blockade began on June 28 and was to last until May 12, 1949, forcing the allies to finally recognize the true face of the Soviets. All the concessions to the Soviets, like the extradition of the Vlasov army and even of old emigrants such as Generals Semenov and Krasnov, had been of no avail. Soon Senator Vandenberg and

Mrs. Eleanore Roosevelt began calling for a halt in the extraditions and forcible repatriations to the Soviet Union, and the United States Congress passed a law to this effect.

One day a British officer told me that I would be transferred to Herford to teach Russian at a school for British officers. The CIC certified that I was a released German prisoner of war and that my home was in East Prussia. I was given yet another cover name, Kazakevich, and my profession was listed as high school teacher. With this certificate I received a room from the city housing office and a card from the employment agency which said that I was employed by the British. My landlady was very proud of my teaching at the intelligence school, and when she introduced me to her visitors she always added that I was working at a "school for intelligent gentlemen." I did not say anything but reflected that some of my students were certainly not very intelligent.

In this connection I would like to say that I had never expected to see such a great difference between two peoples as between the British and Americans. The British were, and this may sound improbable, more democratic than the Americans. The British had only one mess hall for officers and men alike, but the Americans had separate facilities for high-ranking officers, low-ranking officers, non-commissioned officers, and privates. This separation reminded me of conditions in the Soviet Union and may have been justified by the fact that British soldiers behaved much better than and were culturally superior to their American counterparts who showed rather poor table manners and would put their feet up on the table. The British were also more taciturn and understood how to keep secrets much better than the Americans who liked to show off by telling what they had seen or heard of classified matters. This is especially the case with the American press. It is relentlessly hunting for sensational news, and often makes secret matters known to everybody, including foreign governments. For example, a headline would proclaim that a certain company received an order for sophisticated aircraft for so many billions of dollars and that each plane would cost over 25 million dollars. Even a child can figure out how many top secret planes will be produced.

At that time, the British knew much more about the world than the Americans, who often had only the haziest notion of basic geographic facts. My friend Menges told me that an American official bound for Iraq had visited him to learn something about the country. After having been given a long lecture about Iraq, the official asked, "But, professor, aren't Iraq and Iran about the same?" It was also typical of the Americans that they wanted to make other countries happy in the American way even though they knew nothing about those countries. In this respect, the Americans are no different from the Soviets. The Soviets want all nations to have the Russian style of communism, while the Americans want everyone to enjoy life in the American way: Coca Cola, chewing gum, television, and football.

One day I received a letter from Professor Serge Elisseyeff (Sergei Eliseev) who, as I described in Chapter 3, had fled Leningrad in a motorboat and was now at Harvard University. He notified me that I would soon be hired by Harvard, half my salary coming from the Far Eastern department and the other half from the Center for Russian Studies. A short time later, however, the director of the Russian center, Professor Clyde Kluckhohn, informed me that for various reasons, which he did not specify, I could not get that appointment. I could not understand the reasons for this reversal, but they may have had something to do with the same objections Owen Lattimore had already raised to my having stayed in war-time Germany as a refugee from the Soviet Union and worked for the German government.

At the end of January 1949 I received an invitation from the University of Washington in Seattle, and the British CIC in Herford informed me that I would soon be sent to the American zone for transfer to the United States. I was to pack my belongings and be ready on short notice. I was to say nothing to my landlady except that I would return in about a month. I was driven to Lippstadt where we picked up Nataliya and then continued via Frankfurt to a camp surrounded by barbed wire. This was Camp King near Oberursel in the Taunus. We were given excellent food and lived there very well for quite a while. I was interviewed several times and told that Nataliya's general condition made her travel to the United States impractical.

At the beginning of March 1949 I had to go to an UNRRA center in Fulda to register Nataliya and myself as prospective immigrants to the United States. I left my wife at the camp because her multiple sclerosis had reached a stage where she could no longer get up. A few days later her condition took a sudden turn for the worse. When I served her breakfast on March 9 she tried to sit up, but always fell to the side. I called an American woman who was taking care of us and she brought a military surgeon. Nataliya was instantly taken to the American hospital in Wiesbaden, and on March 17 she was transferred to the German hospital Hohe Mark which was near Camp King. From then on she lay quietly in her bed, not uttering a word and showing few signs of being alive. On March 23 Nataliya sank into a coma and on March 26 at 10:10 a.m. she died in my presence. I buried her on March 29 in the Oberursel cemetery, with the funeral services being conducted by a Russian Orthodox priest whom I fortunately managed to find in nearby Bad Homburg. Although Nataliya's sad end did not come unexpectedly, my sorrow was very great. Now I felt utterly alone in Germany, and soon I was about to emigrate to the United States where everyone would be a stranger to me.

Soon after Nataliya's death I was taken from Camp King to the emigration camp in Hanau where I had to wait for an entry visa to the United States. After about three weeks I was summoned to the American consulate in Offenbach for an interview. The vice-consul who conducted the interview was a very nice young man who was more interested in conditions in the Soviet Union than in my background. Our chat was rather pleasant and it was a foregone conclusion that a visa would be issued without further ado.

10 A New Life in America

A few days after my interview with the American vice-consul in Offenbach I was informed that a military car would pick me up to take me to the Frankfurt airport from where I was to fly to the United States. On May 14, 1949 I left Frankfurt on a plane of the MATS (Military Air Transport Service) along with many officers and men on furlough. The sergeant who took me to the airport also gave me two dollars so that I could buy some food en route to the United States. During the night we stopped for several hours in the Azores for refueling and then continued our flight. We landed the next day at Westover Air Force Base near Springfield, Massachusetts. There I was received by a Red Cross official who showed me to my quarters for the night and gave me meal tickets for the messhall. The next morning I was flown to Washington, D.C. The same Red Cross official, when bidding me goodbye, said, "I suppose you still have a few dollars left for a snack during the flight." I replied, "No, I received only two dollars in Frankfurt and I spent them in the Azores." "Oh, how come?" he said, "The sergeant was supposed to give you ten dollars." I did not say anything; perhaps he was to give me ten dollars, but he gave me only two. In any case, the Red Cross official gave me another five dollars.

It was oppressively hot in Washington. As I left the airplane, it felt like walking into an oven. A young government employee took me in his car to the Hotel Brighton at the corner of California and Connecticut Avenues where I was to stay while working for the

State Department. I registered at the hotel under an assumed name. I frequently went to the Library of Congress, probably the largest and richest library in the world, where I could find books necessary for my own research and for the reports which I was to write for the State Department. These reports concerned the sciences in the Soviet Union, the organization of universities and research institutes, and the internal political conditions, particularly the purges in universities and research institutes, many details of which remained unknown to Americans and other foreigners.

In Washington I saw Carmel Offie often. He had already returned from Germany and was working in Washington. He introduced me to his former boss, Ambassador William Bullitt, with whom I had a long and interesting conversation about Moscow and its policies. Mr. Bullitt was very skeptical about the Soviet Union and future relations between the United States and the Soviet Union. I also met Joseph E. Davies, who had also been in Moscow and spoke excellent Russian and was married to a Russian. He was a well-educated person and I was later sorry to hear that he had fallen victim to the McCarthy purges. My most interesting and important acquaintance at that time in Washington was Gustav Hilger, a former councillor to the German ambassador to the Soviet Union. A German born in Moscow, he spoke the elegant Russian of pre-revolutionary Moscow, widely regarded as the finest Russian dialect. He had been brought to the United States in order to help with plans for a future German government, which by the time of my arrival had already been formed under Konrad Adenauer. The existence of the Adenauer government was to a large extent the result of Hilger's activities. He was a brilliantly educated and intelligent person who knew the Soviet Union better than anyone else—even better than I—because while stationed in Moscow, he had gathered much information in meetings with Molotov and many other Soviet officials. I became good friends with the Hilgers and visited them several times in Bonn after their return to Germany.

The famous Mongolist, Father Antoine Mostaert, a member of the Belgian monastic order of the Congregation of the Immaculate Heart of Mary (C.I.C.M.) lived in Arlington, Virginia. Though we had never met we had corresponded regularly from the early 1920s almost until the outbreak of World War II. Our first meeting was very cordial and we had many things to tell each other. I am very proud of our friendship because Mostaert was the greatest Mongolist of our time.[1] Besides, he was friendly, just and helpful, and his impeccable character made him a distinguished member of his religious congregation. When he learned that I had to leave all my books and materials behind in Leningrad, he instantly gave me a copy of each of his publications, among them many of those which he had already sent me many years earlier in Leningrad. That was the start of my own library in the United States. Very soon thereafter I also received offprints and copies of publications of other prominent scholars, first among them Gustav John Ramstedt, the great explorer of Mongolian languages and the founder of the comparative study of the so-called Altaic languages.[2] My friend Professor Erich Haenisch in Germany also sent me some books.[3] Father Louis M. J. Schram, who lived in the same mission house in Arlington as his fellow Fleming Mostaert, also gave me his publications and I could also count him among my friends.[4] I should also mention Francis W. Cleaves, professor at Harvard University, who from the very beginning of my life in America started a lively correspondence, sent me offprints of his publications and even photostats of various ancient Mongolian documents which had never been published.[5] I identified one of them as a brief Mongolian version of the Alexander Romance, and I published it in 1957.[6] For reasons unclear to me, Cleaves eventually stopped sending me offprints, acknowledging receipt of what I sent him and even answering letters. I became afraid that I might have displeased him somehow but, as it soon became evident, my fears were unfounded because Cleaves also broke off all contacts with Mostaert, Schram, and Henry Serruys, C.I.C.M., another outstanding Mongolist.[7]

It was very heartening to acquire such friends in a new and strange country. Actually it was the first time after a long period that I could acquire new friends because in the Soviet Union my only friends were my former classmates. One had to be suspicious of everyone so that new friendships were risky for both parties. A

Russian anecdote illustrates this condition quite well. Once a man went to his physician who asked him, "Do migraines frequent you very often?" "Oh, no," the patient replied, "no one ever frequents us and we don't visit others either."

My stay in Washington passed very quickly. I was fortunate to see many interesting places, like art galleries, monuments, and museums, but I was also very busy. I had to write many reports and answer questions about conditions in the Soviet Union. I was also asked to present several lectures on Mongolia, Sinkiang, and adjoining regions. In the summer of 1949 I went by train to New York for a few days to see the chief of the Russian division of the Voice of America. He was the former Soviet brigadier general A. Barmin who looked rather young and was an interesting conversationalist. He briefly told me about his life and also gave me a copy of his book *One Who Survived* which describes his escape from the Soviet Union.[8] During the years of the Great Purge, 1937-39, he was ambassador to Greece, when one day he was summoned home. He decided to defect because he had known many others who had returned to Moscow only to be arrested and disappear forever. Among many other topics, we discussed the program of the Voice of America. Since I had just come from Germany where there were many Russian refugees, Barmin wanted to know whether they listened to the Voice of America and what they thought of it. I gave him my opinion that some programs were of absolutely no interest to refugees, such as stories about Eleanore Roosevelt's daily routine. Barmin listened attentively and agreed with me that some improvements in the program were in order.

I used my time in New York to do some sightseeing. I went to the New York Public Library, the Metropolitan Art Museum, Central Park, and other famous landmarks. The opulence of the libraries and museums impressed me greatly, but at the same time I was amazed to see the squalid slums of Harlem and other parts of Manhattan. As I was to discover later, life in any large American city—New York, Chicago, or Los Angeles—is most unpleasant. I simply could not understand how such appalling slums could possibly exist in the wealthiest country in the world. I had never seen such filth, decay, and poverty in any Russian or West European cities.

Soon after my return to Washington I left the Hotel Brighton and rented a small apartment at 3068 Canal Street in Georgetown. I had to get in touch with Professor George Taylor at the University of Washington, who had invited me to go to Seattle, but as long as I stayed at the Brighton under an assumed name I could not do so. I wrote to Professor Taylor who promptly replied and urged me to arrive in Seattle before September 15 when students would start consulting professors about their courses. Taylor added that the president of the University of Washington, Dr. Raymond Allen, would soon be in Washington and visit me. Indeed, Dr. Allen came very soon, and we had a long and cordial conversation. I have ever since had a very high opinion of Allen. He held both a Ph.D. and an M.D. degree and, in contrast to all of his successors, he had an abiding interest in East Asia and Russia. He came to our department very often and knew everyone personally. Unfortunately he soon left the University of Washington to become president of the University of Southern California. His successors were Henry Schmitz, professor of forestry, Charles Odegaard, a classicist, and at the time of my retirement, John Hogness, a medical doctor. They were good administrators but never showed the slightest interest in Asian Studies and did not know anybody in the field. Schmitz, for example, once greeted me at a reception by saying, "I'm so glad to see you again. Didn't we meet in the chemistry department some weeks ago?"

I was very happy to return to my scholarly and teaching activities, but it took considerable effort because I had not taught Mongolian and Central Asian subjects since 1943. After a six-year interruption I had to prepare for the following courses at the University of Washington: Introduction to Mongolian, Classical Mongolian, Mongolian texts, the history of Mongolian literature and Mongolian nomadic civilization, and graduate seminars on the hP'ags-pa script and Middle Mongolian. I was also asked to help in the Russian program with courses on Russian syntax and the comparative grammar of Slavic languages. It was a very heavy teaching load of fifteen to sixteen hours spread over a five day week.

In this connecton I must say that an American university professor looked to me then more like a high school teacher. He had to spend much time in the classroom because homework was almost nonexistent. Students were not always, at least in 1949-50, sufficiently prepared for university study. Once when giving a phonetic transcription of Mongolian I wrote γ on the blackboard. "What's this?" one of the students asked. I said, "This is the Greek letter gamma which you probably had in trigonometry in high school." "Oh, no," he informed me, "I never took any trig." Thus I learned for the first time, to my utter amazement, that American high school students were permitted to choose their own subjects, with the result that they often skipped the most important ones. I also found some students to be rather immature. One of them repeatedly mispronounced a certain Mongolian word, and finally I said, "I have corrected you several times. Can't you remember that the word is pronounced this way?" His reaction was quite unexpected. "I don't care how this word is pronounced." I said, "I'm sorry, but don't blame me when you go to Mongolia and people will not understand you." The implications of my remark finally dawned on him and he apologized for his earlier remark. I am absolutely sure that it was not his fault but that of the wretched high school education he had received.

Several years later I had a quite unusual experience. Among my students was a girl of eighteen or nineteen years of age. She had enormous difficulty in studying Mongolian, and I wondered why she had enrolled in the course. She did not have the faintest idea about declension or conjugation even in English, had never heard of a genitive case or a participle, and so I had to teach her basic grammar. One day she came with an elderly gentleman who introduced himself as her father and asked me for permission to sit in on my class. I had no objections, and after class he said, "Professor, this is just too difficult. Can't you teach the language without grammar?" I said, "You can, of course, learn a language without studying its grammar if you live in a country where the language is spoken. When you study it at a university, however, you must first master its basic structure." His reply was that his daughter would drop my course.

I learned that at the root of this problem lay the fact that language study (except for classical languages, French and German) was relatively new in the United States. Even Harvard did not teach Russian until 1920, and the following, possibly apocryphal, anecdote highlights this problem. At the turn of the century German was to be introduced at a certain remote provincial university when one of the regents objected, "Why should we teach German? After all, our Lord Jesus Christ wrote the Holy Scriptures in plain English. Why should we bother with foreign languages?" This is only an anecdote but not all that far removed from the true state of affairs as I found it around 1950. Another anecdote concerns a university where Polish was to be introduced. When the professor arrived for his first class, he found the classroom crammed full of students. Naturally he was pleasantly surprised to find so many students interested in Polish, but after he made a few introductory remarks about the Polish language, he overheard a student mutter, "Gosh, this seems to be about some language." The professor asked him what he thought the course would be about, and the student answered that he had wanted to learn about polish.

These anecdotes, however, should not be interpreted to mean that all my students were naive and childish. On the contrary, some of them were excellent. For instance, John R. Krueger is presently professor at Indiana University. Another was James E. Bosson, now professor at Berkeley. Robert A. Rupen is teaching at the University of North Carolina and has written books on Mongolian history. Another brilliant student of mine was David Farquhar who later became professor at the University of California at Los Angeles. I also had an excellent Mongolian student, Pao Kuo-yi, in Mongolian Ünensechin, who came from Taiwan to get his degree and is now teaching at the University of California at Los Angeles. I also had some excellent Japanese students, like Hidehiro Okada who is now a professor in Tokyo. I should add that my classes were also attended by some prominent scholars, like Li Fang-kuei, a full member of the Academia Sinica and a scholar of world-wide reputation, who was my colleague in the Far Eastern department and who honored me by regularly showing up in my classes and taking Mongolian linguistics.

As a full-time faculty member, I naturally had to attend faculty meetings. I found out, however, rather soon that mostly minor matters, such as grants to students and leaves of absence, were discussed at those meetings. Important problems, such as the hiring of new professors, were often not discussed at all but were solved by the chairman himself. This explains the appearance of some new members who were of little use. I will return to this problem later.

Some meetings were devoted to promotions of faculty members. These promotions were obviously carried out rather arbitrarily, not only in the Far Eastern but also in other departments. For example, in the Department of Romance Languages there was a talented young associate professor named Politzer. His department always turned him down for promotion to full professor, and then Harvard hired him as full professor.

In the Far Eastern and Slavic department, some faculty members who published very little, were easily and readily promoted. On the other hand, there was a scholar who had arrived as a refugee from Russia soon after the revolution. He had published several books which might not have been brilliant but were useful to students. He remained an associate professor until his very last year as an active faculty member, and only then was he promoted to full professor.

Another example was a scholar of Russian literature who remained an associate professor until he was invited as a full professor to one of the East Coast universities. Such practice became routine. I remember that whenever the names of these two professors came up in those promotion meetings, the chairman merely looked at the assembled faculty members and said: "I suppose we vote our usual no." This practice continued until I retired in 1968.

All in all, I can look back at my nineteen years of teaching at the University of Washington with considerable satisfaction. However, the lamentable fact of general illiteracy in the United States cannot be dismissed lightly. Most students made numerous spelling errors in English. I even received letters with spelling errors from university offices. Thus the secretary of a certain university once sent me a letter thanking me for my "patients" in waiting for their answer. I also saw a note written by a professor to his typist who was retyping my manuscript, urging her to complete the job as fast as possible because I was an "imminent" scholar. To my great dismay I must say that such things are utterly impossible at Soviet and European universities.

I was occasionally asked to give talks to students and professors about the Soviet Union. Most of them understood me well, but some colleagues made very naive comments. Thus when I mentioned the lack of political freedom, freedom to read foreign newspapers of one's own choice and, above all, the obligatory study by all of Marxism-Leninism, one professor retorted that absolute freedom did not exist anywhere, and in order to back up his claim he pointed out that in the United States one had to stop at intersections when the traffic light was red. This was, of course, a good example of confusing the lack of political freedom with measures serving the interests of all. Another example of such confusion concerns academic freedom, which is vigorously safeguarded in the United States, and political freedom. A scholar should be free to be, say, a Darwinist or a Mendelian in genetics, or to be a follower or opponent of Chomski in linguistics. His political views or membership in whatever political organizations should be entirely separate matters.

Unfortunately, true *academic* freedom, freedom to adhere to a scholarly theory of one's own choice, is often lacking in American universities, and scholars who do not comply with currently fashionable theories have little chance at a university. This makes an American university somewhat like a Soviet university: in the Soviet Union it is Marxism, in the United States it is, say, a currently obligatory method in linguistics. All of this I learned later.

To return to my first academic year at the University of Washington, I should say that at the very end of January 1950 I received a letter from Ramstedt (Illus. 21). It was his last letter to me, for he died on November 2 of that year. I treasure this letter as a precious memento. His kind and flattering words about me make his letter as valuable to me as an honorary degree from a highly respected learned body. Therefore I reproduce it here in full (Illus. 22).

Illus. 21. Gustav John Ramstedt

Sometime toward the end of 1951, Professor Taylor asked me to come to his office where he introduced me to a Mr. Benjamin Mandel. Professor Taylor told me that Mandel was interested in learning something about Mongolia and that he would like to have a chat with me. The next day Mandel came to my apartment and asked me a number of questions about the Mongolian People's Republic, such as its international position and political organization. I told him that Mongolia was formally an independent nation but in reality a satellite of the Soviet Union. I told him about the Comintern and its role in Mongolia before World War II. He also asked questions

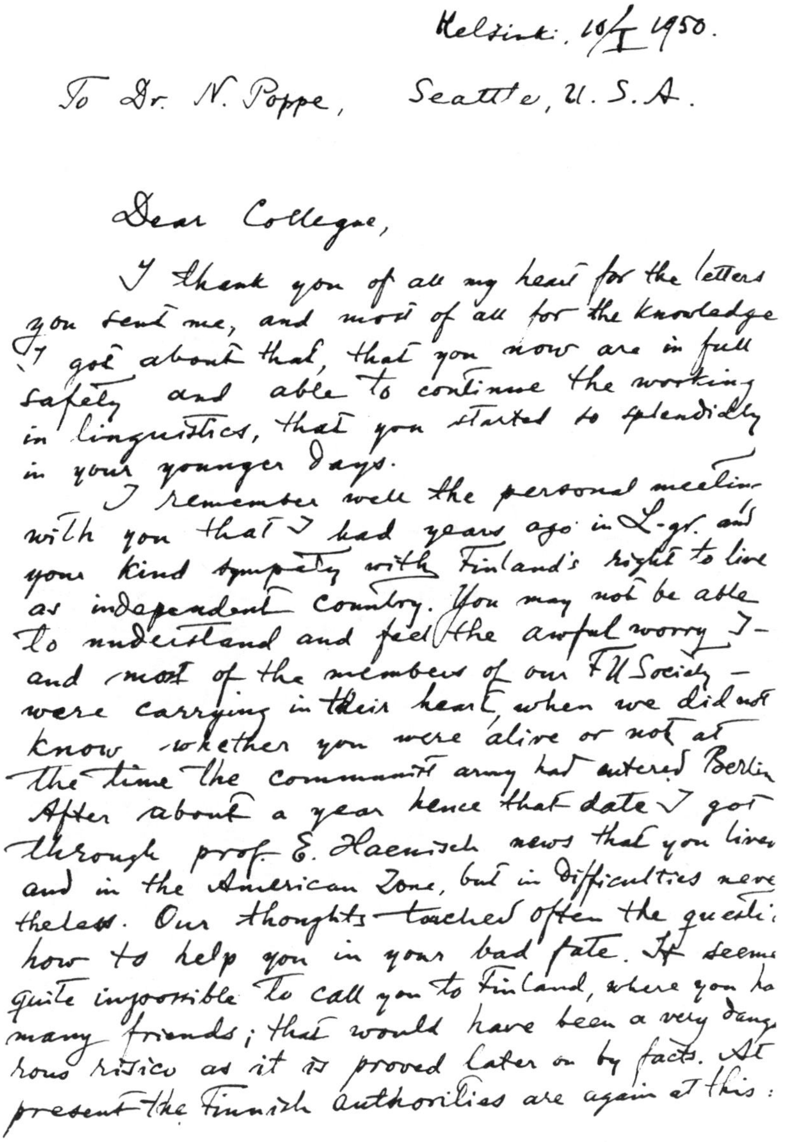

Helsink. 10/I 1950.

To Dr. N. Poppe,   Seattle, U.S.A.

Dear Collegue,

I thank you of all my heart for the letters you sent me, and most of all for the knowledge I got about that, that you now are in full safety and able to continue the working in linguistics, that you started so splendidly in your younger days.

I remember well the personal meeting with you that I had years ago in L-gr. and your kind sympathy with Finland's right to live as independent country. You may not be able to understand and feel the awful worry I — and most of the members of our F U Society — were carrying in their heart, when we did not know whether you were alive or not at the time the communist army had entered Berlin. After about a year hence that date I got through prof. E. Haenisch news that you lived and in the American Zone, but in difficulties nevertheless. Our thoughts touched often the question how to help you in your bad fate. It seemed quite impossible to call you to Finland, where you ha many friends; that would have been a very dangerous risico as it is proved later on by facts. At present the Finnish authorities are again at this:

Illus. 22. Ramstedt's Last Letter to the Author

Gromyko (and whole Sovyet-power) demands 300 persons, said to be in Finland, to be delivered for punishment, as enemies to Sovyet; most of those on the list are from Estonia, Ingermanland and Karelia and some have never been subjects to a & yet state; one has already killed him out of fear, of course. People who have - as far as known - done nothing against Finnish law should be delivered as prisoners to Sovyet, that's what is demanded now. Earlier it was a custom common to all civilized countries to accept fugitives who sought protection, if the whole cause was difference in political questions, that right to protection both Lenin and Stalin have received when the Tsar-regime was looking after them.

Yes, it is something dreadful that demand for delivery of innocent people; some of them are since years Finnish citizens; the list of these 300 is kept secret here and our authorities are trying their best to help the victims - out of the country, I have heard. Hard times are still ahead. - - -

I think you have already received my last book "Studies in Korean Etymology". It is not a book such as I intended it to be. There is no preface and no phonetical explanation about the older and later sound changes. But I will give some details in a following book, Einleitung in die Altaische Sprachforschung (or -wissenschaft) which is almost ready in typed manuscript. I hope to have it clear for print to the end of this year. - My "A Korean Grammar" is selling well and I suppose mostly to U.S.A. because the South of Korea is under American control. Some Americans want to learn a little

about that language also. — I can't complain
my books and articles are sent abroad q.
often, more than most of F.U.S's publication
And the Society (whos president I now am, since 1938
is very kind against my person: I have to live
with my family on the official pension (17.000 -
a month) while any workman, carpenter or daylaborer,
from 40 to 70 thousand a month; the Society (directory of -
gives me 15.000 a month as gratification or stipend

Yesterday I had a letter from A. v. Gabain. She says
it is for her like starting anew with Turkish studies
when she heard my "studies in Korea". But it seems
that she is hesitating in believing, for instance, the
sinokorean kam 'inspector (director) of 'ceremonies' is turc
gam 'shaman'. She finds it alright when slav. ka
'house, family' is the base of turc. qadaš 'a relative'
and that qatun 'Mme' also is from sinokorean source.
It is quite recently. J. Németh wrote that mo-ti. tay,
täyri can't be a Chinese loan and compared it with
Sumerian diŋir (dimir) 'heaven' (suggested by H. Peders
But as the Kitans the Sembi's and others have been
in contact with the Korean (Ko-rye, Ko-ku-rye and
Tiao-Sien = Chosen) in very early times and there was
a beginning civilization developed in South-Manchuria,
(at its height in 400-500 p. Chr.) there can be no
doubt about prehistorical contacts between the
ancestors of the Koreans and those of the Mongols

As it is now, with the stage where the Mon
golian and Turkish studies have reached, I think
the study of Korean is apt to help to go on
farther and clear up many problems. — You are
now, I think, in a position and living in a place
where you have opportunities enough to try to
make acquaintance with Koreans and to penetrate
in their mystical language (mystical because
it is hidden behind Chinese), which can't have

any original source in the Tibeto-Chinese groups of languages. You are still young and capable to much and I hope you — whom I consider my best disciple and my follower, when I am out for ever — I hope you will turn your attention to the Korean question and continue what I have tried to start. I am sickly already — my urinary organs are out of normal order, the ailing of ~~the prostate~~ and don't think I have many years more to live. This year I am 77 and my wife is 74. That is much already.

There is in S Korea now a Cōsen E. hakhŏe (Korean Language-Society), which edits a big Cōsen-mal khin sajŏn (Cōsen-language-big-dictionary) in 6 volumes, 2 of which already are out, printed on the costs of Rockefeller Foundation, I suppose. I have got those 2 volumes and through the Rockefeller Found. I was asked to give some opinion about the "scholarship" of this big enterprise. It is all in Korean and with a quite new "reformed" orthography in Korean letters. I admire the immense work there is done to collect all the content it has; but for linguistical purposes it is dangerous to rely on the new orthography. In South Korea 'language' is mal, and 'horse' is also mal; the old orthography had different a's (mạl 'horse' māl 'speech'). The new orthography has abolished the difference; but in North (Vladivostok and Manchuria?) there is mằr, mŏr 'horse' and māl 'speech'. The exploration of value must keep to a dialect or such dialects, where -r- is heard after vowels and where -ti-, -di-, -thi- are heard for Skor. ćí, ǰi, čǐ, sureička" is in North (in its older shape) tsŭru tiǐnin tsa, but in South tšuril tšǐnan tša ("line-beating ell"). There has been

a diffirence between *ta, tˊa, ča, čˊa* which still is
kept up in the Northern dialects, ~~when~~ the Southern has
ᵗtˊio, ᵗˊča and *ˢˊčia* as *ča* (*tˊǰa*). — Therefore it will be
necessary ~~to keep~~ to dialects spoken as North as
possible, — the are older and more reliable. That
is what I should like you to keep in mind,
if you meet Koreans in Seattle or elsewhere.

I send my best greetings to you and your family
and hope you will have a good and carefree
future on your new path and position. Best
wishes! Good luck! — Greetings ~~from many~~ of you
finnish friends!

yours truly,

G. John Ramstedt

regarding the Institute of Pacific Relations, but I had little information about it. He thanked me and left.

In early 1952 I received a letter from the Senate Committee on the Judiciary and Internal Security of the Congress of the United States requesting that I go to Washington in early February and testify before the committee on matters relating to Chinese Communism, the situation in Mongolia and activities of the Institute of Pacific Relations and other learned institutes in the United States doing research on Mongolia. I participated in a public hearing held by the committee on February 12, 1952. The meeting was opened by Senator Arthur V. Watkins. Then I was asked about my activities in the Soviet Union and the political climate there during my time. He was particularly interested in learning about Chinese and other Asian Communists training in the Soviet Union. I testified about various schools for training Communists in Asia, such as KUTV, the Communist University of the Toilers of the East, and Sun Yat-sen University, both in Moscow, and Tolmachov Political Academy in Leningrad. Next I was questioned about Mongolia, and I explained that country's dependency on the Soviet Union and the NKVD's activities in Mongolia. Finally the committee got around to the main subject: they asked me whether I knew Owen Lattimore. I had never met him but, of course, knew his books. When I was asked whether his characterization of Mongolia as a free and independent country was true, I unfortunately had to answer that this was not quite so. Soon more embarrassing questions were asked: Why is Lattimore giving a false picture of Mongolia? Is he not a secret Communist? Does he not want to mislead public opinion? The only response I could give to any of these questions was, "I don't know." When asked about the quality of Lattimore's writings on Mongolia, I expressed my view that some of them, like *Situation in Asia* and *Solution in Asia*, were superficial due to his lack of knowledge of the true situation in the Mongolian People's Republic whch was closed to foreigners.

Some weeks after my return to Seattle, I received a letter from Lattimore in which he thanked me for not accusing him of secret Communist membership, willful deception of public opinion, and other charges hurled at him by others. He did, however, take exception to my calling his writings superficial. I understand what he means by independence, namely that Mongolia has not been part and parcel of any other nation since 1921. My point, however, was that Mongolia did and still does not have the freedom to conclude agreements with other countries of its own choice or even the relatively innocuous freedom to decide on its own whether to send its scholars to international congresses. A good example of Mongolia's lack of independence was offered in 1964 when the International Congress of Orientalists convened in Ann Arbor, Michigan. At first, the Mongols profusely thanked the organizers for the invitation and sent a list of their delegates and papers to be presented. A month later the Soviet Academy of Sciences refused to participate because of "imperialist aggression in Vietnam," and several days later a similar letter came from the Mongolian Academy of Sciences.

I agree that it is unpleasant to be labeled as the author of superficial statements, but under the circumstances prevailing at those hearings in Washington it was the least harmful thing I could have said. Therefore I regard it as unkind of Lattimore to call me an SS officer in one of his later books.[9]

As I explained in Chapter 9, the Wannsee Institute in Berlin where I was assigned to work in 1943 was a branch of the Stiftung für Länderkunde (Geography Foundation) which, in turn, was an SS organization. However, I was not a member of the SS and, as a foreigner, could not have easily become one. My colleagues at the University of Washington urged me to do something against this accusation. Consequently, I asked the archival office of the Federal Republic of Germany to certify, on the basis of the files of the Wannsee Institute, that I had not been a member of the SS. The archival office replied that whereas all SS members working at that institute are listed together with their SS ranks, I am always referred to as "professor" and "reader" (in German Referent). Moreover, in the section on membership in the NSDAP, there is only a dash after my name whereas party membership of some other employees is indicated after their names. I reproduce the letter here as proof that I have never been an officer in the SS nor a member of the Nazi party (Illus. 23).

All in all, Lattimore's case was rather unpleasant. It reminded me of what I had witnessed on a larger scale in the Soviet Union. To be sure, there were certain differences: in the Soviet Union, scholars were sent to concentration camps, but in the United States Lattimore was merely hounded out of his own country. His case should never have happened because under the provisions of the Constitution of the United States, Lattimore had the right to express any opinions, even controversial ones. It should be added that the Lattimore case involved *academic* freedom but this aspect of it was not generally taken seriously. Fortunately the investigation was discontinued when Eisenhower became president.

In 1952 I remarried. My new wife was the former Edith O. Ziegler, the daughter of one of my father's colleagues at the Tsarist Ministry of Foreign Affairs, Karl V. Ziegler, and she had been one of my childhood friends. She had escaped from Petrograd to Finland in 1920, and soon after my arrival in Berlin in 1943, I met her again. She visited Nataliya and me several times. Marriage necessitated the purchase of a home of our own. The house I bought was small and inexpensive because my meager salary had to support both of my sons who were studying in Europe. Valerian had just enrolled as a geology student at Trinity College in Dublin, and Nicholas was attending the School of Oriental and African Studies of London University. Besides, when I first arrived in the United States in 1949, I had to borrow some money to travel from Washington to Seattle, and at the time of my marriage I was still paying off my debts. To help me out Edith worked as a nurse for six years at Providence Hospital in Seattle.

I incurred these debts because the university did not pay my fare from Washington to Seattle, although I later learned that the Far Eastern and Slavic department did pay the fare for several other new professors. I also became indebted because the university did not pay me my first half-month salary until October 1, even though I had to be on campus at the beginning of September. When I arrived in Seattle I discovered that there was a project on the "Asian mode

BUNDESARCHIV

Az.: 9212 b/Poppe

(bitte bei Antwort anzugeben)

KOBLENZ, den   18. Februar 1963

Am Wöllershof 12
Postfach 320
Fernruf 2411, Ortsnetzkennzahl 0261
Fernschreiber 086816

Herrn
Prof. Dr. Nikolaus Poppe
University of Washington
Far Eastern Department

S e a t t l e 5, Washington

USA

Auf Ihr Schreiben vom 9.2.1963 an Herrn Oberarchivrat Teske.

Sehr geehrter Herr Professor!

Einige, allerdings unvollständige Akten der Gruppe VI G des
Reichssicherheitshauptamtes, der sog. Reichsstiftung für Länderkunde, sind im vorigen Jahr von den USA an das Bundesarchiv
übergeben worden. Speziell Sie betreffende Vorgänge sind darin
nicht enthalten, wohl aber einige Aufstellungen der Angehöri-
gen der unterstellten Institute. Dazu gehört ein Verzeichnis

Illus. 23. Letter from the Archives of the Federal Republic of Germany

217

der Belegschaft des Wannsee-Instituts nach dem Stand vom 4.12.
1943, in der bei den 10 Mitarbeitern, die SS-Ränge bekleideten,
diese angegeben sind, während es bei Ihnen lediglich heißt:
"Prof. Dr. Poppe, Nikolaus, 8.8.1897". In einem Schreiben von
VI G an den Beauftragten für Ausweichquartiere vom 14.6.1944
sind alle Mitarbeiter des Ostasieninstituts aufgeführt, für
die Unterkunft gesucht wurde; Sie werden darin bezeichnet als
"Referent im Institut". Schließlich ist noch ein von Ihnen
selbst ausgefüllter Personalfragebogen vom 13.4.1944 vorhanden.
Darin haben Sie bei den Fragen über Mitgliedschaft in der NSDAP
und ihren Gliederungen jeweils einen Strich gemacht und als
Ihre Stellung im Institut "Referent" angegeben. Daß Sie also
der SS nicht angehört haben, dürfte damit erwiesen sein.

In den USA haben sich die genannten Akten, die auch einigen
Aufschluß über die Tätigkeit des Ostasien-Instituts und der
Gruppe VI G bieten, bei der World War II Records Division in
Alexandria/Va. in Record Group 1010 unter der Signatur 173 -
b - 20 - 05/20 befunden. Es ist anzunehmen, daß sie vor der
Rückgabe im Auftrag der American Historical Association ver-
filmt wurden und ein Mikrofilm unter Angabe der Signatur so-
wohl von Ihnen wie von Mr. Lattimore vom Nationalarchiv,
Exhibits and Publications Branch, Washington 25., D.C., be-
zogen werden könnte.

Mit vorzüglicher Hochachtung
Im Auftrag

(Dr. Müller)

of production" to which I shall return later. A substantial grant had been obtained, and a number of persons were working on that project. The department could have employed me, but did not, as a temporary researcher for the month of September and paid me a salary. This lack of generosity put me in a very difficult position. I was a refugee and did not have anything, so that I had to borrow money to pay for food and other necessities and rent a room on credit.

I have never been treated generously by the University of Washington. My salary in 1949-50 was a little more than $5,000. After taxes and other deductions, only about $4,000 remained. This amount was inadequate because I had to support two sons abroad and pay for their tuition and all living expenses. As neither I nor they were American citizens, I could not claim income tax deductions for them. Consequently, Edith's salary was an important supplement.

In this connection, I would like to point out that at the University of Washington salaries were not paid according to a fixed schedule as in Germany and the Soviet Union. Instead, salaries were determined by the heads of departments. Whether they acted fairly or not is anyone's guess. I, for one, can say that my salary was always among the lowest of full professors' salaries. During my last year of active service, 1967-68, I received $18,000. At that time, those who were often referred to as "the inner circle" received between $22,000 and $24,000 although, from a scholarly point of view, I do not think that they were superior to me.

I was not the only one who did not belong to the most favored group. The outstanding Chinese scholar, the late Hsiao Kung-ch'üan, always received one of the lowest salaries paid to full professors. Li Fang-kuei, another eminent Chinese scholar, was similarly slighted until he finally asked for an interview with the then president, Charles Odegaard, and got the latter's permission to by-pass the head of the department and deal directly with him.

Such great differences in salaries grew even larger under Taylor's successors. In 1980-81, for example, the highest salary of a full professor in the Department of Asian Languages was $47,000 whereas the lowest salary, a mere $27,000, was given to Professor

Paul Serruys, C.I.C.M., internationally recognized as one of the top scholars in Sinology. I am mentioning Professor Serruys's name with his permission.

In this connection I would like to say a few words about my impression of American living standards. When I arrived in Washington, D.C. in May 1949 I was amazed to see the stores crammed with an abundance of goods. After twenty-five years in the Soviet Union, where stores were empty and most commodities could not be obtained at any price, and several more years of acute shortages in war-torn Germany, it was hard to believe one's eyes when seeing this veritable cornucopia. Another pleasant change awaiting me was the politeness of sales personnel; in the Soviet Union, it had always been "I'm alone and you are many; can't you wait?" or "If you don't like it, get out of here!" but now I heard, "Yes, sir," and "Thank you, sir." What surprised me most about life in the United States, however, was that one could buy many things on credit. Thus in 1952 we bought a $5,000 house with a down payment of only $500, and when we sold it in 1956 and bought a better one for $10,000, the down payment again was only ten per cent. We also bought furniture on credit.

I soon discovered, however, that the quality of merchandise was often below pre-war standards. Many houses for sale, especially the newer ones, were poorly insulated, typewriters wore out much faster than those in pre-war Europe, and cameras were not as good as those manufactured by Zeiss. Later it became common knowledge that Japanese tape recorders were superior to those produced in the United States, and Japanese cars became strong competitors to American cars. The obvious problem is quality.

I was much taken by the people's friendliness. It was not only sales clerks who were friendly but people in general. Across the street from our first home lived a certain Mr. Christianson whose job was replacing old utility poles for the city light company. One day he came to us with a truckload of discarded utility poles which he had sawed down to a size suitable for fireplace logs. They were cedar and burned excellently. This was Mr. Christianson's way of welcoming newcomers to his neighborhood. In the streets motorists would stop and offer me a lift and passers-by greeted me with a cheerful "Good morning" or "Good evening," often adding, "Isn't it a beautiful day?" to which I could only reply equally politely, "It is gorgeous!"

I was also greatly impressed by the people's honesty. Once I was returning from the cleaners with a large parcel of freshly laundered shirts. I stopped in the street to tie my shoelaces, placing the parcel on a trash can. After I had resumed my walk and gone on for about ten minutes, at least half a mile, I suddenly remembered that I had left the parcel behind. I retraced my steps and found my parcel still lying on the trash can. This would have been absolutely impossible in the Soviet Union where the parcel would have been stolen the moment I left it behind and where you even had to guard your wash on the clothesline or else the wet wash would have been stolen right off the line. Such honesty as I found in the United States in 1949-1951 I had witnessed in only two other countries, Finland and Mongolia. Something more interesting happened quite recently. In March 1980, I gave my slacks which I had not worn since February 1979 when Edith died, to the cleaners. Another year went by, and in July 1981 I put them on and noticed something attached to the inside of my back pocket with a safety pin. When I took it out, I found four 500-Deutsche Mark bills wrapped in a piece of German newspaper. Then I remembered that I had worn those slacks on my return flight from Germany. Edith's illness and her subsequent death made me completely forget that I had put that unspent money into my pocket when I was in Germany. The slacks with almost $1,000 went to the cleaners who, after discovering the money, neatly secured it to the inside of the back pocket with a safety pin. Times change, of course, and the crime rate has increased enormously since 1949, but the case of my cleaners is proof that honesty has not died out. One reads from time to time in the papers that somebody found a parcel containing somebody else's life savings and returned it to the owner.

The two houses we lived in since our wedding in October 1952 were small and modest but they were our own. I am sure that many Americans took a home of their own for granted, but for those of us who had come from the Soviet Union, where we had lost all our property, by way of war-torn Germany, a home of our own was something out of this world. I need not add that no "Black Maria" ever stopped at our house in the dead of night to take us to the secret police for interrogation about allegedly subversive activities.

Returning to the University of Washington, I should say that I was greatly impressed with American campuses. In Russia, Germany, and many other European countries, universities are housed in a few large buildings containing all or most departments. For example, the old St. Petersburg University consisted of one long, eighteenth-century building to which later, in the early 1900s, were added two modern buildings housing physical and chemical laboratories. There was no park surrounding the university. American campuses, patterned after those in Great Britain, are different. The University of Washington is situated in a large park containing numerous buildings of the same architectural style as well as some newer modernistic buildings. On clear days there is a beautiful view from campus; when standing at the fountain near the administration building one can see Mount Rainier in the far distance. I was also impressed by the Berkeley campus, Harvard University with its colonial-style buildings, Indiana University, and the University of Colorado with its beautiful pink buildings in Spanish-Mexican style. True, some libraries lacked many important books in my fields, but the equipment of the laboratories, the faculty clubs with excellent food, and the students' recreational buildings, such as the HUB of the University of Washington or the Student Union Building of Indiana University, surpassed the imagination of anyone who had been accustomed to the drab Soviet or barrack-like German universities. After I had migrated to the United States, Moscow received a new university, housed in a giant, wedding cake-like building. It is not drab but certainly in poor taste.

What also impressed me greatly was that all professors had their own offices in which they could keep their books and do their research. No professor in the Soviet Union or even in Germany has his own office where he can work all by himself without being disturbed by anyone. Moreover, one was free to choose his subject

222

of research. There was no team work, no "socialist competition," and not even deadlines. There was no obligatory state–enforced theory or ideology, such as Marxist methodology. True, some southern states forbade the teaching of Darwin's theory of evolution, uncomfortably akin to the prohibition of Mendelian genetics in the Soviet Union. However, this excrescence on an otherwise free science did not affect or bother me.

Rich people are of two kinds: some are generous or even extravagant, others are miserly. America could be compared to the former. Waste could be seen everywhere. Generally speaking, during the time from World War II to the early 1970s, American universities and individual scholars received very generous grants from various foundations. I can write, of course, only about the University of Washington and specifically about the Far Eastern and Russian Institute, a research body, and the Department of Far Eastern and Slavic Languages and Literatures whose task was teaching. The institute and department were linked in the person of Professor George Taylor who headed both organizations. I remember the institute receiving during my time $200,000 from the Carnegie Foundation, $500,000 from the Ford Foundation, and $375,000 from the Rockefeller Foundation. Although the research projects, funded by these grants, yielded some results which were later published, the general result was below what one could have expected or, better, demanded in view of the enormous size of these three grants. I am sure that with better organization and a more serious attitude, waste could have been avoided and better results could have been obtained. To give an example of wastefulness, I shall discuss the project on the Asian mode of production.

When I first arrived in Seattle, the Far Eastern and Russian Institute had already begun to work on this project. The Asian mode of production plays a role in certain Marxist theories about the various stages of social development. As is well known, Marxists allege that all human development is principally based on the "mode of production," i.e., on economic factors. Thus ancient society is said to be based on slave labor, feudal society on agricultural serf labor, and so forth. The Asian mode of production was supposedly

223

centered around huge irrigation works and serf labor, and societies having such a mode of production were subjected to a particular form of government which Karl Wittfogel called "Oriental despotism."[10] In the 1930s a discussion of the Asian mode of production was held in the Soviet Union. Stalin opposed this theory, and most scholars involved in the discussion, such as Godes, Safarov, and others were arrested and some of them were shot. The reason for Stalin's opposition was that Lenin had stated that a feudal society could move toward socialism bypassing the capitalist stage, especially when helped by the victorious proletariat of a socialist country. Stalin applied this theory to China, and in order to make Lenin's prophecy come true, Chinese society had to be declared feudal rather than as having an Asian mode of production because the latter could not bypass capitalism. Anyway, the Seattle group studied these problems and translated huge amounts of literature from Russian into English. Then the entire project was suddenly discontinued and no results were ever published. The grant was thus wasted.

Rampant waste was also evident in students' stipends. I know of several cases where girls received scholarships, but after attending the university for one or two years, got married and never returned to finish their studies. In other countries they would have had to hand back the entire amount of their scholarships. Thus my general impression of American society was one of unbelievable waste. In restaurants I saw people leaving large steaks on their plates after having eaten a few mouthfuls. Cars were parked in front of diners with their motors running while their drivers were having their lunch. Walking in forests near Seattle, I sometimes came across abandoned railroad tracks, all rusty and overgrown. I was told that they led to now abandoned mines some twenty or thirty miles away, and I remembered how the Soviets had dismantled the railroad from Mineral'nye Vody to Kislovodsk, a distance of about fifty kilometers, transported the tracks to Kizlyar and built a new railroad from there to Astrakhan along the shore of the Caspian Sea, thus compensating for the railroad cut by the Germans in the Northern Caucasus and securing an uninterrupted supply of oil from

Baku. Another example of waste were the large heaps of discarded boxes lying in front of food stores. In Europe such boxes would be reused many times, but in the United States they were simply picked up the next day and burned at the city dump.

In this connection I should say that my remarks concerning waste have often been misinterpreted as criticism, and the reaction of some persons was quite unexpected. "Why don't you go back to your old country if you don't like it here?" they would ask. My intentions, however, were merely to voice a well-intentioned warning that the national interest demanded frugality in the use of natural resources. Nowadays, with an oil shortage, inflation, and high prices, most people would probably agree that my remarks were not made maliciously. To my satisfaction I no longer see brightly lit offices and classrooms in deserted university buildings at night, and I no longer expect to see thermostats set at 75 degrees and all windows open because of suffocating heat.

I would now like to turn my attention to my colleagues at the University of Washington. The chairman of the Department of Far Eastern and Slavic Languages and Literature, and the director of the Far Eastern and Russian Institute was Professor Taylor whom I mentioned earlier. He was British and specialized in the modern history of China. He was well informed but also very critical of communism and skeptical about the possibility of establishing normal relations with the Soviet Union and China (the latter at least as long as Mao lived) so that it was quite natural that several government agencies frequently consulted him. Student protesters in the 1960s misinterpreted these consultations, accusing the institute and department of serving the interests of the CIA. As the head of our institute and department, he was also interested in attracting as many students as possible to courses we offered on the Soviet Union and China. Thus one day he addressed a group of high school principals in Seattle urging them to encourage their seniors to consider studying Russian or Chinese or, even better, both languages when they entered the university. A short while later, however, Taylor started getting desperate letters lamenting "Why have we listened to you? Now all the parents come and accuse us of trying to force their children to study the languages of communist countries!" To this I can only say: "To deal with the enemy, one has to know him." At that time, both Russia and China were enemies.

Taylor made several trips to Taiwan and other countries, especially in Southeast Asia, and later became a member of the Presidential Committee on Education. He was a good organizer and had connections with various foundations which gave the Far Eastern and Russian Institute generous grants. These enabled me in 1958 to visit Japan and do research there and publish several of my books, such as *Mongolische Epen*, *Khalkha-mongolische Grammatik*, Krueger's English translation of my *Mongolian Monuments in ḥP'ags-pa Script*, *Twelve Deeds of Buddha*, and *The Diamond Sutra*, a translation of three Mongolian versions of a Buddhist philosophical work whose original is in Sanskrit. After his retirement in 1969, Taylor became the head of the Washington state trade commission for the Far East.

The deputy director of the institute was Professor Franz Michael who was German and had received his doctoral degree from Freiburg University. His field was also the modern history of China.[11] He had been in the German foreign service in China, but when he lost his job under Hitler he stayed in China doing research. He was friendly and very pleasant, and both he and Mrs. Michael became my and Edith's best friends. Unfortunately, Michael did not remain long at our university but moved to George Washington University in Washington, D.C. One of the main reasons was serious disagreements with the department's chairman. A scholar in the field of ancient and medieval China and Chinese philosophy was Hellmut Wilhelm, the son of the well-known German Sinologist Richard Wilhelm and himself a student of Erich Haenisch. Wilhelm was an active member of the Chinese history project, and some works were completed under his supervision.

The most important member of this project, however, was the well-known Karl August Wittfogel, an expert in Marxist philosophy and communism, himself a former member of the German Communist Party, who knew many inside details about that party unknown to most other people. His book on the history of the Liao is a remarkable work.[12]   His other book on Oriental despotism, mentioned earlier, contains unacceptable statements, for instance, that Oriental despotism had been introduced into medieval Russia by the Mongols who had become acquainted with it after their conquest of China. Arnold Toynbee, among others, has criticized this book, but the fact remains that Wittfogel was an outstanding scholar.

The two most prominent members of the Far Eastern department and institute were Professors Li Fang-kuei and Hsiao Kung-ch'üan respectively, both of them full members of the Academia Sinica. Li was a brilliant linguist in Chinese, Tai, and Tibetan, and even some American Indian languages were the subjects of numerous first-rate scholarly works by him.[13]   He was also a well-educated person, spoke excellent English, French, German and even Russian. As mentioned earlier, he did me the high honor of attending my classes in Mongolian which he mastered perfectly. We became good friends and I am proud of his friendship. Unfortunately Li did not stay at the university but left for the University of Hawaii where he spent about ten years until his retirement. Professor Hsiao was probably the greatest authority on the history of Chinese political thought,[14] a field alien to me so that my opinion of his work is based entirely on comments by specialists. Professor Hsiao's high merits are commonly recognized, and I should add that he was one of my most pleasant colleagues.

A scholar equal in qualifications to Li and Hsiao was Edward Conze, a brilliant British Sanskritist and Buddhologist.[15] He came from England as a visiting professor, and we became close friends very soon after his first arrival, and remained friends until his death in 1979. He was to become a permanent member of the faculty, but most unfortunately nothing came of it for two basic reasons. One of them was political in nature, and I am sorry to say that it was used successfully against him. Like Wittfogel and thousands of others, Conze had been a Communist Party member but later quit and became an outspoken enemy of communism. The purges and murders of innocent people in Stalin's Soviet Union, the concentration camps in which millions perished, the criminal pact with Hitler and the rape of Poland had forced many Western Communists to leave a party which no longer pursued the ideals of Marx and Engels. It was many years after he quit the party that Conze came to our department. However, while Wittfogel, who also had been a party member, was never attacked for it, Conze was not only attacked but requested by the federal authorities to present a list of all Communists personally known to him. He refused on the grounds that as a subject of Great Britain he could not be expected to collaborate with a foreign government. Those in our department who wanted to get rid of Conze had counted on his refusal because they knew that the United States would strip Americans of their citizenship if they were to collaborate with a foreign government under similar circumstances. It was clear that the real reason for the opposition to Conze becoming a tenured member of our department was not his former membership in the Communist Party.

The real reason for hostility towards Conze was purely personal. Conze had a very difficult character, and it was by no means easy to deal with him. He made himself most vulnerable by living with a British woman while not yet divorced from his wife. Once he came to my office and told me that the department threatened to make his common-law marriage known to everyone if he did not agree to the promotion of a professor who, in Conze's opinion, did not deserve it. He called it blackmail. Soon, however, he obtained his divorce and married his companion in Vancouver, B.C., so that the threat could not be carried out. At that time, such things as living with a woman out of wedlock were considered immoral, but today Conze's common-law marriage could not be used against him. After Conze left Seattle for good, he retaliated by mentioning all this--and much more--in his memoirs.[16]

A scholar of high standing was Professor Vincent Shih whose special field was the history of Chinese literature and philosophy.[17] Like all the others mentioned so far, he retired several years ago. With the exception of Conze, all of them were scholars in the Chinese field which was represented much better than any other field. In fact, it would be no exaggeration to say that some fields were even neglected. At the time of my arrival, all Japanese studies were conducted on a much more modest scale, and Korean had only one native teacher with no professor who could give more than practical teaching of the language. Strangest of all, Russian and other Slavic languages were not taught in a separate department but were treated as a kind of appendage to East Asian Studies.

The only professor was Victor Erlich, a talented scholar in the field of Russian literature and the author of a book on Russian formalism. [18] Victor Erlich was from Poland and spoke also very good Russian. Later Russian literature was taught by George P. Ivask, an Estonian who had lived most of his life in Moscow and naturally spoke an excellent Russian and was himself a poet. After he left for the University of Massachusetts, he was succeeded by lecturers who spoke a rather poor Russian. Such a situation was the exact opposite of what I had experienced at Petrograd/Leningrad University where the professors of foreign literature spoke superb German (V. M. Zhirmunskii), French (V. F. Shishmarev) and Spanish (D. K. Petrov). The situation at the University of Washington became as intolerable as someone reciting Keats's poetry in strongly mispronounced English. At the time of my arrival, most instructors offered practical teaching of colloquial Russian. This is why I was also given the task of lecturing in Russian syntax, comparative grammar of Slavic languages and the history of the Russian language.

The Far Eastern and Russian Institute and its successors (see below) have had several excellent scholars in the Russian and East European fields. In my opinion, its most outstanding members included Professor Marc Szeftel from Poland, a specialist in the history of Russian law and judiciary system and the author of important works in French. Another excellent scholar is the Hungarian Imre Boba, a specialist in the history of Eastern Europe and the author of significant monographs. Besides, he is an affable person and a good friend of mine. The list would not be complete if I did not mention Professor Herbert Ellison, who is an expert on Soviet history, a talented scholar and an excellent teacher. It has always been a pleasure to me to meet and talk with him.

A Russian proverb says that "there is no family without a monster," and our department also had a member who created problems. In 1952 I received a letter from a young Austrian scholar, the Turcologist and Mongolist Udo Posch, who taught at the University of Graz. He asked me whether he could obtain a Fulbright Fellowship to work at the University of Washington. I talked this over with Professor Taylor, and arrangements were made for Posch's coming. He arrived in the fall of 1953. From the very beginning he appeared a strange person. He often was, or pretended to be, ill and missed many classes. One could often see on the blackboard of his class the notice "No Turkish today." Finally this notice became permanent, and a note to the janitor was added which told him not to erase it.

Posch was irascible and unfriendly to his students. His unpublished doctoral dissertation was on Tibetan verbal prefixes, and he often showed it to his students as if wanting to say that they would never be able to produce a scholarly work like this. Once a student who was not studying under him asked him for help in translating an obscure passage in a Tibetan text. Posch flew into a rage and declared that he did not know and did not want to know "all those monkey languages," and ordered the student out of his office. The student went to the student lounge and while he was sadly reflecting on his clash with Posch, another student entered and asked what the matter was. He related his experience with Posch and his listener said that he was utterly puzzled because Posch had always boasted about his dissertation on Tibetan verbal prefixes. The two students then decided to solve this puzzle, and one day when they found Posch's office open and empty, they took Posch's dissertation which lay on his desk and microfilmed it. They then went to the university library and discovered in the catalog the title of a book on Tibetan verbal prefixes by von Koerber, published in Los Angeles in 1939. After obtaining a copy of that book, the students quickly discovered that Posch's dissertation was a verbatim translation of that book. Armed with this evidence, they marched to Professor Taylor and showed it to him. Posch was immediately fired and Vienna University was notified and it declared Posch's doctoral degree null and void. When I asked Posch why he had done it, he answered that he had been Professor Duda's doctoral candidate in

Turkish but that he had a quarrel with him and changed over to become a graduate student of Professor Robert Bleichsteiner, the Tibetanist and Mongolist. Bleichsteiner allegedly suggested that he write his dissertation on Tibetan. I suspect that Bleichsteiner knew perfectly well that Posch's dissertation was simply a translation of von Koerber's book because Bleichsteiner was too good a scholar not to be acquainted with that book. Being a kind person, he obviously wanted to help Posch who was in a difficult position after his clash with Duda.

Professor Taylor suggested to Posch that he get a valid doctoral degree, but Posch had become addicted to drugs in the meantime and died in the 1960s. Posch's case was unique. I had never before encountered a plagiarist quite like him, and I was surprised to learn that a plagiarist could be as naive as to show his manuscript to everybody and to brag about it. At the very least, he should have destroyed the manuscript after having obtained his degree.

Posch was unfortunately not the only unpleasant case during my years at the University of Washington. I remember several instances in which persons claimed to be what in truth they were not. For example, I was once asked to examine a man who claimed to have graduated from the Leningrad Polytechnical Institute and who was looking for a job as a qualified engineer. Of course I could not investigate his qualifications as an engineer but only his general background. I found out immediately that he could not remember the name of the rector, i.e., president, of his institute nor the names of the dean of his faculty, i.e., department, and his professor of sopromat, the Russian academic abbreviation for resistance (or strength) of materials. When asked where he had lived in Leningrad, he replied Nevskii Prospect, Leningrad's main street, which is mentioned in hundreds of novels and is as well known to everyone, even to those who had never been there, as is Park Avenue in New York or Piccadilly Circle in London. He was vague about the nearest intersection, and when asked about the number of the streetcar he took from his apartment to the institute, he answered that he had always walked which is absolutely impossible because the distance was about twelve miles, something like from the Battery to the

Cloisters in New York. I told him so and added that I was sorry to be unable to recommend him for a job. Unfortunately, there were untrustworthy elements among refugees, and this is reflected in an anecdote which made the rounds among displaced persons. There was, so the story goes, a mongrel the size of a Pekinese in a refugee camp who listened to some fugitives from the Soviet Union boast about having been ministers of the Czarist government or of having held some other eminent position, so when his turn came the mongrel proudly declared that under the old regime he had been a Great Dane.

In 1955 Nicholas graduated from the School of Oriental and African Studies and received his B.A. degree with honors in Turkish. In December of that same year he came to the United States and after spending a month with us in Seattle, he went to Washington, D.C. where he had obtained a temporary job at one of the research institutes and also started teaching Russian at a language school. Two years later Valerian graduated from Trinity College with a B.S. degree in geology and went to Canada where he got a job at the Kerr-Addison gold mine in Virginiatown, Ontario. I visited him in that beautiful area covered with dense forests interspersed with large and small lakes. In later years he worked in Kingston on Lake Ontario, close to the region known as the Thousand Islands, and he finally moved to Ottawa where he got a position at the National Research Council of Canada.

Valerian's case is a good example of the importance of connections. After he had graduated from Trinity College, Valerian went to look for a job in Ottawa, Canada. He visited the offices of many mining firms but all of them politely turned him down, claiming they had no vacancies. At the same time I wrote to my friend, Earl R. Hope in Ottawa, about whom I will say more shortly, asking him to help Valerian find a job. A short time later, one of Hope's acquaintances took Valerian to the office of a mining company which Valerian had visited unsuccessfully only the previous day and, to his great surprise, he received a job immediately. The gentleman recommending him happened to be one of the company's major stockholders. This episode proves that the answer, "We are sorry that we have no openings, but will keep your name on file," is often untrue.

I became acquainted with Earl Hope in the early 1950s when he sent me a paper he had written in which he severely criticized the famous Sinologist Karlgren's reconstruction of the glottal stop in ancient Chinese.[19] The paper was published as an open letter to scholars who, in Hope's opinion, adhered to Karlgren's theory. I wrote Hope thanking him for the paper, but pointed out that what I had actually done in my book on the Mongolian monuments in ḩP'ags-pa script was to quote widely from Dragunov's work on Old Mandarin which relied heavily on Karlgren.[20] Hope's response was very friendly and our correspondence gradually developed into friendship. I visited him many times in Ottawa and count him among my best friends. Hope is a very gifted and learned man who worked for the Canadian government as a translator of scholarly and technical literature from Japanese and many other languages. He knows not only Japanese but also Chinese, German, Russian, French, and Spanish and is very well informed about linguistic literature, particularly on the Celtic languages. He also published a number of his own scholarly works, e.g. on Western calendar reform and problems of English spelling.

Returning to persons deserving mention I would like to start with the Mongol Dilowa Khutuktu (Illus. 26). He was a reincarnated saint of the Lamaist Church who had been the abbot of the Narobanchin monastery in the Mongolian People's Republic. He was arrested by the Mongolian secret police in the 1930s and tried. However, his alleged subversive activities could not be proven. He was released and sent home. Fearing still greater trouble in the future he decided to escape abroad. Dilowa went to China from where in 1948 Lattimore took him, together with two young Mongols, to the United States where he worked on Lattimore's research project at Johns Hopkins University in Baltimore. In the summer of 1951, upon the invitation of the Far Eastern department, Dilowa came to Seattle for a meeting in which he answered questions from some professors, among them Paul Kirchoff, and the graduate student Robert Miller, now a professor at the University of Wisconsin in

Madison. Since he did not know any English, I acted as his interpreter. After the session one of my colleagues said he was greatly
impressed with the way I handled the interpreting because he had
always thought that my Mongolian was a kind of self-invented
gibberish which I passed off for Mongolian! The following day we all
went to Mount Rainier National Park where Dilowa was delighted to
see tame deer whom he could feed.

Illus. 24. The Author and the Dilowa Khutuktu, August 1951

Dilowa was a learned man, although I had met more learned
Buddhist priests before. He was also an unusually pleasant, witty,

and amiable person. We became close friends and continued to correspond after his departure. I met him several times later in Berkeley and New York and I was very sad when in 1965 he died of cancer.

I also became acquainted with scholars at other universities in the United States. In 1951 I met for the first time Professor V. A. Ryazanovskii, the well-known historian and author of books on Mongolian customary law as well as on the history of Russian culture, at the University of Oregon in Eugene.[21] At the time of our meeting he was already crippled by polio which he had contracted many years before, but his mind was clear. I met him later once more in San Francisco. He had originally been a professor at Moscow University, but after the revolution moved to Harbin in Manchuria where he became president of Harbin University. At a meeting of the Far Eastern Association, held at Harvard University, I met Professor S. G. Eliseev, mentioned earlier, and Dr. Rudolph Loewenthal, who has translated some works on Mongolian subjects into English and published a bibliography of works on Turkic languages.[22] Our friendship has lasted until now.

In Berkeley, California, I made the acquaintance of several scholars. First of all, Professor F. D. Lessing, the well-known Sinologist, Mongolist, and Buddhologist who had worked at the Völkermuseum in Berlin and left Germany after Hitler came to power. He was a good scholar and exceptionally knowledgable but not particularly prolific and the number of his publications is not impressive. In 1950 he started to compile a Mongolian-English dictionary, and in 1953 I spent part of the summer in Berkeley helping Lessing with his dictionary which was eventually published at the end of 1960.[23] On the whole, it is a good dictionary, but its main defect is the indiscriminate rendition of *o* and *u* in the non-initial syllable as u and the rendition of *ö* and *ü* in the non-initial syllable as *ü*. I tried to persuade Lessing to use the transcription applied in Mostaert's *Dictionnaire Ordos*, as for example in the word *Mongol* instead of his own incorrect *Mongul*. But he was adamant and insisted on using his peculiar and incorrect transcription. Although a successful scholar and a professor at a prestigious university,

Lessing never looked happy to me. I had the impression that his feelings were hurt because no German university had ever offered him a chair, thus causing him to emigrate to another country.

In Berkeley I also met Professor Wolfram Eberhard, a prolific scholar in the field of Chinese history and society as well as in fields outside Sinology. He, too, had left Nazi Germany and spent World War II in Turkey where he acquainted himself with Turcological matters and even published a book on the various types of Turkish folktales. Another interesting person was Maenchen-Helfen who, as a German press agent in the Soviet Union made a journey to Tuva, on which he wrote an interesting book, and later became the author of numerous other works of which a particularly valuable work was on the Huns.[24] Maenchen-Helfen had an excellent knowledge of Eastern Siberia, Tuva, Mongolia, and everything concerning the Huns and tribes somehow affiliated with them.

The scholar most interesting to me undoubtedly was Peter A. Boodberg, a brilliant Sinologist and Altaicist, son of a Baltic Russian baron who was the director of the Russian-built Chinese Eastern Railroad in Manchuria. Boodberg received his high school education in Harbin and his Ph.D. degree in the United States. Like most people he had his oddities. For example, he never cared to publish his articles in professional Orientalist journals but instead published them in dittoed student publications. He neither sent offprints of his publications to his colleagues nor acknowledged receipt of publications sent to him. He was very meticulous in his translations from Chinese, and he even coined many neologisms to translate Chinese expressions verbatim. Some scholars criticized him for this, but I sided with him because I regarded it as important to render foreign expressions as accurately as possible. I was very glad when some years after Boodberg's death, his students and friends published a volume of his articles.[25]

I found Berkeley a much more interesting university than my own, where for some time I had no colleagues in my fields of interest. Later, after Posch's dismissal, the Ukrainian scholar Omeljan Pritsak, a talented Turcologist and Altaicist, was invited to join the faculty in Seattle. He hailed from the western Ukraine which the

Soviet Union annexed from Poland during World War II. He finished his university training in Germany and received his Ph.D. at the University of Göttingen after defending his dissertation on the Hunnic-Bulgarian words attested in the ancient Bulgarian list of rulers. Pritsak first went to Harvard University as a visiting professor in 1960-61. There he was promised a permanent position at some later date, but until that position became available he had to find a temporary job elsewhere. As a result, Pritsak came to the University of Washington. Professor Taylor, our departmental chairman, was elated about getting Pritsak, especially at the low salary he offered him. Taylor once said to me: "Boy, did I get him cheap!" I did not respond because I knew Pritsak would not stay long with us. Besides, in retrospect, I must say it was a good thing, too, in view of the precarious conditions which began soon after Taylor's and my retirements.

Once again a search was conducted for a replacement. I recommended the well-known Hungarian Turcologist János Eckman who at that time was a visiting professor at the University of California at Los Angeles. Eckman accepted our invitation, but at the very last moment, only two weeks before the start of the new academic year, he changed his mind and remained in Los Angeles. He had used our university's invitation to obtain tenure from his own university which it had previously been reluctant to give him. I must say that Eckman's change of mind put our department in a very difficult position because it now obliged us to inform our students, some of whom had come from some distance, that no courses in Turcology would be offered and they then had to leave our university. Not surprisingly, the head of our department, Professor Taylor, regarded Eckman's action as morally objectionable, even though I had a high respect for his scholarly achievements. I mention this here although *de mortuis aut nihil aut bene*. Eckman died a few years later. Consequently, even if he had come to the University of Washington, he would not have been able to serve for long.

In this connection, I should point out that an invitation by another university often helps a professor in the United States to improve his position at his own university. For example, during my first three years at the University of Washington, I was only a visiting professor. Not long after I began teaching there, I asked Professor Taylor for tenure, but my request was not acted upon. This stalling tactic added to my financial problems, discussed above, because as long as I remained in a visiting status, neither deductions from my salary nor, more importantly, contributions by the university could be made toward my retirement fund. Then one day in 1952, Professor Sebeok at Indiana University invited me to move to his university. I showed his letter to Taylor and promptly received tenure. If Indiana University had not sent me that invitation, I might have remained a visiting professor for many more years.

Eventually we found a replacement for Pritsak in the person of Professor Ilse D. Laude–Cirtautas, a professor at Indiana University and a former student of Annemarie von Gabain at Hamburg University. Indiana University had hired her in 1965 to teach Turkish but, strangely enough, when she arrived in Bloomington someone else was already teaching Turkish, and so she was asked to teach Uzbek and other Turkic languages of the Soviet Union which had never been taught in the United States. She had to begin from the very beginning because no books in or about these languages were available in libraries and no English-language manuals of these languages existed. She not only built up a fine collection of Turcological books for the university library. Several research trips to Soviet Central Asia enabled her to collect valuable language materials. The result was the introduction of courses which had never been taught anywhere outside the Soviet Union. These courses study what is generally called Turcology, in contradistinction to the study of Turkish spoken in Turkey, which is taught at many universities in the United States and Europe. Her research is centered on the spoken Turkic languages of the Soviet Union and Chinese Turkestan (Sinkiang), i.e., Uzbek, Kazakh, Kirghiz, and Turkmenian, and on the old literary Turkic languages such as Chaghatai, Uighur, and Ancient Turkic (Orkhon Turkic of the eighth and ninth centuries). Since joining the University of Washington, she has taught not only these languages but also courses on the literature and culture of the nationalities speaking these languages.[26]

238

However, strange as it may seem, Professor Ilse Laude-Cirtautas has never been appreciated at the University of Washington. Her application for full professorship was supported by excellent recommendations from internationally known authorities in Turkology, such as Annemarie von Gabain, Karl Jahn, Gunnar Jarring, and Omeljan Pritsak. Nevertheless, her colleagues voted her down. It should be noted that none of them was a Turkologist nor had the slightest idea about Turkology.

Professor Cirtautas's courses were not the only new courses. Shortly before my retirement, the Department of Asian Languages and Literatures added courses in several Indian languages and in Thai, although it was very uncertain how many students would enroll in these courses. Moreover, instructors with the same high qualifications that our old Far Eastern department maintained were hard to find. Languages such as Thai and the Dravidian languages of India had been taught only at very few universities. The result was that, with the addition of the instructors in South Asian languages, the general quality of the department declined. Only those sections which had existed in the old Far Eastern department, namely, Chinese, Japanese, Korean, Tibetan, Turcology, and Manchu, retained a high level of excellence.

Moreover, the Department of Asian Languages and Literatures has been unable to make the newly introduced South Asian courses anything more than additions loosely attached to the old core of the Far Eastern department. The latter represented an area of organic unity: China with its minorities—Mongols, Turks, and Tibetans—; Korea, historically and culturally firmly related to China; and Japan, the second great nation in East Asia which is culturally akin to China and which has played an important role in East Asian history.

Under these circumstances, it is perhaps not surprising that the new programs are rather motley and fragmentary. According to the university catalog for the academic years 1980-1982, the Department of Asian Languages and Literatures offers Thai language but no Thai literature nor graduate courses in Thai. The program in Indian studies offers a large number of courses in

Sanskrit but only very few in modern spoken languages. In fact, the department offers only Hindi of all the Indo-European languages, along with Tamil and Tagalog. Linguistically, culturally, and historically, these three languages are totally unrelated to each other.

A year before my retirement, which was due in 1968, Professor Taylor asked me to find a successor to myself. First I offered my position to the British Mongolist Charles R. Bawden, but he declined the offer on the grounds that he wanted his children to get a good education in British schools. Then I wrote to Heissig's former student, Professor Klaus Sagaster, in Bonn, but he also declined because he did not want to be separated from his elderly parents.

Finally, my former student, the Japanese Mongolist Hidehiro Okada, was offered and accepted my chair. He is a brilliant scholar and highly educated person, speaking excellent English, German and even Russian. Unfortunately his wife disliked life in the United States and was homesick for Japan. In order not to sever his ties with Japan, Okada refused tenure and insisted, instead, on the position of a visiting professor. After two years of teaching at our university, Okada returned to Tokyo and became a professor there.

In any event, the fate of Mongolian Studies had already been sealed. Even if Bawden or Sagaster had accepted, even if Okada had remained, Mongolian and Altaic comparative studies had no future at the University of Washington. The university came under severe financial pressure which, ten years later, has still not abated. At the end of 1981 the university's president warned that even tenured faculty members might have to be dismissed. At the time of Okada's departure, the University of Washington adopted a new policy whereby a position was eliminated when it became vacant and the courses associated with it were discontinued. Theoretically, this policy could lead to such anomalies as courses in a particular language being abolished while courses in the literature of the same language are continued. Okada's departure had another sad aspect. The Mongolian native teacher Yidamjab Meng, a Chahar Mongol who had conducted practical seminars in the colloquial language, was dismissed. He was placed in a desperate situation because being in his late fifties he was too old to get some other job but too young to draw social security. I should add that the university had hired him from Taiwan where he held a very secure government job, but after his arrival in Seattle he received American citizenship and thus forfeited the right ever to be employed again in Taiwan. Obviously this new policy completely disregarded the human factor. Besides, the university's financial woes which had prompted the adoption of this policy had to some extent been brought about by bureaucratic proliferation. To cite just one example, when I joined the University of Washington in 1949, it had only one vice president and 9,000 students. Now that there were 36,000 students, four vice presidents should have been enough but instead there were ten or perhaps even more. This phenomenon is found at all universities in the United States and is another illustration of the rampant wastefulness in American society which I described earlier.

At about the same time as Mongolian Studies were terminated, a major reorganization took place. The Far Eastern and Russian Institute became the Institute for Comparative and Foreign Area Studies, and soon thereafter it, in turn, was renamed the School of International Studies. It retained the high level of excellence of the old Far Eastern and Russian Institute, partly because it was ably directed, first by Professor Herbert J. Ellison and later by Professor Kenneth B. Pyle. By contrast the Department of Far Eastern and Slavic Languages and Literatures, renamed the Department of Asian Languages and Literatures (with Russian and East European languages placed in a separate department) deteriorated enormously. In all the years since Taylor's retirement in 1969, the department has never had a chairman with the requisite abilities.

The inglorious end of Mongolian Studies and Altaic comparative linguistics, which I had organized, was a severe blow to me. In addition, the moment I retired I was shunted aside. When I had still been on active duty, it was a university policy that retired professors were not required but had the right to attend faculty meetings. After I retired, however, I was told by the University Association of Retired Professors that this policy no longer existed and that it was now up to the discretion of the chairman of each department whether to invite retired professors to meetings. I was

241

never invited and was not even admitted to certain meetings, such as those dealing with promotions. This struck me as being discriminatory. At German and Soviet universities, retired professors are welcome at all meetings and their advice is always eagerly sought.

Fortunately there is a bright spot in the darkness that has surrounded me. My friend, Professor Henry G. Schwarz, of Western Washington University in Bellingham, whom I have known for many years, has introduced Mongolian Studies at his university. He established the Center for East Asian Studies in 1970 and directed it for six years. In the face of even more severe financial cuts than those faced by the University of Washington at the same time, he built up programs not only for China and Japan, but also for Korea and Mongolia. He is now teaching, *inter alia*, an introductory course on Mongolian culture and society and two upper-division courses on Mongolian history. At his insistence, every East Asian survey course also includes Mongolia. In addition, Schwarz published a very useful bibliography on Mongolia[27] and edited a collection of translations of Mongolian short stories.[28] In 1978, the most difficult year of my life, he organized the North American Conference on Mongolian Studies in Bellingham which was attended by scholars from the United States, Canada and Japan. The proceedings of this conference were later published by him.[29] In summer 1981 he led a group of Western Washington University students to Inner Mongolia where they studied Elementary Mongolian. It marked the first time ever that American students were given formal Mongolian language instruction in any part of Mongolia. Thanks to his efforts, Mongolian Studies are not quite dead.

In this connection I shall permit myself a brief digression and make a few remarks on the situation of universities and learned bodies not only in the United States but in the entire world. The rapid growth of population and of attendant problems forces the attention of persons in charge of education and research more and more in the direction of practical tasks. This is quite natural and no objection to it can be made except that the humanities have suffered in the process. The world seems to have forgotten that culture is more than technology and the manufacture of goods. On more than one occasion, while speaking about modern Mongolian society and culture, I remarked that the fact that the Mongolian Academy of Sciences started collecting and publishing folklore was a more significant sign of cultural progress than the construction of, say, airports in that country. After all, it is easier to build anything with the help of blueprints obtained abroad than to train scholars for the collection and study of folklore. One should never forget the great truth in the words "Not by bread alone." One should also keep in mind that countries where much attention is paid to the humanities are also the most developed industrial countries. An example is Germany, a country of great philosophers, linguists, and historians, which is also a country with the most developed industry in Western Europe.

I would like to add that in 1980 I taught again during spring and fall quarters. I was invited to substitute for Professor Laude-Cirtautas who was on leave of absence at Bonn University. In spring quarter I taught a course on Altaic comparative linguistics which Professor Laude-Cirtautas's students and other students had requested. I must say that my students were exceptionally well prepared. Those from the Department of Asian Languages and Literatures had studied Uzbek, comparative grammar of Turkic languages, Uighur, Old Turkic, Middle Turkic, Kazakh, Kirghiz, Korean, Japanese, or Manchu. Other students came from the linguistics and anthropology departments. They were intelligent, and it was a real pleasure to work with them. My courses in fall quarter were Beginning Mongolian and Tatar.

While living in the United States I had ample opportunities to travel around the country and abroad. In addition to trips already mentioned, I spent the entire spring semester, February–May 1961, as a visiting professor at Columbia University where I had been invited by Professor John Lotz who headed the Department of Uralic and Altaic Languages. Edith and I lived in Butler Hall, an apartment house owned by the university on West 117th Street. I conducted research seminars on Altaic comparative linguistics and Khalkha Mongolian, and my students included the then beginning scholar John

C. Street, who later became a well-known linguist specializing in Altaic languages and became highly proficient in Japanese, and John Gombojab Hangin, a Chahar Mongol, at that time a graduate student working toward his Ph.D. degree and who later became a professor of Mongolian at Indiana University. In New York I had the opportunity to work at the New York Public Library which has a fine collection of Russian books, and to visit the Metropolitan Art Museum and various other museums and galleries in the city.

I also worked as a research scholar at the Hoover Library of War and Peace in Palo Alto in 1951 where I collaborated with Professor Vucinich on a book about the Soviet Academy of Sciences.[30] At that library I discovered Lenin's letter to Herbert Hoover in which the Soviets expressed their gratitude for the generous food donations from the United States after half the population of the Volga region had died of starvation in 1921. People had nothing to eat but some herbs and clay, and even cannibalism flourished. I remember someone from the Volga region telling me at that time that when in a certain village an old man had died of starvation, his family went to the priest and asked him, "Father, will you bless us to consume the body?" and the priest answered, "The good Lord will forgive you." Seeing that letter from the Soviet government to President Hoover made me reflect on the ingratitude of Lenin's epigones who were saved from defeat by the Lend-Lease program and the Allied landing in Normandy. Unlike Lenin, they burned with hate for the country that was their benefactor and which, by the way, unfortunately had also been the first of the great powers to recognize the Soviet government in 1933.

I also took several other trips. In 1951 I went by train from Washington, D.C. to New Orleans, a city I liked very much except for the strict racial segregation prevailing there at that time. I found it strange to see even buses segregated. On one occasion a driver did not let me board his bus because it was for blacks only, and I protested that I was in a hurry and did not care for their stupid local rules. On another occasion I was really puzzled when I saw a red cross blazing in the night sky and beneath it the inscription, "Jesus Saves Blacks Only." Actually, a Black Jehovah's Witnesses church had two signs. One read "Jesus Saves," commonly found throughout the United States. Directly beneath it was another sign, reading "Blacks Only," a reminder of the segregationist policy in Southern states. At night, however, these two signs appeared to be one, and the unintended claim struck me as being grotesque.

Edith and I traveled to Yellowstone Park in the late 1960s and we were impressed by Old Faithful and other scenic landmarks such as the beautiful lake on which we took a sail and later the road from the park to Cody and Billings, Montana. We also visited Alaska by taking a ship from Vancouver, B.C. in 1972 or 1973. The trip was paid for as a gift by my sons. It was very interesting and made a great impression on both of us. In Juneau we saw street names like Zimovie which in Russian means "winter camp," obviously left from the old days when Alaska was Russian. I remember a church which we particularly liked. Instead of an altar painting, it had a window looking out on a beautiful glacier-capped mountain. What altar painting could have been more impressive!

I went to Canada many times to visit my elder son. I familiarized myself with the scenes on both sides of the railroad from Vancouver to Ottawa, and also visited some places far removed from the transcontinental trunkline. I have already mentioned Virginiatown in northern Ontario near the Quebec border. To get there I had to take a local train from North Bay to Swastika. The name Swastika calls for an explanation. I was told that during World War II the Canadian government wanted to change the name to Kitchener because the swastika was the sign adopted by the Nazis as their emblem, but the plan was dropped when the miners living in that area protested. They said that they did not care for Kitchener or anybody else but wanted to keep the old name because of an old superstition that the swastika sign brings good luck.

I also went to Europe many times. In 1956 I received a grant from the Guggenheim Foundation to do research in the library of the British Museum which possessed a small but very good collection of Mongolian manuscripts and xylographs. One of the manuscripts was a Buryat treatise, written in the second half of the nineteenth century, which dealt with medicinal mineral waters and is of

Illus. 25. Edith Poppe, née Ziegler

Illus. 26. Nicholas and Edith Poppe

interest as a sample of Buryat balneological literature in Script Mongolian. I published it with a translation and commentary in the Orientalist journal *Asia Major*[31] which was still edited as it had been in the 1920s by the late Bruno Schindler, a fine scholar and a fine man. I also worked in the archives of the India Office which possessed some fragments of Mongolian manuscripts found by the famous traveler Sir Aurel Stein. They proved to be fragments of astrological books and calendars, and later I published them with translations and commentaries in the *Central Asiatic Journal*.[32]

While in London I made the acquaintance of Professor Walter Simon, the well-known Sinologist and Tibetanist, who had to flee Hitler's Germany although he had been a decorated officer of the Imperial German army. I also met for the first time the Turcologists Professors Wittek and Fahir Iz, the latter a Turk whose classes at the London School of Oriental and African Studies my son Nicholas attended. I used my stay in Great Britain to travel and visit friends, some of whom were former officers of the BAOR, the British Army of the Rhine. I made trips to Evesham, Gloucester, Oxford, and Cambridge. In Cambridge I visited Professor D. M. Dunlop, the well-known author of the book *The History of the Jewish Khazars* and other works,[33] and Dr. Ethel John Lindgren who had been in Mongolia and Manchuria in the 1920s when I was in Mongolia. As I described in Chapter 9, after the war in 1945, while I was still in Germany, Dr. Lindgren had been instrumental in having me invited to join the faculty of Cambridge University. When I visited Dr. Lindgren in 1956, she gave me copies of some of my own works which I no longer possessed in my own library. In other words, she acted as a true friend. At Cambridge University I also met Professor Denis Sinor whom the university had invited after it realized that nothing would come of its invitation to me. We talked very amiably for quite a while and ever since our relations have been friendly. I also visited the great Russian scholar V. F. Minorskii who was a historian of the Islamic countries and who has published very important works in that field.[34] Later, I learned that he had willed all his books and manuscripts to Leningrad University. After his death his books were shipped to Leningrad but, for lack of space, were stored in a shed. Soon afterwards that area was flooded, and most of his books and manuscripts were damaged, some beyond repair.

I also took the opportunity to visit the city of Wellington in Shropshire (Salop) where my sons had lived and worked from 1947 to 1951. It is a pleasant town nestled among very beautiful hills. Not far from Wrekin Hill, which commands a magnificent view of the surrounding countryside, lie the ruins of the ancient Roman town of Ureconium. The present name Wrekin is certainly another grammatical or phonetical form of Ureconium. I also visited my elder son Valerian who was studying in Dublin. I went via Holy Head across the Irish Sea to Dun Laoghaire, the port of Dublin, visited Trinity College and its famous Beatty Library which possesses, among other treasures, an excellent collection of Mongolian books which were later catalogued by my friend Walther Heissig. I took sightseeing trips to several beautiful areas outside Dublin. Particularly noteworthy were the Avoca Valley and Glendalough, which means "Forest of Two Lakes," where an ancient cemetery, a church with grey Irish round towers, and St. Kevin's home are located. On the way to Glendalough the driver of the sightseeing bus pointed to a small house with only two windows at the side of the road and said that it had only one room but seven kitchens. After a brief pause, the driver then explained that in that single room Mr. and Mrs. Kitchen and their five children lived. Soon thereafter Valerian went with a group of students on a geological excursion to Switzerland and I returned to London.

After completing my work at the British Museum, I went to Copenhagen to meet for the first and, alas, the last time the Danish Turcologist and Mongolist Kaare Grønbech, the author of several important works, like a Coman dictionary and a book on Turkic structure,[35] the former written on the basis of a manuscript dictionary compiled in the fourteenth century by Venetian merchants and missionaries who conducted trade with the Comans, a Turkic people living at that time in southern Russia. I had been corresponding with Kaare Grønbech for many years and was anxious to meet him in person. This distinguished scholar received me with typical Scandinavian hospitality and in order to facilitate my work at the Oriental Division of the Royal Library of Copenhagen, which has a fine collection of Mongolian books collected by Grønbech in Mongolia, he gave me the keys to the Oriental Division rooms and to the main gate so that I could come and go at any time, a privilege bestowed on very few people. The Mongolian collection contains numerous old manuscripts which Kaare Grønbech acquired in Mongolia by an ingenious trick. He offered neat, beautifully executed new copies in exchange for the old soiled originals. The ignorant Mongols willingly accepted the deal, probably deriding the "foolish" foreigner behind his back. I have absolutely no misgivings about Grønbech's ruse because in this particular case, with war soon to be raging between China and Japan, these manuscripts would probably have perished. After ten days in Copenhagen I returned to London with microfilms of numerous manuscripts. Unfortunately I never saw Grønbech again because shortly after our meeting he died of a brain tumor. In Copenhagen I also met Grønbech's student Kaare Thomsen who looked promising but actually published almost nothing.

Copenhagen is a beautiful city and I spent some time sightseeing. I went to the National Ethnographic Museum which has a better collection of Salish Indian objects than the museum in Seattle and the best Eskimo collection in the whole world, the Armory, the Torvaldsen Museum, the famous Tower, Tivoli Park, and also visited the famous Elsinore Castle where Hamlet had lived.

While in Copenhagen I also met for the first time the German Mongolist Walther Heissig who ever since has remained my best friend. Heissig's name became known to me soon after my arrival in Berlin in 1943. I read his interesting book on the cultural changes among the Mongols and also a dictionary of modern Mongolian, compiled by him and Robert Bleichsteiner.[36] I also learned that Heissig was at that time in China where he had been since shortly before the outbreak of the war. I learned many years later that after Japan's surrender, the Americans arrested him as an enemy agent. It was obviously beyond the military men's comprehension that Heissig could have been a scholar instead of a spy, but thinking is not a virtue of military people. In all the world's armies the first commandment is "A soldier must not think." Heissig spent several years in jail and soon after his release, we began to correspond. After everybody realized that Heissig was absolutely innocent he was released from prison. He first found a position at Göttingen University, and later he moved to Bonn University where he organized an excellent Central Asian institute under the title Seminar für Kultur- und Sprachwissenschaft Zentralasiens. Mongolia and Tibet are represented by numerous scholars including a learned Tibetan and a Mongol. To do full justice to its title, the institute should also include Turcology which so far has been lacking, if we do not take into consideration Professor Cirtautas's recent stay there as a visiting professor. A Central Asian institute without a permanent chair of Turkology is actually unthinkable because the Turks have played a very important role in the political and cultural history of Central Asia. At an institute with four or five Mongolists and an equal number of Tibetologists, there should be at least one Turcologist.

In addition to Heissig, I must also mention my personal meetings with Herbert Franke, the leading European Sinologist, Annemarie von Gabain, whom I had not seen since 1944, and Professor Hamm, the Tibetologist and Sanskritologist, a very pleasant person and an excellent scholar who unfortunately died a few years ago of a disease which could not be diagnosed by the physicians. Finally, mention should also be made of Heissig's gifted students Klaus Sagaster, Michael Weiers, Rudolf Kaschewsky, Veronika Veit, Rainer Kämpfe, and others who have performed a tremendous task in helping German Oriental studies to take a leading position in the world of scholarship.

While I was teaching at Bonn University, I also became acquainted with Professor Otto Spiess, a specialist in Near Eastern languages, a learned and very pleasant person. Another scholar I met was Werner Schulemann, professor of pharmacology and an outstanding expert of Central Asian art, author of an important work on this subject,[37] and a very friendly and helpful man. He died a few years after my stay in Bonn. I shall always remember him as an outstanding person.

At some meetings held at Bonn University, Professor Herbert Franke, probably the foremost Sinologist of our time, was also present. A serious scholar and a good organizer, he had been responsible for the International Congress of Orientalists, held in Munich in 1957, where I first met him. Ever since we have been good friends.

The following year, 1957, I received a travel grant for work in Germany. I spent most of my time in Munich where I worked in libraries and attended the meetings of the International Congress of Orientalists. At that congress some Soviet scholars were also present. I met N. V. Pigulevskaya, the well-known specialist in Syriac and Byzantium. She was very surprised and obviously very frightened to see me, and after a brief greeting she hastily withdrew into the crowd. I do not blame her for her conduct because she had been arrested and spent years in Soviet jails and her husband even died in jail. On the other hand, the young Turcologist A. S. Tveretinova, in my time a member of the Communist Youth League, was very happy to see me and to my remark that I had seen her from the distance the day before and had been doubtful whether she would be pleased to see me she retorted, "But, why, I'm so happy to meet you, and how is Nataliya Valerianovna [my first wife] and what are your boys doing?" I told her about my wife's death in 1949 and about my sons. She was sorry to hear about my wife's death, expressed her sympathy but was glad to hear that the boys were all right. I appreciated Tveretinova's friendliness very much. Unfortunately, she died some time later in Leningrad. At the congress I also spoke with the well-known Soviet scholar I. M. D'yakonov, specialist in Cuneiform scripts in Assyrian and Babylonian. We talked about his brother Mikhail Mikhailovich, the Iranist, whom I had known and liked very much. D'yakonov was very upset because some emigré newspaper had published articles shortly before the opening of the congress in which D'yakonov's brother was accused of being an NKVD informer. I doubted it very much because I knew him as a pleasant and decent man and I said so to D'yakonov adding that he should not pay much attention to such articles because the emigrés, who had suffered much from the Soviets, often suspected innocent persons. The system, of course, was to be blamed for making them so suspicious in the first place.

When I turned sixty in August 1957 the German Academy of Sciences and Literature in Mainz elected me as a corresponding member. I felt very honored and accepted with great satisfaction, not with the kind of fear which had filled me many years earlier when the late Willi Bang planned to nominate me for membership in the Berlin Academy of Sciences. At the same time, a Festschrift in my honor was published by the Societas Uralo-Altaica upon Pritsak's initiative.[38] Thinking of the election and the Festschrift, I could not help remembering the disastrous consequences for Beneshevich of membership in the Bavarian Academy of Sciences and for Zhebelev of participating in the *Seminarium Kondakovianum* volume.

In the summer of 1958 I made an interesting trip to Japan in order to work at the Tōyō Bunkō (Oriental Library) in Tokyo. Edith and I sailed on the cargo ship "India Mail" of the American Mail Line from Seattle to Yokohama and took the same ship back again. The ship had six spacious cabins. Ours was as large as an average living room in a good apartment. The food was served in the crew's dining room and was of excellent quality. In the evenings we were permitted to enter the kitchen and make sandwiches for ourselves. Both ways the weather was very good but sometimes foggy so that the ship had to blow its horn all the time. Whales could be seen at a distance, and porpoises trailed the ship in anticipation of garbage thrown overboard, and large flocks of birds enlivened the picture. My wife and I enjoyed that voyage tremendously and retained many happy memories. On our return trip we had an interesting fellow passenger in the person of the former British High Commissioner of Malaya who was returning with his family to Great Britain because Malaya had just gained its independence. Among other interesting things he told me regretfully that Malaya had great economic difficulties. While he was still High Commissioner, the United States offered the colonial government economic aid in the form of credits with which to buy American industrial products. What Malaya really needed, however, was to find markets for its rubber.

In Tokyo we found a suitably furnished apartment in a house of Western style near Sugamo station and close enough to walk to work at the Tōyō Bunkō. There, in collaboration with Leon Hurvitz, an assistant professor at the University of Washington, who had accompanied us from Seattle, and the Japanese scholar Hidehiro Okada, who later came to our university to study Mongolian with me, I catalogued the Mongolian and Manchu xylographs and a few manuscripts. The results of our labors were later published.[39]

In Japan I had the opportunity to again see my friend from my wartime days in Germany, Professor Shichirō Murayama, and also the well-known linguist Professor Shirō Hattori whom I had met for the first time in Washington, D.C. in 1950. I also got acquainted with a number of other prominent Japanese scholars like Egami, Enoki, Jirō Ikegami, Shinobu Iwamura, Kobayashi, and Masayoshi Nomura. Edith and I visited many famous and beautiful places such as Kamakura, Nikko, Nara, and Kyoto. A particularly interesting place was Tenri, the center of the Tenri religion and the site of a university with an excellent library. There I had the pleasure of being introduced to the head of the Tenri religion, the Shimbashira, whose family name was Nakayama and who invited Hurvitz, Murayama, Edith and me to dinner. In the Tenri library I had the pleasure of meeting Professor Shunju Imanishi, a prominent scholar in the Manchu field who showed me many precious books, among them the Zirni manuscript which contains a Moghul-Persian dictionary discovered by Professor Iwamura in Afghanistan. It was later published with my introduction.[40]

In 1960 I attended the meeting of the Permanent International Altaistic Conference in the castle Liebenstein on the Rhine in West Germany. At this conference I met for the first time my friend, Professor Karl Jahn, the founder and editor of the prestigious *Central Asiatic Journal*. Our correspondence and ensuing friendship started long ago. I received his first letter when I was still in Leningrad, some time in the late 1920s. Jahn is an excellent scholar and a great specialist in the history of Central Asia. I also met, after a long interruption, Erich Haenisch and got acquainted with the Polish Turcologist Ananijasz Zajączkowski.

After the conference I visited my Finnish friend, Professor Pentti Aalto, a student of Ramstedt, at his summer cottage in Vestanfjärd near Turku. I had met him, along with his wife and their three-year-old son Martti, for the first time in Munich in 1957 during the International Congress of Orientalists. Now in 1960 the Aaltos had another son, Erkki, which is Eric in English. Aalto is primarily a scholar in the classical field and of comparative linguistics. As Ramstedt's student he is also a highly competent scholar in the field of Altaic linguistics, and he edited and prepared for publication Ramstedt's posthumous three-volume work on Altaic comparative linguistics.[41] From Vestanfjärd, Aalto and I made a trip to Parikkala and saw my family's former summer villa which I had not seen for forty-three years. During my childhood it was 270 kilometers from the Russian border, now it was only nine kilometers away. The villa was still standing, and the ice-cold water in the well was as refreshing as a half a century ago. We took a taxi to the nearby border where we were met by the oppressive sight of watch-towers and rolls of barbed wire. I remarked to the Finnish driver, "Look how afraid they are of you!" to which he replied, "Not of us they are but of their own citizens who might try to escape." I thought about how good Fate had been to me. I was not standing on that accursed farther side of the barbed wire fence but on this side among free men enjoying the greatest gift life can bestow upon a human being, namely the gift of freedom.

From Parikkala, Aalto and I continued our trip to Savonlinna, a beautiful town famous for its medieval castle, then by steamer across Lake Saimaa to Lappeenranta, now a sizeable city, and from there we returned by train and bus to Vestanfjärd. Aalto and I also paid a visit to Ramstedt's widow, Mrs. Ida Ramstedt, in her apartment in Helsinki where we also met her daughter and the latter's husband, Mr. Järnefelt, who had been in the diplomatic service and served for a long time as ambassador to Poland. Mrs. Järnefelt spoke very good Polish. After spending another few days with the Aaltos, I returned to the United States, first by ship to Stockholm, then by train to Hamburg via Copenhagen, and finally by plane to Seattle.

Speaking of my Finnish colleagues, I should add that in that same summer of 1960 I met for the first time the well-known scholar Aulis Joki, professor of Finno-Ugric languages at Helsinki University. He is the author of an excellent book on the loan words in Sayan-Samoyed which include numerous Altaic words, and another interesting book on the relations between the Indo-European and Uralic languages.[42] Later in 1976 at the reception given by the Permanent International Altaistic Conference in Helsinki I also met the well-known linguist, Professor Erkki Itkonen, whose brother Ilmari Itkonen, lived in Parikkala and was married to Enni, née Innanen, whom I had known long before. Among the young Finnish scholars, Harry Halén made an excellent impression on me. He has published a number of articles and a catalog of Oriental books and manuscripts in Finland,[43] and a chapter in a book on Finnish travelers in Asia.

In 1968, after my retirement from the University of Washington, I was invited as a visiting professor to Bonn University where I spent the academic year 1969-70 lecturing at the Central Asian institute headed by Professor Heissig. Edith and I took the "Bremen" from New York and returned on the same ship a year later. The voyage was very pleasant and everything was perfect except that the food, while good, was served in such small amounts that we were often hungry. My lectures at Bonn University were on comparative studies of the Mongolian languages, comparative Altaic linguistics, reading the Mongolian text of the Diamond Sutra and comparing it with the Tibetan translation and the Sanskrit original, and reading the Mongolian text of the Twelve Deeds of Buddha, a biography of the Buddha written by Choskyi 'Odzer in the fourteenth century and translated at that time into Mongolian by Shesrab Senge.

While in Germany I attended a reunion of my former classmates which took place in 1969 in Oberstaufen, a beautiful place in the Allgäu where the organizer of the meeting, my friend Wilfried Strik-Strikfeldt, lived. As mentioned earlier, he had played an important role in the Vlasov movement. Besides being a good poet, he wrote the book *Against Hitler and Stalin* about the Vlasov movement,[44] and he was also organizer and *spiritus movens* of the book

Russia Enters the Twentieth Century, edited by G. M. Katkov, E. Oberländer, and me and containing a number of articles, one of which, written by me, deals with the economic and cultural development of Siberia.[45] Strik-Strikfeldt died in 1977. In December 1969, I fell gravely ill and was hospitalized at the clinic of Bonn University. It was appendicitis which the physicians, strangely enough, had not diagnosed in time, thinking that it was food poisoning. The result was a ruptured appendix.

In the summer of 1970 I went with Edith to Strasbourg to attend the meeting of the Permanent International Altaistic Conference where I met many colleagues from France, Hungary, Great Britain and other countries. It turned out to be a most interesting conference devoted to the religious and parareligious beliefs of the Altaic peoples. It was of particular importance to me because I was awarded the Gold Medal of Indiana University for Altaic Studies. The conference was attended by an unusually large number of persons. There was also my friend Karl Jahn, the editor of the *Central Asiatic Journal*, and most of my German friends. Hungary was strongly represented by Louis Ligeti, András Rona-Tás, Lajos Bese, Lásló Lőrincz, Alice Sárközi and others. Ligeti was the senior among the Hungarians, a brilliant scholar of Paul Pelliot's school, the author of very detailed articles including numerous footnotes. There was also István Kecskeméti who, as Martti Räsänen's assistant, helped him publish his huge etymological dictionary of the Turkic languages.[46] Kecskeméti died a few years later. French Mongolists were represented by Roberte Hamayon, the author of interesting ethnographic works, and British Altaicists were represented by Charles Bawden, the author of many important works on Mongolian subjects. There were also some Turkish scholars but, just as at most previous and subsequent PIAC meetings, Soviet scholars were not present.

On our way back to Bonn, Edith and I had a most delightful trip through the Black Forest. The dense forests, the rushing waters of mountain brooks, and the shimmering serenity of large lakes was just overwhelming. We stayed in Bonn until the end of July and then traveled by train via Denmark to Stockholm and from there by ship to Turku where our friends, the Aaltos, met us and we spent a delightful week with them in their cottage in Vestanfjärd. We continued our trip to Helsinki, stayed in Aalto's apartment, made sightseeing excursions in the city, including the National Museum and the Suomenlinna (Finland's) Fortress, and went by train to the place of my childhood, Parikkala. Later we also visited Savonlinna, went by steamer across Lake Saimaa to Kuopio and many other beautiful places, returned to Bonn and then back to the United States.

In 1973 I was one of four scholars especially invited as guests of the Turkish government on the occasion of the fiftieth anniversary of the Turkish Republic. The Permanent International Altaistic Conference also convened there at the same time. The other three scholars were Annemarie von Gabain, Gyula (Julius) Németh, and Martti Räsänen. Németh and Räsänen could not attend because of ill health. All four of us were awarded honorary diplomas of the Turkish government which also paid for our rooms, board, and transportation.

I attended other meetings of the Permanent International Altaistic Conference in Bad Honneff near Bonn in 1974, in Bloomington in 1975, and in Helsinki in 1976 where I presented a paper on the affinity of the Uralic and Altaic languages.[47] Some Soviet scholars also attended. One of them, Mukhamed'yarov, a Tatar, in his paper on Tatar historiography sang the praises of the Soviet Union, allegedly the only country allowing full freedom of historical research. It was a ridiculous and primitive performance. By contrast, the other Soviet scholars, including a Kazakh, two Turkmenian ladies and N. Z. Gadzhieva, the wife of the well-known linguist, B. A. Serebrennikov, presented serious, absolutely scholarly papers. Of the other participants, Gunnar Jarring, Ilse Cirtautas, and Karl Menges presented interesting papers.

Our Finnish hosts took all conference participants on several sightseeing trips around Helsinki. I was much impressed by a church built in a niche carved out of a rocky hillside and by Mannerheim House which had on display, among other things, a Finnish coat of arms made of birchbark which had been presented by Soviet prisoners of war to Marshal Mannerheim during the war of 1939-40. It was dedicated, according to the caption, "to Marshal Mannerheim from grateful Soviet prisoners of war." No comment is necessary. Equally impressive was a monument to members of the Finnish Red Guards killed during the civil war in 1918. The inscription read: "To our fallen comrades, former members of the Red Guards of Finland." This, to me, represented the quintessence of democracy and fairness. Would a similar monument for the officers and men of the anti-Communist armies killed during the civil war be conceivable in the Soviet Union? Never! Only a mature democracy can afford the recognition that the vanquished enemy had the same right to fight for his cause as the victors.

After the conference I spent a few days with the Aaltos in their cottage in Vestanfjärd and then proceeded on a round trip to Oulu, Kajaani, Joensun, Parikkala, and back to Helsinki. In Parikkala I stayed at a vacation house where I made the acquaintance of a very friendly Finnish family from Helsinki. We spent several days together during which we spoke only in Finnish. Leaving Finland, I went to Viken in Southern Sweden to visit my friend, Ambassador Gunnar Jarring, and his wife Lillan who were spending their summer vacation there. Gunnar Jarring is not only a distinguished Turcologist, author of numerous important works on Eastern Turkic but he and his wife speak excellent Russian which they had studied at the university. All who know Jarring will agree that he is a very pleasant person of high culture and a great expert on world affairs. He is an unusual combination of a distinguished scholar and a broadminded and excellently informed diplomat. He is certainly one whose friendship is a high honor for me.

My stay in the United States during the past thirty years allowed me, *inter alia*, to become a member of numerous learned societies and accept awards without those doubts which haunted me at the time the late Willi Bang had asked me to send him my curriculum vitae. While in the Soviet Union I had this freedom only in the 1920s. When I helped the Finnish scholar Kai Donner to obtain a Lamut, a Ket and a Samoyed to go to Finland where he and some other scholars intended to investigate the respective languages, the three native informants, students at the Leningrad Institute of the Peoples of the North, were sent for a whole summer to Finland. For this help I was elected a corresponding member of the Finno-Ugric Society in Finland. I had also published some articles in the *Keleti Szemle* and *Kŏrösi-Csoma Archivum* and was elected a member of the Kŏrösi-Csoma Society, the Oriental Society of Hungary. But after 1930 acceptance of membership in foreign learned societies became dangerous. I have mentioned earlier what happened to Beneshevich when he was elected a corresponding member of the Bavarian Academy of Sciences.

In 1950 I was elected a member of the Royal Asiatic Society of Great Britain and Ireland; in 1951 a corresponding member of the Finnish Oriental Society; in 1957 corresponding member of the Tŭrk Dil Kurumu (Turkish Linguistic Society) in Ankara; in the same year, corresponding member of the Academia Scientiarum et Litterarum Moguntina; in 1963, an honorary member of the Société Finno-Ougrienne; in 1968 honorary member of the Deutsche Morgen-ländische Gesellschaft (German Oriental Society) and received an honorary doctorate *(doctor philosophiae honoris causa)* from the Philosophical Faculty of Bonn University; in 1977 I became a corresponding member of the Finnish Academy of Sciences; and in 1978 a fellow of the British Academy. In addition, as I mentioned earlier, I received the Gold Medal of Indiana University for Altaic Studies and in 1973 an honorary diploma from the Turkish government. I should also mention that in 1957 a Festschrift was published on the occasion of my sixtieth birthday, and in 1978 a bibliography of my publications was published by the University of Washington.

I have listed these honors not in order to boast. My sole purpose is to show how much can be achieved in a relatively short time when one is free to concentrate on one's work. Thus freedom to travel, to attend conferences and congresses in other countries, freedom to publish his articles and books in other countries, and freedom to join foreign learned societies and accept awards bestowed by them were unthinkable before I had left the Soviet Union. I can only compare this to a treasure chest falling open in front of a pauper. It just overwhelmed me. I should point out that this productivity has been the result of many favorable circumstances. Probably the most important of them is the American attitude of minding one's own business. I have been absolutely free to write as I please. No censors have imposed their ideas on me, no party members have "edited" my works nor "helped" me ideologically. I have never had any reason to protect my work from infringement, and there is no one in the United States whom I would have to admonish *"Noli turbare circulos meos."*

11

My Publications

This chapter, dealing with my publications, will represent a kind of brief annotated bibliography. I will arrange my works into two categories, linguistics and philology, and I will briefly describe their contents. Readers who are specialists in Altaic Studies will probably have my bibliographies. The latest and most complete bibliography is Arista Maria Cirtautas, *Nicholas Poppe: Bibliography of Publications from 1924 to 1977.*[1] However, this one, like previous bibliographies, gives only titles without any annotations, thus making it difficult for readers unfamiliar with Altaic Studies to get a good idea about my research fields.

Another reason for discussing my publications is the fact that science does not stand still but is in constant motion, discovering new facts and leading to new conclusions. Today's facts and theories may not be valid tomorrow, and to be honest I must admit that today I would write several of my works in a different way. I am certain that my predecessors, too, would have written their works differently today had they lived long enough. It is, therefore, unfair to speak contemptuously about their mistakes, but we should always remember that without their works, our task of improving science would have been harder.

I will proceed on the assumption that the reader will expect me to point out my own mistakes but also to say something about the validity of some views expressed in my publications. I will also try to demonstrate to what degree my respective works have

261

enriched our knowledge and advanced Asian Studies in general and Mongolian Studies in particular.

I shall begin with works on linguistics. I mentioned at the beginning of this book that I became fascinated by languages when I was only a boy. Perhaps it was only natural that when I started my scholarly career I continued to be interested in spoken languages. At that time universities taught only literary languages, neglecting the spoken languages. When I began my university studies of Mongolian in 1918, there were not only no grammars of Khalkha, the main language spoken in what is now the Mongolian People's Republic, but almost no other scholarly works on that language. The sole exceptions were Ramstedt's comparative phonology of Khalkha and Written Mongolian, i.e., the old literary language, and his Khalkha conjugation.[2] Since these two books were unsuitable as teaching aids, I resolved to create teaching materials on Khalkha as soon as I had an opportunity to do so. That opportunity came in 1926, 1927, and 1929 when I traveled to the Mongolian People's Republic. There I collected much material, including some folklore texts which I published with German translations in 1955.[3] I used these and other materials for my manual of Khalkha in Russian which was published in 1931.[4] This was a graded reader with exercises, combined with a grammatical outline and an index of forms. Much later, in 1951, I published a theoretical grammar of Khalkha, with texts and a glossary.[5]

This book was the first complete grammar, including phonology, morphology, and syntax. The grammar gives all the necessary facts and is free from errors. It closed the enormous gap that existed at the time when I was a university student. In subsequent years I also published a Mongolian handbook,[6] which is based partly on the grammar just discussed and partly on Street's *Khalkha Structure.*

An important major Mongolian language is Buryat which is spoken in Eastern Siberia, particularly in the area around Lake Baikal, and in Northwestern Manchuria. It is a language particularly interesting to linguists because it is divided into numerous dialects and has preserved some ancient traits. Some of these traits are personal endings at verbal forms, like *yerebeb* 'I have come' (cf. Middle Mongolian *irebe bi* same) and ancient words like *zükheli* 'the hide of a sacrificial animal with head and legs, hanging from a long pole' (cf. *jügeli* in the *Secret History,* written in 1240).

Before I started my study of Buryat in 1928, there existed Castrén's excellent grammar (1857),[7] but it deals only with the Selenga and Nizhneudinsk dialects. There was also Rudnev's work on the Khori dialect which is also good but still leaves many dialects uninvestigated.[8] I started my Buryat studies with an investigation of the Alar dialect spoken west of Lake Baikal. I collected a number of texts, mostly folklore, such as epics, tales, songs, and riddles. Part of this material was incorporated in my two-volume work on the Alar dialect.[9] Two years later I went to the Aga Buryats who live close to the Manchurian border. There I collected interesting materials such as tales about everyday life, songs, riddles, fairy tales, and shamanist incantations. The results were published in the form of an article on the phonological features of the Aga dialect,[10] While in Ulaanbaatar in the summer of 1929, I collected, *inter alia*, material on the Bargu dialect spoken in Northwestern Manchuria. This dialect has preserved some ancient features, e.g. the ablative case ending $-\bar{a}ha$ (= $-h\bar{a}$ in other dialects) and the affricate *j* (= *dzh*).[11] In 1931 I investigated the Tsongol dialect in the Selenga region, and in 1932 the dialect of the Ekhirit in the Barguzin area.

These investigations culminated in a complete grammar of the Buryat language, published in 1938.[12] It takes into account most dialects of the Buryat language and is, to a certain extent, a comparative grammar of the Buryat dialects. Later, in 1958, I wrote a structural grammar of the modern literary Buryat language and published it in 1960.[13]

In consequence of all these studies, the Buryat language as early as 1938 became one of the best explored Mongolian languages. However, many other Mongolian languages still remained almost unexplored. One such language was Dagur in Northern Manchuria. It had been commonly regarded as a Tungus language, and Ramstedt called it a "mixed Manchu-Mongolian dialect." I investigated it in 1927 and published a book in 1930[14] and an article in 1934.[15] As a result of these publications Dagur was recognized as a conservative, archaic Mongolian language which had preserved some Middle Mongolian (twelfth to sixteenth centuries) features. For example, it preserved *e which has developed in some positions into $\ddot{o}$ in Modern Mongolian, like *emes-* "to dress oneself, to put on" to Khalkha $\ddot{o}ms$-. It also preserved *au* and *eü* which became $\bar{u}$ and $\ddot{\bar{u}}$ respectively in Modern Mongolian, as in *aula* "mountain" to Khalkha uul.

Mongolian was not the only Altaic language I was interested in. Another Altaic language group is Manchu-Tungus. It comprises a large number of languages, each spoken by relatively few people. Some of them are about 2,000 speakers of Manchu in Manchuria, 10,000 Nanai (or Goldi) on the Amur River, 5,000 Solons in Northwestern Manchuria, and 30,000 Evenki in Eastern Siberia. With the exception of Manchu which is very well known and is represented in excellent dictionaries and grammars, this language group was scarcely explored.

I was particularly interested in Evenki, one of whose dialects had been investigated by Castrén. I became first acquainted with Evenki, one of the relatively widespread Tungus languages, in 1925 in Leningrad where I had found a young Evenki man who was studying at the Institute of the Peoples of the North. I published the material gathered in 1927.[16] Later, in 1932, I made a trip to my informant's homeland, the area called Derēn to the east of Lake Baikal, to collect more material, but this has remained unpublished.

In 1929 I met several Solons in Ulaanbaatar. The Solons call themselves Evenki, live in northwestern Manchuria, and speak a Tungus language close to Evenki but not identical with it. A book, containing texts with Russian translations, a Solon-Russian glossary, and a grammar, was published in 1931.[17] It supplements A. O. Ivanovskii's obsolete and rather unreliable *Mandjurica* published in 1894, considerably.[18]

In connection with my linguistic research, I should also mention the grammars I compiled for students. Although they are based on older works done by other scholars, the interpretation is often mine, and the methods applied are those of modern linguistics. In 1937 I published in Russian a grammar of Written

Mongolian.[19] What was new in it was the phonemic distinction between short and long vowels, e.g. *daγa-* "to follow," *dayā-* "to be able to lift; "*baγa* "small", *baγā* "to empty one's bowels." Some grammatical forms are treated in a manner different from older grammars (Bobrovnikov, Kotwicz, Rudnev and others). In 1954 I published a grammar of Written Mongolian in English,[20] and two newer editions appeared in 1964 and 1974. This grammar is more complete than its predecessors. Word formation is discussed in more detail, and suffixes, missing in my Russian edition, are given.

The very first grammar for students I ever wrote is a Yakut grammar, which my professor, A. N. Samoilovich, recommended I compile for teachers of Yakut in Yakut schools.[21] I based it on the older grammars by Böhtlingk (1851)[22] and S. V. Yastremskii (1900),[23] but my treatment of some grammatical forms is different, e.g. the form with -ta (*ūta* "some water") is called *partitive* instead of *indefinite accusative*.

At a later time I wrote a Tatar and a Bashkir manual for university students.[24] These manuals are structural grammars. They make a strong distinction between phonemes and allophones, the grammatical terms are treated in accordance with their forms which is not done in traditional grammars. Thus the Tatar word *kəm* "who" is not classified as an interrogative pronoun but as an interrogative noun because its declension is nominal and it also has the same plural form as any noun. An example would be *kəmnär* "who" when referring to more than one person. Likewise, the negative *yoq* is not classified as a negative particle but as a negative noun which actually means "absence" and can be declined.

As for linguistic works based entirely on my own research, I should like to mention works on the history of languages. My very first work in this category dealt with the list of animal names in the work of Ḥamd'ullāh Qazwīnī, compiled in 1339. This work was written in Arabic, and in one of its chapters there is a list of animal and plant names in Mongolian. V. V. Bartol'd had excerpted this list and given it to Vladimirtsov who passed it on to me. I investigated those names and, with Bartol'd's kind permission, published it in 1925.[25]

A work dealing with two glossaries, namely a Mongolian-Persian and an Arabic-Mongolian of 1343 was investigated by me later. I received photostats of the two glossaries, which are contained in a manuscript at the Leiden Library, from Professor Willi Bang-Kaup, and wrote an article for the Bulletin of the Russian Academy of Sciences in 1927-28.[26] The Turkic part of the manuscript had been investigated by M. Th. Houtsma[27] but he misread the date as 1245. I took this date from Houtsma without checking it and, therefore, the date in my article is wrong. It is strange that such a great scholar as Houtsma could misread a date.

The largest collection of Middle Mongolian words including numerous sentences, written in Arabic script, with Chaghatay Turkic, Arabic, and Persian translations is a manuscript of the famous dictionary *Muqaddimat al-Adab*, compiled by al-Zamakh-shari who died in 1156. Later Chaghatay Turkic and still later Mongolian equivalents of Arabic words and sentences were added. The copy containing the Chaghatay and Mongolian materials dates from 1492 but the original must have been older, going back to the fourteenth century. This copy had belonged to the palace library of the Emir of Bukhara whose librarian had been the well-known Uzbek writer and scholar Abd ar-Ra'uf Fitrat. After the revolution the library became a state library and was renamed the Avicenna Library.

With Fitrat's help I received an excellent copy of the library manuscript and was in a position to do my research on this valuable material. I arranged all words and sentences in alphabetical order and made indexes of the non-initial words in sentences, translated the Mongolian and Chaghatay Turkic words and sentences into Russian, and wrote a grammar in which the Mongolian words and forms are compared with Written Mongolian and Modern Mongolian forms.

A more specialized article on the functions of the Mongolian case forms occurring in the dictionary *Muqaddimat al-Adab* was published by me in 1953,[28] and an analysis of the Chaghatay Turkic materials in that work appeared in 1951.[29]

The medieval Arabic-Mongolian glossaries mentioned above have greatly increased our knowledge of Mongolian of that time.

Before the publication of these sources, only a few brief lists of Mongolian words in some Armenian and Georgian manuscripts and Ibn Muhauna's glossary of the fourteenth century were known. The Mongolian material contained in Moslem sources represents either colloquial Mongolian or Written Mongolian as read at that time. The Arabic alphabet contains letters for sounds which cannot be rendered precisely in the Mongolian alphabet. The Mongolian words written in Arabic transcription are, therefore, an important primary source for the history of the Mongolian language. It is a known fact that foreigners often render the words of another language better in their own script than the native speakers who keep to the traditional orthography.

In 1269 the Emperor Kublai Khan (Qubilai) introduced a new script for all languages spoken in the Mongol empire. That script had been created by a Tibetan named the ḥP'ags-pa Lama "The Venerable Lama" and, therefore, the script is called ḥP'ags-pa script, or square script after the shape of its letters which were based on the Tibetan alphabet. The script was used until the end of the Yüan dynasty in 1368. I published a monograph on the ḥP'ags-pa script and the language of the texts written in that script in Russian in 1941. The book appeared a few days after the German invasion of the Soviet Union on June 22, 1941, and therefore never reached the Western world. I have one copy in my possession. It was translated into English in 1955–56 by John R. Krueger, who was at that time my graduate student, and was published in 1957.[30] The texts are mostly inscriptions on steles, granting the clergy exemption from taxes. It is interesting to note that on one stele the Mongolian and Chinese texts clearly differ. The latter says that the monks of a particular temple are free from all taxes after which words there is a gap on the stele. The Mongolian text says, however, that they are free from all taxes except some particular tax. It is clear that the gap in the Chinese inscription on the same stele is the result of erasure of some characters, presumably by the monks. The Chinese tax collectors did not know Mongolian and, therefore, the monks did not bother to change the Mongolian text. As for the language of the documents in ḥP'ags-pa script, it is Written Mongolian, but in a rendition approaching the colloquial pronunciation of Middle Mongolian.

One of my minor works dealing with Middle Mongolian is an article on the passive constructions in the *Secret History* (1240). The constructions in question resemble English expressions like "I was shown a beautiful picture," i.e. the passive verb governing a direct object. English has a few expressions like "I was given a book," and "I was told a story," but no constructions, frequently found in Mongolian, like "we were driven away our cattle," meaning we have become victims of somebody's driving away our cattle. I should note that the use of such constructions seems to be limited to unpleasant experiences suffered by the grammatical subject. At least I have not encountered sentences of the type "we were given precious gifts." My article on this subject appeared in 1964.[31] Another article on the identity of the language of the *Secret History* and that of the ḥP'ags-pa script appeared in 1944.[32]

The method of reconstructing older forms of a language on the basis of its loan words in another language is widely used. A good example is so-called Sino-Korean which reflects the Chinese sounds of the eighth and ninth centuries and, therefore, is an excellent source for reconstructing the Chinese finals -p, -t, and -k.[33] An example from Europe would be the Germanic loan words in Finnish. They are so archaic that their forms could have never been reconstructed on the basis of Germanic data alone, e.g., Finnish *rengas* 'ring' < Germanic **hrengaz* (cf. Gothic *hriggs*, German *Ring*, Old English *hring*).[34]

The Middle Mongolian period started around the beginning of the twelfth century. There are no texts from the preceding Ancient Mongolian period because the Mongols did not have a writing system then. However, Ancient Mongolian can be reconstructed on the basis of Ancient Mongolian loan words extant in Evenki and Jurchen. Some Mongolian borrowings in Evenki have preserved *t* and *d* before **i* whereas the respective words in Middle Mongolian have *č* and *j*, e.g. Ev. *gutin* "thirty," *kadiwun* "scythe," etc. My articles on Ancient Mongolian loan words in Tungus were published in 1966 and 1972.[35] Additional material was presented in my article on Jurchen and Mongolian.[36] Jurchen is the language of the Manchus' predecessors and is actually an older form of Manchu. The Jurchen first appeared prominently on the historical stage in 1115 when they set off on the campaigns which led to their conquest of Southern Manchuria and then North China. They remained in power there until 1234 when the Mongols defeated them. The Jurchen language has many borrowings from Mongolian, most of which entered into the language during the Ancient Mongolian period, i.e., before the twelfth century.

One of the tasks involved in studying a language group is the investigation of the relationships of sounds and grammatical forms among the members of that group. The comparative study of languages which belong to any specific language group is of great importance, because such a study enables linguists to distinguish loan words from the words of the old stock common to all members of the language group in question. Then, loan words can shed light upon the ancient history of the peoples by revealing contacts for which there may be no historical evidence. Books discussing the sound correspondences and grammatical forms of related languages are called comparative grammars. The only previous comparative grammar of the Mongolian languages had been Vladimirtsov's book which appeared in 1929.[37] It very soon became obsolete because of Antoine Mostaert's works on Ordos Mongolian and Monguor.[38] My works on Dagur and Middle Mongolian appeared after Vladimirtsov's book had been published, and they contained much new material which had not been known to Vladimirtsov.

My comparative study appeared in 1955.[39] It sets forth the sound correspondences among Khalkha, Ordos, Buryat, Kalmuck, Dagur, Moghol in Afghanistan, Monguor in Kansu, the language of the ḥP'ags-pa script and *Secret History*, Middle Mongolian, and Written Mongolian, and it gives a brief comparative morphology. It also deals with both vowels and consonants, while Vladimirtsov's work had neglected consonants. It is in the main still usable, with one serious reservation: when it was published the existence of primary long vowels in Common Mongolian was still unknown. Therefore my later articles on the long vowels in Common Mongolian[40] must be taken into consideration when using my earlier comparative study. The disappearance of the consonants *b*, *g*, *y*, ŋ, and *m* occurs only before a long vowel, e.g., Common Mongolian *dabāri-* "to pass by, to attack," Written Mongolian *daɣari-*, Buryat *dāri-*, etc. It should be added that the two articles mentioned were instantly criticized by the German Altaicist Gerhard Doerfer who refused to accept Common Mongolian long vowels, although he does not offer any other explanation for such correspondences as ā = ā and a = a in various Mongolian languages. Thus Dagur *tāun* 'five' corresponds to Monguor *tāwen* and Moghol *tăbun*, Dagur (from Ivanovskii's work) *gāɣ* 'hog' corresponds to Mogh. (from Ramstedt) *ɣōq* ε*i*, and Dagur (Ivanovskii) *gāli* 'fire' corresponds to Moghol *ɣāl*. On the other hand, the following correspondences should be noted: Dag. *am* 'mouth' = Monguor *ama*, Mog. *aman;* Dag. *bari*, 'to take' = Monguor *bari-*, Mogh. *bari-* and Dag. *xari-* 'to return' = Monguor *xari-* and Mogh. *qari-*. It is quite obvious that we have here two different vowels, namely, a long *ā* and a short *a*. One must be blind not to see the pattern in these correspondences.

The Mongolian language group is, in its turn, related to the Turkic and Manchu-Tungus language groups, and to Korean. This larger group is called the Altaic family of languages. The history of Altaic comparative studies is old and begins with Mathias Alexander Castrén's scholarly activities which impressed me when I was a teen-ager, but it was the other Finnish scholar, Gustav John Ramstedt, who applied the methods of modern comparative linguistics, introduced by the neogrammarians, to Altaic comparative studies. Ramstedt made comparative studies of Mongolian, Manchu-Tungus, Turkic, and Korean, and he was among the first to believe that Japanese was also related to the Altaic family of languages.

I shall mention here only a few of my works in Altaic comparative linguistics. Like Ramstedt and his Finnish students Pentti Aalto, Aulis Joki, and Martti Räsänen, like Vladimirtsov and contemporary Soviet scholars such as Baskakov, Tsintsius, Novikova, Kolesnikova, like Karl H. Menges, and Omeljan Pritsak, I strongly believe in the genetic affinity of Altaic languages, and I am glad to have strong supporters in my work. The argument that the Altaic languages do not have numerals in common is not serious. Negative evidence is not proof. If we used lack of something as a criterion, English should be excluded from the Indo-European family of languages, because it lacks the category of gender *(magnus, magna, magnum)* and has no personal conjugation *(amabam, amabas, amabat)* except for third person singular. Yet English is a Germanic language and rightfully belongs to the Indo-European language family because it shares many phonological and morphological features with other languages belonging to this family. What matters is that there are numerous features common to most Altaic languages. There is the negative verb, as in Evenki *e-si-m dukura* 'I do not write' and Mongolian *e-se medemüi* 'I do not know.' There are possessive suffixes denoting the owner of an object, as in Ev. *amin-mi* 'my father,' Buryat *esege-mni* same, and Turkish *ata-m* same. There is the cumulation of suffixes, as in Ev. *jū-du* 'at home,' *jū-lā* 'to the house,' *oror-du-lā* 'to the reindeers'; Mongolian *ax-īn* 'of the elder brother' and *ax-īn-da* 'at the elder brother's' (i.e., at his home), Turkic Karakhanide (eleventh to thirteenth century) *biz-iŋ-dä* 'at our's' (i.e., at our home) where *-iŋ* is the genitive suffix and *-dä* is the locative suffix. In addition, the Altaic languages have numerous regular sound correspondences.

I agree, however, that these relationships among Altaic languages are not as close as those among most of the Indo-European languages. Mongolian and Turkic are not related in the same manner as Latin to German but rather like Swedish to Modern Greek.

I presented my observations of the relationship of the Altaic languages in a book published in 1960,[41] which received some good reviews, like Aalto's, but mostly negative ones. The detractors found fault with almost everything in the book. Thus, Doerfer regarded all words common to Altaic languages as borrowings, and Sinor criticized the book because I work with reconstructed forms. This latter criticism came as a great surprise to me because in comparative linguistics only reconstructed, older forms are compared. Thus, English *head* cannot be connected directly with Proto-Indo-European **kap-ut* 'head' but, together with correspondences in other Germanic languages, ancient and modern, it goes back to the *reconstructed* common Germanic form **haub-u δa*, the latter going back to Pre–Germanic **kaup-ut* and Proto–Indo–European **kap-ut*. Therefore Sinor's objections are absolutely unacceptable, and I must say that even Doerfer, the most outspoken objector, has never criticized my reconstructions. Instead he regards my reconstructed Proto–Altaic forms as Proto–Turkic loan words in Mongolian and Tungus.

Besides the comparative grammar mentioned above, I have published an *Introduction to Altaic Linguistics*[42] which gives classifications of the languages, the history of their investigation, and biographies of the most important scholars in the field of Altaic Studies.

In the field of comparative linguistics, I studied the Chuvash language and its relation to Turkic and Mongolian. Chuvash is spoken by 1.5 million people in the Middle Volga region of the Soviet Union. Formerly it was regarded as a language of Finno–Ugric origin, but which had been Turkicized. It is close to the Turkic languages but not so close as to be grouped together with such languages as Tatar, Kazakh, and Uzbek. In an article written in 1924-1925 I stated that Chuvash was an language intermediate between Mongolian and Turkic,[43] but later I gave a better definition of both Chuvash and Turkic by going back to two dialects of Pre–Turkic, Proto–Chuvash and Proto–Turkic, and arguing that the Turkic languages are descendants of the second of these.[44]

Ramstedt has been mentioned above as believing that Japanese is related to the Altaic languages. It cannot be denied that it is structurally almost identical with Altaic and there are also some words which might be of common origin with Altaic correspondences. However, Japanese is by no means as close to, say, Mongolian as Tungus is. If Mongolian, Manchu–Tungus, Turkic, and Korean are descended from one common language, Japanese may go back to a proto–language which has an ancestor common with Proto–Altaic. I am inclined to accept, as far as Japanese is concerned, Street's scheme reproduced on p. 147 of my *Introduction to Altaic Linguistics*:

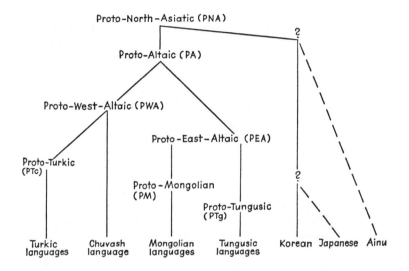

Consequently, I accept the respective works of Roy Andrew Miller and Karl Menges on Japanese and Dravidian, only with the same reservation, namely, that these languages are not Altaic but, together with Common Altaic, may go back to a still older proto-language. In other words, the relation of Japanese or Dravidian to the Altaic languages is possibly the same as the relation of the Uralic to Altaic languages. To this I might add that there is still so much work to be done to solve all problems revolving around the Altaic languages that I, for my part, cannot go into still wider fields such as Japanese-Dravidian-Altaic Studies.

The second group of my publications are philological works, i.e., text editions, translations, grammatical and other commentaries. Of the numerous old Mongolian literary sources only a few have been investigated. This is a serious gap. Most of them had not even been published until recently. During the past twenty years or so, the Hungarian scholar Louis Ligeti has published a number of them in the series *Monumenta Linguae Mongolicae Collecta*, but philological investigation of older texts has so far made little progress. The texts in question are of great importance to language study. They contain words and expressions no longer found in newer literary works, and they are also grammatically different from texts of subsequent periods. In order to establish the history of the Written Mongolian language, the investigator must follow all changes in the language which occur from time to time. Mongolian Studies must include philology which has played a significant role in the investigation of the older stages of European languages.

Speaking of my works belonging to this category, I should point out that the earliest of these works, which is also one of my very first works published, deals with the linguistic features of the epic *Geser Khan* as published in I. J. Schmidt's edition of 1836.[45] This article was published in *Asia Major* in 1926.[46] The most interesting feature of this text is that the direct speech of the *dramatis personae* appears in a dialect, in other words, it does not follow the rules of the written language.

While I was still a student under Vladimirtsov I read the manuscript *Arban qoyar jokiyangγui* (The Twelve Deeds of Buddha), a biography of the Buddha. This manuscript was Shesrab Senge's fourteenth-century translation of an abbreviated Tibetan version of the famous Sanskrit work *Lalitavistara* (The Great Game). I prepared a text edition, but it remained unpublished and was lost in Leningrad during World War II. Later I obtained a microfilm of the manuscript, prepared a text edition in transcription, made a translation, and added linguistic commentaries. This work appeared as a book in 1967.[47] I also published one of the jātakas, i.e., rebirth stories, namely the Mongolian and Oirat versions of *Vessantara-jātaka*.[48]

Another important Buddhist work is the *Vajracchedikāprajñā-pāramitā* (The Diamond Sutra), which was translated into Mongolian several times. There is an anonymous version believed to go back to an original of the fourteenth century. Another version is a translation made by the famous Shiregetü Güshi Chorji in 1612, and the third translation was done by the no less famous Zaya Pandita between 1650 and 1662. The main idea going through the whole work is that each one of the Buddhist concepts is equivalent to its contradictory concept. Besides texts, translations, and commentaries, my book also contains two glossaries which give the Sanskrit and Tibetan equivalents of the Mongolian terms.[49]

Among the numerous manuscripts in the archives of the Institute of Oriental Studies of the Soviet Academy of Sciences in Leningrad there are several Buryat historical works. They were practically unknown to Mongolists during my student years. I published two texts of the chronicles of the Khori Buryat, one by Tuguldur Toboev (1863) and the other by Vandan Yumsunov (1875) in 1935.[50] The text of the chronicle of the Selenga Buryats by Lombo Tserenov (1868) followed in 1936.[51] A translation of the chronicles of Toboev and Yumsunov was prepared by me and published in 1940.[52] I also translated and published, together with my colleague A. I. Vostrikov, the chronicles of the Barguzin Buryats by Sakharov (1869–1887).[53]

Work on some of my philological writings amounts to detective work, for I had to identify to what literary work certain manuscript fragments belonged. For example, when deciphering some fragments published by Shirō Hattori, I noticed that the text, as far as it could be read, resembled that of the Buddhist work known under the Sanskrit title *Bodhicaryāvatāra* (Entrance into the Practice of Bodhisattvas). When I compared the fragment with the passage in question, the two were almost identical.[54] I have also identified several badly damaged pages of a manuscript as fragments of a Mongolian version of the Alexander Romance. The manuscript is part of the Turfan collection preserved in the Völkermuseum in Berlin. Professor F. W. Cleaves of Harvard University had photostats of several manuscripts of that collection and kindly gave me copies. When reading those fragments, I noticed that in one of them the name *Sulqarnai* occurred many times. It resembled very much the Arabic name of Alexander the Great, *Zū'l-qarnain* which is literally "The Two-Horned." Comparison of the Völkermuseum text with the original text of the Alexander Romance produced the evidence that the various sections were indeed pieces of the Mongolian text of that name.[55] Later Cleaves published a long article on the subject.[56] The text is, however, so fragmentary that reconstruction of it is impossible. The important point is that the fragments are valuable because they prove that the Mongols, like many other peoples, had known of the Alexander Romance.

In 1930 a team of collective farm workers was digging a hole for a silo in the former Volga German Autonomous Republic, when they found pieces of birch bark with characters on them. They were so thrilled that they took their findings to the party secretary to obtain an explanation. Of course, he could not explain the writing, so he sent it to a local museum. There was no one there who could do anything with the birch bark manuscript either, so they sent it to the Hermitage Museum in Leningrad. There the manuscript was given to Zhamtsarano for decipherment. He had succeeded in deciphering a few pages when he was arrested and murdered, and the photographs of the manuscript were given to me. The badly damaged text proved to be a song, a dialogue of a mother with her son. I succeeded in deciphering most of it and reconstructed a large portion of the poem. This was not so difficult because the Mongolian verse is characterized by two main features. One is parallelism, i.e., repetition of what is said in the first stanza in a modified way in the following stanza. The second is the alliteration of the initial syllables of a quatrain. My article on this manuscript appeared in 1941[57] shortly before the Germans invaded the Soviet Union, although still in time for it to become known in the West. I was told that the American press mentioned that finding and my work. As a matter of fact, my work evoked great interest because in the preface I pointed out that subsequent archeological excavations had shown that the place where the birch bark fragments were found had been a cemetery at the time of the Golden Horde, and the grave in question had been that of a Mongolian warrior or scribe. A brass inkpot had also been found with the birch bark fragments.

To conclude this section on my philological works, let me mention that besides old Mongolian texts I also edited and investigated an old Turkic text of the fifteenth century. This is a Middle Turkic text of the Christian Confession of the Faith with parallel Armenian, Arabic, and Latin translations. The original document belongs to the Medici Library in Florence and is part of the collection of materials related to the seventeenth Ecumenical Council which took place from 1438 to 1445 under Pope Eugene IV. Also known as the Florentine Council, it was originally convened to discuss the spread of the Catholic faith in the Orient, but instead spent most of its time on debates about whether the pope's power was superior to that of the council or vice versa. It is interesting to note here that the text of the Confession of the Faith in question consists of only two articles, although its text refers to things mentioned in all three articles. It also contains details which are missing from the Apostles' Creed, such as Christ's ascension to Heaven as witnessed by the Apostles.[58]

As I mentioned in Chapter I, I have always been interested in folk poetry. The fascination caused by Karelian folk singers when I was still a schoolboy is possibly responsible for my determination to study little-known languages and oral literature. When later I chose Mongolian as one of my main subjects, this choice happened to be very fortunate because the Mongols have a rich oral literature, including tales, riddles, proverbs, songs, and even epics. In Mongolia (both the People's Republic and Chinese Mongolia) and Buryatia, oral epic literature is still alive. Work on collecting folk poetry was started at the end of the nineteenth century. The first collectors were M. N. Khangalov, a Buryat teacher, G. N. Potanin, the well-known traveler and explorer of Mongolia and Eastern Siberia, and Ts. Zhamtsarano, already mentioned in this book. They had collected much, but still more remained to be recorded, translated and investigated.

In the summer of 1931 I collected folklore material among the Tsongol Buryats in the Selenga region of Buryatia.[59] The texts were translated by me and long after published in English.[60] I had earlier published another collection of the folklore of various Buryat areas in 1936.[61] These texts are quite interesting because some of them represent shamanistic incantations, ancient songs, and tales.

In more recent years I made German translations of a number of Mongolian and Buryat epics. This work has been organized by Walther Heissig's Central Asian Institute of Bonn University with financial help from the German foundation Forschungsgemeinschaft.

I have published seven volumes to date.[62] The total number of epics contained in them is forty-four. Some of the epics are rather long and occupy up to 250 pages of printed text.

These epics have as their central theme the hero's struggle with his enemies and his ultimate wedding. It is interesting to note that the hero usually appears at the home of his future father-in-law in the shape of a ugly runny-nosed boy. Some Buryat epics sometimes contain episodes found in European epic literature. For example, the epic *Bükhe Khara Khübüün* contains an episode identical to the one about the Cyclops in the *Odyssey*. The main hero of the epic *Yerensei*, resembles very much the ancient Greek Orestes who kills his mother and her lover as revenge for their murdering his father.

I have also written in Russian a book on the Mongolian heroic epics[63] which was later translated by Krueger into English.[64] Although written long ago, it is still useful, though nowadays much more material is available to the investigator. This book discusses the contents of epics, the *dramatis personae*, the structure of the epics, and the figures of speech they employ. The general conclusion is that the Khalkha Mongolian epics took their present shape during the period of feudal wars, from the fourteenth to the seventeenth centuries.

By way of conclusion, I would say that the works I have discussed in this chapter have closed some gaps in Altaic Studies. New materials have been investigated, older stages of the history of the Mongolian language have been worked on, and the relationships among Altaic languages have become better understood. As a result, we can now see more clearly what has been known until now and discover new aspects of and establish new relationships between objects and phenomenons. At the same time, we have also become aware of new gaps in our knowledge. The process of learning goes on forever. It is wrong to think that any work can ever give us ultimate knowledge. However, among the works a scholar produces there are always some which he likes more than others, which satisfy him more and which he believes will preserve their validity longer than others. My translations of Mongolian epics and collections of Khalkha, Buryat, Dagur, Solon, and Barguzin-Tungus texts will probably be used by scholars for a long time. Likewise, my grammar of Written Mongolian will be used until a better and more complete one appears.

As to works which I regard as more important than some other writings of mine, I would choose my books on Mongolian monuments in ḥP'ags-pa script and on the Mongolian dictionary *Muqaddimat al-Adab* and the article on the Mongolian material in a Leiden manuscript. These three works contain materials which will always be needed and used. Together with the Buryat chronicles and their Russian translations, they are to me the most interesting books I have written because they contain important material such as linguistic samples not previously studied and aspects of Buryat history that had been previously unknown.

As for my interpretations of facts, my works in comparative Altaic linguistics will be superceded by works of other scholars. I have been one of the pioneers in this field, and what I have done is merely lay the cornerstone of an edifice that is still abuilding. Pioneering works always suffer the fate of quickly becoming obsolete, but I have no regrets. What I have achieved has to a large extent been made possible by my predecessors. This does not mean that they were, as scholars, inferior to me. On the contrary, it only means that by their achievements they paved the way for me. Without their life works, I would have achieved nothing.

12 Conclusions

Life is sometimes compared to a journey. If I may accept this comparison, I am now, in the last week of December 1981, on the final stage of my journey. From the preceding narration, the conclusion can be drawn that my life has been rather turbulent and frequently even dangerous. The Boxer revolt in my early childhood, the Russo-Japanese War in my boyhood, the First World War when I was a teenager, the subsequent Civil War, the atrocities of the Stalinist regime and, especially the purges and mass executions under Stalin, World War II and the danger of being discovered by the Soviet occupation forces in postwar Germany, all this is a little too eventful for one man's life. However, I am not complaining and indulging in self pity because this has been the fate of all the people in the Soviet Union and in many other countries as well. On the contrary, I must frankly say that, in spite of the prevailing conditions during my life, I have been very fortunate and rather successful. I have never experienced the horrors of a Soviet jail or concentration camp, did not have to fight in World War I, the Civil War, or World War II. Therefore I was not wounded or crippled for life and I did not die on the battlefield. Moreover, I got my first academic position in 1919 when I was not yet 22 years old and since then have never been jobless. I became a full professor at Leningrad University in 1925 at the age of 28, and in 1932 I became the second youngest corresponding member of the Soviet Academy of Sciences.

I do not mention all this in order to show off. I only want to acknowledge how fortunate I was. I am sure the kind of person who always suspects everybody else of wrongdoing must wonder about me, since I had done so well in the Soviet Union. They must suspect this might have come as a reward for being an informer of some kind. After all, one should not forget that the people of the Soviet Union divided all non-informers into three categories: those who were in jail, those who are in jail, and those who will be in jail. I had not been in jail, consequently it is not surprising that one of the dissidents living in the Soviet Union, a certain Voznesenskii, when discussing in an article the purges and the arrests of persons working in the Institute of Oriental Studies of the Academy of Sciences mentions, *inter alia*, Grum-Grzhimailo's ordeal, described in Chapter 5, and depicts me as Grum's "evil genius," implying that I was a Communist who reported to the party committee.[1] This is simply untrue. My scholarly disagreement with Grum's historical views, which did no political harm to him at all, does not make me an evil genius, otherwise anyone disagreeing with somebody else's theories would be also an evil genius. This shows that Voznesenskii, like so many otherwise admirable Soviet scholars, has no concept of academic freedom and the right of a scholar to form his own ideas. As for my membership in the Communist party, it is also untrue, and to prove it, I reproduce here my military card which clearly states that I was not a party member (Illus. 27). This is another example of how easy it is to become a victim of slander. In this connection, one can imagine what will happen in the Soviet Union after the fall of the communist regime. Everybody will report on everybody else, taking revenge on those suspected of some evil actions against fellow citizens.

To conclude this section, I can say that my emigration from the Soviet Union was by no means motivated by lack of success and bleak prospects for ever achieving anything. The reason I left was my fear that a new wave of political terror might ultimately plunge me into a concentration camp and destroy my family. This is my answer to those who sometimes ask me why I left the Soviet Union where I had already achieved so much. I must add that I could not

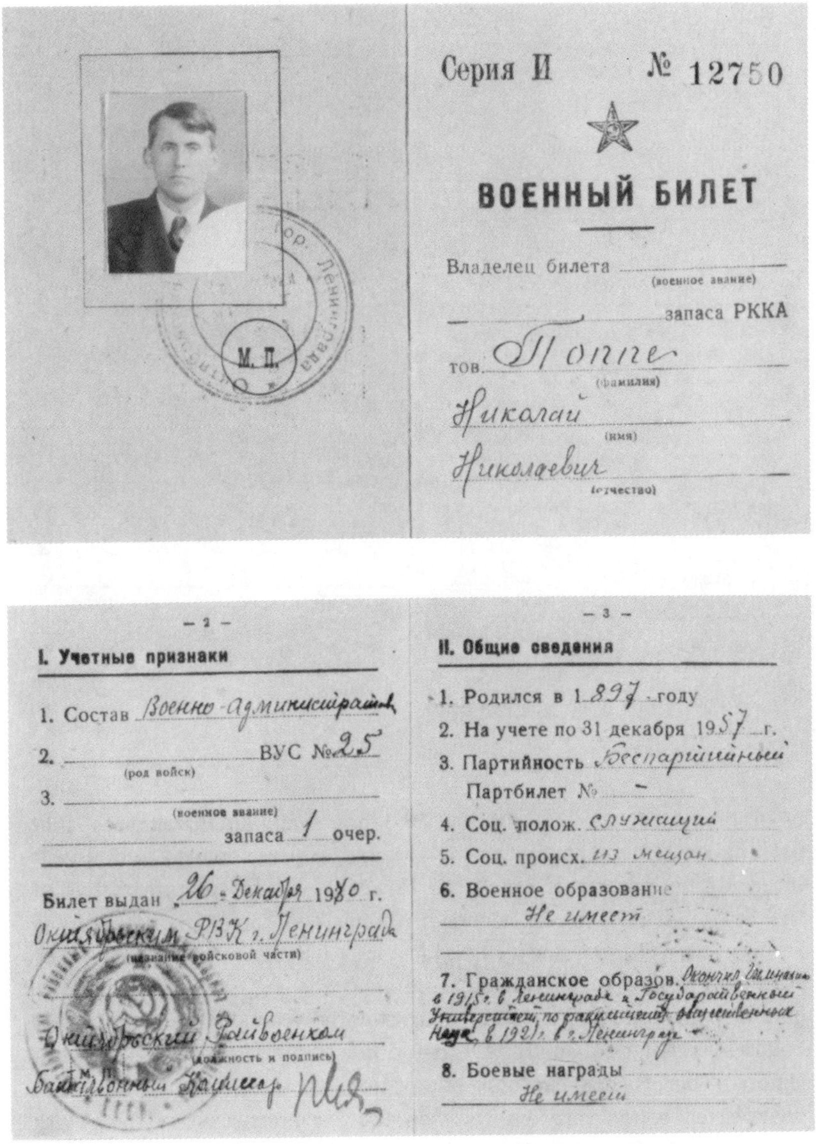

Серия И № 12750

ВОЕННЫЙ БИЛЕТ

Владелец билета ______ (военное звание)

______ запаса РККА

тов. Поппе (фамилия)

Николай (имя)

Николаевич (отчество)

М. П.

— 2 —

I. Учетные признаки

1. Состав Военно-административный
2. ______ (род войск) ВУС № 25
3. ______ (военное звание)

запаса 1 очер.

Билет выдан 26 декабря 1940 г.

Октябрьским РВК г. Ленинград (название войсковой части)

Октябрьский Райвоенком (должность и подпись)

М. П. Батальонный Комиссар

— 3 —

II. Общие сведения

1. Родился в 1897 году
2. На учете по 31 декабря 1957 г.
3. Партийность Беспартийный

   Партбилет № —
4. Соц. полож. служащий
5. Соц. происх. из мещан
6. Военное образование

   Не имеет
7. Гражданское образов. Окончил гимназию в 1915 г. в Ленинграде и Государственный Университет по факультету общественных наук в 1921 г. в Ленинграде
8. Боевые награды

   Не имеет

Illus. 27. The Author's Military Card

have remained there even if I had had ironclad guarantees that nothing would ever happen to me and my family, because I am a very international person, if I may use favorably a term of opprobrium of the Soviet era. I have friends in many countries. I like reading foreign newspapers and magazines and listening to foreign radio stations. I like to travel and I demand the right to have my own opinions and exchange them with equally free people from other countries. All this would have been impossible for me in the Soviet Union. Therefore, I had only one option, namely, to emigrate. The unexpected opportunity came when the Germans invaded the Soviet Union and occupied the town of Mikoyan Shakhar in the Caucasus on August 13, 1942 where I happened to be living. I was offered an escape. Of course, Germany was not my final destination but only a stopover on my way to freedom. The way was long, with many delays and disappointments.

I have described in Chapter 10 my life in the United States, a life full of success. No one, however, is spared from grief. The recent unhappy period of my life began in 1977. On July 15, three weeks before my eightieth birthday, a colleague of mine and his wife visited us at home. My wife was in good spirits, and everything seemed fine. After our friends had left, my wife suddenly was unable to speak at all. The next morning I took her to the hospital, where the physicians diagnosed a mild stroke with subsequent aphasia. She remained in the hospital for almost a week and underwent thorough treatment. A specialist in speech disorders treated her, and her speech slowly returned. She soon learned to speak quickly, but was never again to achieve perfection in speech. She often confused words or could not remember a word she was looking for. It was frustrating for her because she had always been active and independent. Such was fate's first warning to us that worse was yet to come.

On August 8, however, I celebrated my eightieth birthday. My colleagues at the School of International Studies, University of Washington held an official lunch in my honor, which took place in the hall of the Faculty Club. In the evening, a party organized by our Turkish students was celebrated in my honor. Those Turkish students were actually young Turkish scholars who had come from Turkey to do postdoctoral research under Professor Ilse Cirtautas's guidance. They had also invited Turkish friends to the party.

I still remember one particular detail. On that day a certain Solomon Ioffe had come to Seattle. He had left the Soviet Union and had only recently come to the United States. I knew him by name because we had been writing to each other for almost ten years. Now he had finally arrived, but his luggage had not come with the same plane. Consequently, I had to lend him one of my suits so he could attend the party. Subsequently, Ioffe enrolled as a graduate student at the University of Washington.

Later that year, on December 13, Solomon Ioffe came to see

me. When I answered the doorbell and let him in, he was holding in his hand something looking like a letter. It was a telegram and it had been hanging on the doorknob when he rang the bell. I opened the telegram. It was unsigned and came from Leningrad. The text was brief: "Elizaveta Nikolaevna died suddenly on December 12." A few days later, a letter came from my sister's colleague, a scholar at the Hermitage Museum in Leningrad. It gave some details, stating that the cause of my sister's death was heart failure and that she had been buried "according to the rites of the Christian Church" in a certain cemetery, and that later a tombstone would be erected, paid for by my sister's savings which, for this purpose, had been released by the pertinent government agency.

My sister's death was, of course, a very grievous shock to me and to Edith, who had known Elisabeth as a young girl. Elisabeth's death saddened us, but what was even more tragic was that I had not even seen her for thirty-six years, i.e., since the summer of 1941. Edith and I had invited her several times to Seattle and formally promised to pay her fare from the Soviet Union and back, pay all her expenses while in the United States, and be responsible for medical care in the event of an illness. She applied for an exit visa but never got an answer, even though there is a law saying the government is obliged to answer any application or inquiry made by a Soviet citizen within one month. An empty declaration on paper! The Soviet constitution and its laws, its treaties and agreements are just paper. We never knew why they had not let her out and she herself was afraid to apply for a visa again. They must have been afraid she would talk—talk about the lack of towels, coffee, lemons, eau de cologne in shops, lack of nylons and bras for ladies, shorts for men, and many other basic goods. The Soviets lack everything except a cornucopia of police measures limiting the already meager and appallingly curtailed individual rights. Elisabeth's death brought an end to hopes that my wife and I would ever see her again. My elder son who often went to the Soviet Union as a member of groups of Canadian scholars doing research on an exchange basis was luckier. He met her at least six times after I had settled down in the United States.

Before proceeding to other events, I would like to say a few more words about my sister. As I mentioned in Chapter 1, she was born in 1903. Later she graduated from the School of St. Peter and Paul from which both our parents and our maternal grandfather had also graduated. Before the revolution the school was organized into two divisions, each housed in its own building, one for boys and the other for girls. After the revolution the school became coeducational.

Elisabeth studied history and art history at Leningrad University and graduated around 1925. She also graduated from the Leningrad Conservatory and was an excellent pianist. In 1927 she married my first wife's, Nataliya's, childhood friend Konstantin I. Gindus, a talented architect. He was shot in 1930 because a house he had designed was built in the wrong location. One would certainly think that the blame should have been placed on the contractor but not on the architect. Later Elisabeth remarried. Her second husband was the engineer Nenarokov, but they divorced rather soon. She became a historian of painting specializing in engravings at the Hermitage Museum in Leningrad and published a book on Italian colored wood engravings of the sixteenth to eighteenth centuries.[2]

Thus ended 1977. The next year was to be the most disastrous year of my life, the accursed year 1978. It began peacefully and pleasantly enough. In March, on Easter, my elder son Valerian and his wife Barbara, née Schneider, who is a doctor of mathematical chemistry, came from Ottawa to visit us. Their arrival was always a happy event for Edith and me. He was, as always, friendly and happy. As usual he brought lavish gifts—this time it was an expensive camera—and told many interesting stories about his recent trip. Valerian and Barbara spent several happy days with us and the time passed all too quickly. One day Valerian suggested that I go with them on a vacation. He knew that in autumn I had to participate in a conference at Bonn University. After that, he suggested that I should join them on their vacation in Austria. Of course, everything sounded fine, but for some reason I felt reluctant to have a joint vacation. Something just seemed amiss. Since I could not explain my misgivings, I called myself an old fool and promised to join them. After the conference was over on September 30, I would go straight to Graz to meet them.

In the summer I had a pleasant surprise. I was elected a corresponding fellow of the British Academy. This was the most prestigious membership I had ever held with any learned body and I felt highly honored. I wrote to Valerian and he was greatly impressed with the honor bestowed on me. So, after all, things seemed to be moving along nicely, bringing me only satisfaction and joy.

Valerian was having a very busy summer, working in Alberta with a group of Canadian and Soviet exchange scholars. In August Valerian returned home from his expedition utterly exhausted and felt nauseous. He attributed this to a dinner party organized by the Indians in Northern Canada in honor of his expedition. On August 12, he felt chills, pains in the upper right part of the abdomen, and began to vomit. He entered Riverside Hospital in Ottawa. The x-rays showed nothing and the doctors suspected duodenitis. Valerian was afraid his illness might frustrate the plan of our joint vacation and explained this to the physician, who agreed with him that since no malignancy had been discovered he might take the vacation and even try to get a good rest. Valerian and Barbara did not go to Austria directly but first to Munich, where Barbara's mother lived. I was to leave for Germany on September 15, but a few days before that Valerian telephoned from Munich to say that the German physician suspected gall stones and had sent him to the hospital. When I arrived in Frankfurt on Saturday, September 16, I took a rest in a local hotel, and on the next day I went to Munich where, that afternoon, I visited the hospital. Valerian did not feel any discomfort but was very tired. The initial tests in the Munich hospital, undertaken on September 13, showed only the presence of duodenitis. No malignant growth anywhere was discovered on the following day either, but on Monday, September 18, a sonogram of his upper abdomen showed a malignant growth. A computergram taken on September 19 revealed a multiple metastisization of the liver, and finally, test surgery exposed numerous large and small tumors covering most of the liver. Valerian was doomed. He did not feel any pain as he was being treated with pain-killing drugs, but he was drowsy and mostly slept. At the times when he was awake, I talked to him and tried to minimize the seriousness of his condition, assuring him that recovery would soon begin. Lying to him made me terribly unhappy. Suddenly I understood the poor harlequin who had to amuse idle onlookers while his child was dying. Did Valerian suspect anything? I think he did. Leaving him at the end of visiting hour I said, "Get well fast, my dear!" He looked at me and said, "I think I am no longer *your* dear."

On the other hand, Valerian paid attention to what people were doing, and obviously tried to find out the truth. Thus when I did not leave on September 25 for the conference on the day of its opening, Valerian grew worried: "Why don't you go?" he asked. I answered that the first day was of no importance and I wanted to stay with him, but that I would leave the next day. "So you will go tomorrow." he said, obviously relieved. I left and was away for two days. He seemed very pleased.

We also had the problem of letting my younger son Nicholas come and be with his brother. One difficulty was that Nicholas visited his brother very rarely even in good times. How could we explain Nicholas's presence in Munich at the beginning of a new academic year, when Valerian would know he should be missing his classes at the University of British Columbia where Nicholas was professor of Slavic languages. It would be quite out of the ordinary, and Valerian would certainly recognize the terrible truth.

Soon after a laparotomy on September 20, Valerian lapsed into a coma. Now there was no problem about Nicholas. We telephoned to Vancouver and Nicholas came. He was the only one of us who was present in the sickroom on October 8, 1978 when Valerian died.

Thus ended the short but very active and fruitful life of my elder son. His death was a terrible blow to me and I was utterly devastated. I am so much older than he was, and even as I write now, a little more than three years after ths tragedy, the pain caused by his loss has not lessened. On the contrary, the more time passes, the greater my longing for him becomes.

Edith had known Valerian since he was a teenager, and his death made a devastating impression on her as well. Her health worsened from day to day. Two weeks after Valerian's death, we rushed her to the hospital with a severe kidney malfunction. Soon she returned home but in November she was again hospitalized because of water in her lungs. I remember it was November 18, the fortieth day after Valerian's death, when I visited her at the hospital after Nicholas and I had attended memorial services in the Russian Orthodox Church in Seattle. It was a cold and snowy day, and traffic in the city was greatly impeded. She came home in December. We had a modest Christmas celebration at home with a small tree and some gifts, and Nicholas came from Vancouver. Edith wanted all of us to go to a nearby Chinese restaurant, but it was closed for the holiday. She was very disappointed, but still did not feel like trying another Chinese restaurant which was farther away. I was sorry that I was unable to fulfill this wish, which may have been the last in her life.

On January 8, 1979, we celebrated her eighty-first birthday. A few of her friends came, and we had a quiet celebration with coffee and cake. It was a far cry from previous birthday celebrations.

On January 18 Edith and a lady from the neighborhood drove to a beauty salon. When the two of them came back, I was helping my wife up to the porch when she suddenly fell against me and slowly sagged down. As far as I could judge she was unconscious. We called an ambulance which arrived in less than two minutes. The physician pronounced her clinically dead and started resuscitating her. After a while, her heart began to beat and she started to breathe again but remained unconscious. She was taken to the intensive care unit of the Group Health Hospital. She remained in a coma for three days and suddenly came to. The doctors warned me, however, that her heart might fail again. Edith was surprised to be in the hospital. She did not remember anything and started crying when she had heard what had happened—"I died without pain and suddenly. Why did you bring me back to life? I am a sick person and I shall die anyway, possibly in great pain and suffering." She returned home on February 8. She was very weak and spent most of her time lying or sitting and sleeping. The night of February 12 to February 13 was very stormy. The wind lashed the trees and bushes in our backyard, and the branches beat against the walls and windows. Edith had always been sensitive to wind and storms and always had difficulties with breathing at such times, for she had chronic emphysema. I got up several times during the night in order to help her if she needed anything, but she was peacefully sleeping. The next morning I made breakfast for her and brought it to her bed, but she was dead and had probably died an hour or so before morning.

Funeral services were performed on February 24, eleven days after her death, because my daughter-in-law, Valerian's widow, had to come with her mother, Mrs. Schneider, from Ottawa. Edith was cremated and her remains were placed into our common grave in Washelli cemetery. Thus, four months after Valerian's burial, Edith left this world. And a year before my sister had died. All went exactly according to an old Russian superstition that great grief comes by threes. With Edith's death a third person had left me after a long time of togetherness. We had been friends from my ninth year of age until 1920 when she left Russia, walking across the frozen Gulf of Finland from the Russian shore. We were later to meet again, in Berlin in 1943. Our marriage had lasted just over twenty-six years.

I remained alone, living in our house at 3220 N.E. 80th Street. It was strange to be alone and see no one the whole day, but there was much work to do. The house needed cleaning, the garden needed care, and I had my books and was in the middle of translating a volume of Buryat epics. In September 1979 I went to Germany to attend the annual conference on Mongolian epics at Bonn University. Thus the year 1979 also came to an end.

Living alone in a large house and all the work connected with it were too much for me. In February 1980 I moved into an apartment. It was a quiet and convenient place. I gave away all books I did not urgently need to Western Washington Unviversity in Bellingham, which has a fine Center for East Asian Studies of which my friend, Professor Henry G. Schwarz, is an active member. I took the rest of my books along to the apartment. In summer 1980 the seventh volume of my translations of Buryat epics appeared. I dedicated it to the memory of Valerian, for he had always pursued my research with great interest.

I resumed my studies in my new apartment. First I wrote an article on cities in Mongolian epics. I was to present it as a paper to the annual Permanent International Altaistic Conference in Vienna. I was also invited to attend a conference on the origin of the Japanese language, organized by my friend, Professor Shichirō Murayama, which was to convene in Kyoto. The third conference to be attended was on Mongolian epics, which was again to convene at Bonn University. The University of Washington had asked me to conduct regular courses of Mongolian and Turkic languages during the spring and autumn quarters of 1980. Thus, suddenly I had more work than I could possibly do. I cancelled my attendance at all three conferences and accepted only the teaching position at the university.

That teaching assignment came up because Professor Ilse Cirtautas was given a leave of absence, and a substitute was needed to take over her students during her absence. I agreed for several reasons. I had not taught since 1970, the year I spent as a visiting professor at Bonn University, and I liked the idea of doing it again for a while. Besides, I wanted to make sure that my friend's students would not lose time in their studies. There were no other professors of Turkic languages spoken in the Soviet Union in the United States who would agree to teach for one or two semesters on a ridiculously low salary. For me, however, it was a welcome supplement to my rather less than munificent pension. In spring quarter of 1981 I taught Professor Circautas's students again, this time a course in Old Uighur, using a Buddhist text, probably of the tenth century, Kazakh grammar and reading of a chrestomathy for Kazakh schools.

In July 1981 I took my vacation with the Aaltos at their summer cottage in beautiful Vestanfjärd in Southern Finland. I also had the opportunity to visit the home of Jean Sibelius, the great composer, which is not very far from Helsinki, and do some other sightseeing.

At present I am translating the Kalmuck epic cycle Jangar,

starting with the second volume of the Moscow edition of 1978.[3] I have already translated nine epics, totaling 252 pages. The reason I did not start with the first volume is because most of the epics in that volume have already been transcribed by Baatar Basangov and excellently translated into Russian by Semen Lipkin.[4]

My other research is of a linguistic nature. There are still many unsolved problems concerning relationships among Altaic languages. I am collecting material from G. Doerfer's and Semih Tezcan's Khalaj dictionary.[5] It contains, *inter alia*, a long list of words with initial *h* (<*p*-), such as *här* 'man' and *hat* 'horse' which can be reconstructed only as **per* and **pat*, respectively. This finding invalidates previous reconstructions and comparisons. It is quite obvious that Altaic comparative linguistics would have developed quite differently if we had had Khalaj materials long ago. This is another example of science's dynamic nature. A scholar's work is only done when he dies or is incapacitated for the rest of his life.

These lines are being written at the beginning of January 1982. It has been announced that this year's meeting of the Permanent International Altaistic Conference will be held at Uppsala in June. If nothing unexpected happens, I plan to attend it. Being in good health, I assume that the "unexpected" could be either lack of travel funds or some international political trouble. The latter has frustrated many of my plans, but I hope that I will be able to go to Sweden.

I conclude my reminiscenses with the Sanskrit benediction *svasti* which is traditionally put at the end of Mongolian Buddhist writings.

Notes

Chapter 1

1. For another eyewitness account, see B. L. Simpson (Putnam Weale, pseud.), *Manchu and Muscovite* (London, 1907), Chapter 14, "Tsitsihar," pp. 196-209.
2. G. Z. Yrjö-Koskinen, *Suomen kansan historia* (Helsinki, 1881-1882).
3. Matthias Alexander Castrén, *Reiseerinnerungen aus den Jahren 1838-1844.* 1853; *Reiseberichte und Briefe aus den Jahren 1845-1849.* 1856; and *Ethnologische Vorlesungen über die altaischen Völker nebst samojedischen Märchen und tatarischen Heldensagen.* 1857. Published in St. Petersburg as volumes 1, 2, and 4 of *Nordische Reisen und Forschungen.*
4. Juhani Aho (1861-1921) was the author of numerous novels and tales from Finnish life, such as *Panu,* a novel on the Finns during the pre-Christian era, and *Heränneitä* (The Revivalists), a novel about that religious sect who lived mainly in the northern part of the country. Alexis Kivi (1834-1872) wrote *The Seven Brothers* and other works on the life of Finnish peasants. Franz Eemil Sillanpää (1888-1964) wrote *Silya, the Maid* and other works describing life in Finland. Minna Canth (1844-1897) was the author of *Agnes* and other novels about Finnish intellectual society.

5. Wilfried Strik-Strikfeldt (tr. David Footman), *Against Hitler and Stalin: Memoir of the Russian Liberation Movement 1941-1945.* New York: John Day, 1973.

Chapter 2

1. "Beiträge zur Kenntnis der altmongolischen Schriftsprache," *Asia Major* 1 (1924), 668-675.
2. *Dagurskoe narechie.* Leningrad, 1930. 176 pp. (Materialy Mongol'skoi Komissii, v. 6).
3. A. V. Burdukov, *V staroi i novoi Mongolii, vospominaniya i pis'ma* (Moscow, 1969), 21.
4. A. N. Samoilovich, *Kratkaya uchebnaya grammatika sovremennogo osmanskoturetskogo yazyka.* Leningrad, 1925. For a list of his articles, see *Sovietico-Turcica* (Budapest, 1960), items 2056-2114.
5. Wilhelm Radloff, *Die Sprachen der türkischen Stämme Süd-Sibiriens und der Dsungarischen Steppe.* 6 vols. St. Petersburg, 1866-1885.
6. Abu'l Gazi Bahadur Khan, *Histoire des mogols et des tatares.* Tome 1: Texte. St. Petersburg, 1871.
7. *The Báber-Náma* (ed. Annette Susannah Beveridge). Leiden-London, 1905.
8. *Uchebnaya grammatika yakutskogo yazyka.* Moscow, 1926. 120 pp.
9. S. E. Malov, *Yazyk zheltykh uigurov* (Alma-Ata, 1957); *Uigurskii yazyk* (Moscow-Leningrad, 1954); *Pamyatniki drevnetyurkskoi pis'mennosti* (Moscow-Leningrad, 1951); *Lobnorskii yazyk* (Frunze, 1956); and *Eniseiskaya pis'mennost' tyurkov* (Moscow-Leningrad, 1952).
10. F. I. Shcherbatskoi's major works include *Teoriya poznannya i logika po ucheniyu pozdneishikh buddistov* (2 vols; St. Petersburg, 1903-1909); *Nyāyabindu: Buddiiskii uchebnik logiki* (2 vols; St. Petersburg, 1904-1909); *Tibetskii perevod sochinenii Saṃtanantārasiddhi Dharmakīrtī i Saṃtanantārasiddhitīkā Vinītadeva vmeste s tibetskim tolkovaniem, sostavlennym*

Agvanom Dandar-Lkharamboi (Petrograd, 1916); *Tibetskii perevod Abhidharmakoçakarikaḥ i Abhidharmakoçabhāṣyam sochinenii Vasubandkhu* (2 vols., Petrograd, 1917-1930); *and Buddhist Logic*, Volume I (Leningrad, 1932).

11.   The Soviets abolished the week and replaced it with a five-day period *(pyatidnevka)* in which every fifth day was a day off. This lasted for about a year, and then the normal week was restored.

12.   He is perhaps best known in the West for his works *Four Studies on the History of Central Asia* (Leiden, 1956-58) and *Turkestan Down to the Mongol Invasion* (London, 1958).

13.   Among Ol'denburg's better-known works is *Russkaya Turkestanskaya èkspeditsiya 1909-1910 gg.* (St. Petersburg, 1914).

14.   L. V. Shcherba, *Yazykovaya sistema i rechevaya deyatel'nost'.* Leningrad, 1974.

15.   Two of Marr's works were "Rasselenie yazykov i narodov i vopros o prarodine turetskogo yazyka (The separation of languages and peoples and the problem of the original home of the Osmanli Turkic language]," *Pod znamenem marksizma* 1927:6, pp. 18-60; and *Zametki o turetskom yazyke okrestnostei Abastuman* [Remarks on the Turkic Language of the Abastumani region]. Moscow-Leningrad, 1937. For a discussion of Marr's theories, see L. L. Thomas, *The Linguistic Theories of N. Ja. Marr* (Berkeley, 1957).

16.   Polivanov's many works include *Vvedenie v yazykoznanie dlya vostokovednykh vuzov* [Introduction to Linguistics for Orientalist Institutes] (Leningrad, 1928), *Kratkaya grammatika uzbekskogo yazyka* [A Concise Uzbek Grammar] (Tashkent-Moscow, 1926), and *Za marksistskoe yazykoznanie* (Moscow, 1931). See also the collection of some of his articles in *Stat'i po obshchemu yazykoznaniyu* (Moscow, 1968).

17.   V. A. Kaverin, *Skandalist* (Moscow, 1928).

Chapter 3

1. L. Ya. Shternberg, *Gilyaki* (= *Étnograficheskoe obozrenie*, vols. 60, 61, 63), 1905. On Shternberg, see N. I. Gagen-Torn, *Lev Yakovlevich Shternberg*. Moscow, 1975.
2. G. N. Prokofiev's major works are "Énetskii (eniseisko-samoedskii) dialekt," *Yazyki i pis'mennost' narodov severa*, Vol. 1 (1934); "Nenetskii (yurako-samoedskii) yazyk," *ibid*.; *Sel'kupskaya grammatika* (Leningrad, 1935); and "Materialien zur Erforschung der ostjak-samojedischen Sprache," *Ungarische Jahrbücher* 11 (1933).
3. One of her major works is *Sravnitel'naya fonetika tunguso-man'chzhurskikh yazykov*. Leningrad, 1949. For a description of her life and work, see N. I. Gladkova, "O nauchnoi i pedagogicheskoi deyatel'nosti Very Ivanovny Tsintsius," in *Voprosy yazyka i fol'klora narodov severa* (Yakutsk, 1980), pp. 3 ff.
4. Vasilevich wrote many works on the Evenki, including an Evenki-Russian dictionary (Moscow, 1940, new enlarged edition, 1958), a collection of folklore materials (Leningrad, 1936), a grammar (Leningrad, 1940), and a work on the dialectology of the Evenki language (Leningrad, 1949).
5. She wrote three grammars and one collection of folklore, to wit, *Grammatika oirotskogo yazyka* (Moscow-Leningrad, 1940); *Grammatika khakasskogo yazyka* (Abakan, 1948); *Grammatika shorskogo yazyka* (Moscow-Leningrad, 1941); and *Shorskii fol'klor* (Moscow-Leningrad, 1940). See also Nicholas Poppe, *Introduction to Altaic Linguistics* (Wiesbaden, 1965), 109.
6. For a description of the museum and its activities, see *Aziatskii muzei: Leningradskoe otdelenie instituta vostokovedeniya AN SSSR* (Moscow: Nauka, 1972). An older work is *Aziatskii Muzei Rossiiskoi Akademii Nauk, kratkaya pamyatka* (Petrograd, 1920).
7. "Zum Feuerkultus bei den Mongolen," *Asia Major* 2 (1925), 130-145.

8. A. M. Pozdneev, *Lektsii po istorii mongol'skoi literatury.* 2 vols. St. Petersburg, 1895, 1897.

9. *Sokrovennoe skazanie: Mongol'skaya khronika 1240 g. pod nazvaniem "MongYol-un niɣuča tobčiyan"* Yuan' chao bi shi *Mongol'skii obydennyi izbornik.* Tom 1. *Vvedenie v izuchenie pamyatnika.* Moscow, 1941. (Trudy Instituta Vostokovedeniya AN SSSR, v. 34).

10. A. A. Shakhmatov, *Mordovskii ̇etnograficheskii sbornik.* St. Petersburg, 1910.

11. "Mongol'skie nazvaniya zhivotnykh v trude Khamdallakha Kazvini," *Zapiski Kollegii Vostokovedov* 1 (1925), 195-208.

12. The author contributed four items to the journal's first volume: "Beiträge zur Kenntnis der altmongolischen Schriftsprache," pp. 668-675; "Russische Arbeiten auf dem Gebiet der Mongolistik 1914-1924," pp. 676-681; "Neues über den Tanjur in mongolischer Sprache," p. 682; and "Die tschuwassischen Lautgesetze," pp. 775-782.

Chapter 4

1. Georg Huth, *Die Inschriften von Tsaghan Baišin: Tibetischmongolischer Text mit einer Übersetzung sowie sprachlichen und historischen Erläuterungen.* Leipzig: F. A. Brockhaus, 1894.

2. "Otchet o poezdke na Orkhon letom 1926 goda," *Materialy Mongol'skoi Komissii* 4 (1929), 1-25.

3. *Dagurskoe narechie.* Leningrad, 1930. 176 pp. (Materialy Mongol'skoi Komissii, v. 6); "Skizze der Phonetik des Bargu-Burjätischen," *Asia Major* 7 (1931), 307-378.

4. *Alarskii govor.* Leningrad, 1930-31. 130 + 216 pp. (Materialy Mongol'skoi Komissii, v. 11 and 13).

5. B. B. Baradiin, *Statuya Maitrei v Zolotom khrame v Lavrane.* Leningrad, 1924.

6. *Buddist palomnik u svyatyn' Tibeta* (Petrograd, 1919). An English translation by Roger Shaw, entitled *A Buddhist Pilgrim at the Shrines of Tibet,* was published by Human

Research Area Files in 1956. Cited in N. L. Zhukovskaya, "Izuchenie lamaizma v SSSR (1917-1976)," as translated by Tracy Schwarz in *The Canada-Mongolia Review* 5:1 (1979), p. 39 and footnote 6.

7. Moscow-Leningrad, 1936. Obraztsy Narodnoi Slovesnosti Mongolov, v. 5. 167 pp.

8. Edige Kirimal, *Der nationale Kampf der Krimtürken, mit besonderer Berücksichtigung der Jahre 1917-1918.* Emsdetten, 1952.

9. T. A. Bertagaev's major works are *Sintaksis sovremennogo mongol'skogo yazyka v sravnitel'nom osveshchenii* (Moscow, 1964); *Morfologicheskaya struktura slova v mongol'skikh yazykakh* (Moscow, 1969); *Sochetaniya slov i sovremennaya terminologiya* (Moscow, 1971); and *Leksika sovremennykh mongol'skikh yazykov* (Moscow, 1974).

10. Cf. George Kennan, *Siberia and the Exile System* (New York: Century, 1891), Part 2, Chapter 3, "A visit to the Selenginsk lamasery," pp. 60-97; and A. A. Bestuzhev, *Gusinoe Ozero* (Verkhneudinsk, 1925).

11. *Yazyk i kolkhoznaya poèziya buryat-mongolov Selenginskogo aimaka.* Leningrad, 1934. 132 pp. (Obraztsy Narodnoi Slovesnosti Mongolov, v. 4). English translation *Tsongol Folklore* (=*Asiatische Forschungen* 55). Wiesbaden, 1978.

Chapter 5

1. K. M. Cheremisov (with G. N. Rumyantsev), *Mongol'sko-russkii slovar' (po sovremennoi presse).* Leningrad, 1937; and *Buryatsko-russkii slovar'* (Moscow, 1973).

2. *Mongol'skii slovar' Mukaddimat al-Adab.* Moscow-Leningrad, 1938-39. 3 parts. Reprint: *Mongolian Dictionary Mukaddimat al-Adab* (Farnborough: Gregg International Publishers Ltd., 1971).

3. The most extensive study in English of Pokrovskii is George M. Enteen, *The Soviet Scholar-Bureaucrat: M. N. Pokrovskii and the Society of Marxist Historians* (University Park, Pa., 1978).

4.   *Mongol'skii slovar' Mukaddimat al-Adab*, pp. 1–88.

Chapter 6

1.   The Russian words are *moloko* (milk), *myaso* (meat), *maslo* (butter), and *muka* (flour).

2.   *Gulag Archipelago* (New York, 1973), I, 5 and II, 644.

3.   Ts. Zh. Zhamtsarano, *Mongol'skie letopisi XVII veka* (Moscow-Leningrad, 1936); translated by Rudolf Loewenthal as *The Mongol Chronicles of the Seventeenth Century* (Wiesbaden, 1955).

4.   His doctoral dissertation was devoted to the *I Ching*. It later appeared in English translation as *Researches on the I Ching*, by Ioulian K. Shchutskii, translated by William L. MacDonald and Tsuyoshi Hasegawa with Hellmut Wilhelm and an introduction by Gerard W. Swanson (Princeton, 1978). Mr. Swanson obtained some information from me, but obviously his notes contained some errors, such as the false claim that I had tried to cross the frontier illegally into Finland.

5.   G. K. Papayan and M. Kokin, *Tszin-Tyan'.   Agrarnyi stroi drevnego Kitaya*. Leningrad, 1930.

6.   M. G. Bulakhov, *Evfimii Fedorovich Karskii.   Zhizn', nauchnaya i obshchestvennaya deyatel'nost'* (Minsk, 1981). This book does not say under what conditions Karskii died.

7.   For a description of the Seminarium Kondakovianum and its activities, see L. Hamilton Rhinelander, "Exiled Russian scholars in Prague: The Kondakov seminar and institute," *Canadian Slavonic Papers* 16 (1974), 331–351.

8.   Alexander Pushkin (tr. Walter Arndt), *Ruslan and Ludmila*. Ann Arbor, 1974.

Chapter 8

1.   "Die Sprache der mongolischen Quadratschrift und das Yüan-ch'ao pi-shi," *Asia Major*, N.F., 1 (1944), 97–115.

301

Chapter 9

1. Hertha Koenig published several novels, such as *Emilie Reinbeck, Die kleine und die grosse Liebe*, and *Die Letzten*, and collections of poems, such as *Sonnenuhr, Sonette, Blumen, Die alte Stadt*, and *Alles ist Anfang geworden*.

Chapter 10

1. In addition to works cited in note 38 of Chapter 11 (below), Mostaert wrote "Sur quelques passages de *l'Histoire secrète des Mongols*," *Harvard Journal of Asiatic Studies* 13 (1950), 285-361, 14 (1951), 329-403, 15 (1952), 285-407, and numerous other articles. For a full list of his publications, see his obituary by Nicholas Poppe, "Antoine Mostaert, C.I.C.M., August 10, 1881-June 2, 1971," *Central Asiatic Journal* 15 (1971), 164-169.

2. Ramstedt's major works include *Einführung in die altaische Sprachwissenschaft*, posthumously edited by Pentti Aalto and published in three volumes from 1952 to 1966 *(Mémoires de la Société Finno-Ougrienne* 104: 1-3); a compilation of *Kalmückische Sprachproben* in two volumes in 1909 and 1919 *(Mémoires de la Société Finno-Ougrienne* 27: 1-2): *Kalmückisches Wörterbuch* (Helsinki, 1935); a collection of *Nordmongolische Volksdichtung*, translated by Harry Halén and published in Helsinki in 1973 and 1974; and *Über die Konjugation des Khalkha-Mongolischen* in 1903 *(Mémoires de la Société Finno-Ougrienne 21)*.

3. Haenisch was a distinguished Mongolist who reconstituted the original Mongolian text of the Secret History of the Mongols from its Chinese transcription. A preliminary work was published under the title *Untersuchungen über das Yüan-ch'ao pi-shi, die Geheime Geschichte der Mongolen* in 1931, followed by a three-volume work (1937, 1939, 1941) entitled *Die Geheime Geschichte der Mongolen*. The final version was reprinted in 1962.

4. Schram was an expert on the T'u or Monguors, a Mongolian-speaking nationality in Western China. His earliest work was *Le mariage chez les T'ou-jen du Kan-sou* (Shanghai, 1931). After World War II, he published three volumes on *The Monguors of the Kansu-Tibetan Border* (Philadelphia, 1954, 1957, 1961), dealing with history and social organization, religion, and genealogy, respectively.

5. Cleaves contributed many articles to the *Harvard Journal of Asiatic Studies*, dealing with Sino-Mongolian inscriptions of the fourteenth century and other philological problems.

6. "Eine mongolische Fassung der Alexandersage," *Zeitschrift der Deutschen Morgenländischen Gesellschaft* 107 (1957), 105-129.

7. Henry Serruys, one of the most prolific Mongolists, has written several major works, including *Genealogical Tables of the Descendants of Dayan-qan* (The Hague, 1958), *Kumiss Ceremonies and Horse Racing* (Wiesbaden, 1974), *Sino-Jürčed Relations During the Yung-lo Period (1403-1424)* (Wiesbaden, 1955), and a three-volume history of *Sino-Mongol Relations During the Ming* (Brussels, 1959, 1967, 1975).

8. A. Barmin (Barmine), *One Who Survived: The Life Story of a Russian under the Soviets* (New York, 1945).

9. Lattimore characterized the author as "a Soviet defector to the Nazis during the war and an officer in the Nazi S.S. [who] is even more anti-Soviet than anti-Mongol." See *Nomads and Commissars* (New York, 1962), 125.

10. Karl A. Wittfogel, *Oriental Despotism: A Comparative Study of Total Power* (New Haven, 1957).

11. Michael's specialty was the Taiping rebellion, on which he wrote a three-volume work by the same title (Seattle, 1965).

12. Karl A. Wittfogel and Feng Chia-sheng, *History of Chinese Society: Liao (907-1125)* (Philadelphia, 1949).

13. Li's main area of specialization was the Sino-Tibetan languages, particularly Tai and Tibetan. North American languages also attracted his interest: his first publication was *Mattole, an Athabaskan Language* (Chicago, 1930), followed by works on Chipewyan.

303

14. K. C. Hsiao was the author of such major works as the six-volume study of *Chungkuo chengchih ssuhsiang shih* (Taipei, 1954), *Rural China* (Seattle, 1960), and *A Modern China and a New World* (Seattle, 1975).

15. Author of many books, Conze became most widely known for his *Buddhism: Its Essence and Development* (New York: Harper and Row, 1951) and *Buddhist Scriptures* (New York: Penguin Books, 1959).

16. Edward Conze, *The Memoirs of a Modern Gnostic.* 2 parts. Sherborne, England: Samizdat Publishing Co., 1979.

17. Shih's main work is *The Taiping Ideology* (Seattle, 1967).

18. Victor Erlich, *Russian Formalism* (The Hague, 1955) and *Twentieth-Century Russian Criticism* (New Haven, 1975).

19. Earl R. Hope, *Karlgren's Glottal Stop Initial in Ancient Chinese, with Particular Reference to the hPhags-pa Alphabet and to Certain Points of Linguistic Psychology* (Ottawa, 1953). 88 pp.

20. A. A. Dragunov, "The hPhags-pa script and ancient Mandarin," *Izvestiya Akademii Nauk SSSR* 1930, 627-647, 775-797.

21. V. A. Riasanovsky (Ryazanovskii), *Customary Law of the Mongol Tribes* (Harbin, 1929), *Customary Law of the Nomadic Tribes of Siberia* (Tientsin, 1938), and *Fundamental Principles of Mongol Law* (Tientsin, 1937).

22. Rudolf Loewenthal, *The Turkic Languages and Literatures of Central Asia: A Bibliography* (The Hague, 1957). His major translations are Pokotilov's *History of the Eastern Mongols During the Ming Dynasty* (Chengtu, 1947), and Zhamtsarano's *Mongol Chronicles* (see Chapter 6, note 3).

23. Reprinted in 1973 by the Mongolia Society at Bloomington, Indiana.

24. Otto Maenchen-Helfen, *Reise ins asiatische Tuwa* (Berlin, 1931); *The World of the Huns: Studies in Their History and Culture* (Berkeley, 1973).

25. *Selected Works of Peter A. Boodberg* (Berkeley, 1979).

26. Her latest work is *Chrestomathy of Modern Literary Uzbek* (Wiesbaden, 1981).

27. Henry G. Schwarz, *Bibliotheca Mongolica*, Part I: *Works in English, French, and German*. Bellingham, 1978. (Studies on East Asia, v. 12.)

28. Henry G. Schwarz, ed., *Mongolian Short Stories*. Bellingham, 1974. (Studies on East Asia, v. 8).

29. Henry G. Schwarz, ed., *Studies on Mongolia*. Bellingham, 1979. (Studies on East Asia, v. 13).

30. Alexander S. Vucinich, *The Soviet Academy of Sciences* (Stanford, 1956).

31. "An essay in Mongolian on medicinal waters," *Asia Major*, n.s. 6 (1957), 99-105.

32. "On some Mongolian manuscript fragments in the Library of the India Office," *Central Asiatic Journal* 5 (1959), 81-96.

33. D. M. Dunlop, *The History of the Jewish Khazars* (Princeton, 1954).

34. See *Iran and Islam: In Memory of the Late V. F. Minorsky* (Edinburgh, 1971).

35. Kaare Grønbech, *Komanisches Wörterbuch* (Copenhagen, 1942) and *Der türkische Sprachbau* (Copenhagen, 1936).

36. Walther Heissig, *Der mongolische Kulturwandel in den Hsingan Provinzen Mandschukuos* (Vienna, 1944); *Wörterbuch der heutigen mongolischen Sprache* (Vienna, 1941). The introduction to the dictionary was written by Heissig's friend, W. A. Unkrig, a well-known author of numerous works on various Mongolian subjects. Unkrig was German but professed the Russian Orthodox religion and was an ordained priest after completing his studies at the Russian Orthodox Academy. I met him in Berlin in 1943. See his obituary in Walther Heissig, "W. A. Unkrig †," *Central Asiatic Journal* 3 (1957), 19-22.

37. Werner Schulemann, *Die Kunst Zentralasiens als Ausdruckform religiösen Denkens* (Opladen, 1967).

38. *Studia Altaica: Festschrift für Nikolaus Poppe zum 60. Geburtstag* (Wiesbaden, 1957).

39. *Catalogue of the Manchu-Mongol Section of the Toyo Bunko* (Tokyo and Seattle, 1964).

40. Iwamura Shinobu, *The Zirni Manuscript: A Persian-Mongolian Glossary and Grammar* (Kyoto, 1961).

41. G. J. Ramstedt (ed. P. Aalto), *Einführung in die altaische Sprachwissenschaft* (Helsinki, 1952, 1957, 1966). For a list of Aalto's other works, see Harry Halén, comp., "Bibliography of Professor Pentti Aalto's publications 1938-1976," *Studia Orientalia* 47 (1977), 287-311.

42. Aulis Joki, *Die Lehnwörter des Sajansamojedischen.* Helsinki, 1952 (Mémoires de la Société Finno-Ougrienne, v. 103); *Uralier und die Indogermanen: Die älteren Berührungen zwischen den uralischen und indogermanischen Sprachen.* Helsinki, 1973 (Mémoires de la Société Finno-Ougrienne, v. 151).

43. Harry Halén, *Handbook of Oriental Collections in Finland* (London, 1978).

44. See Chapter 1, note 5.

45. "Die wirtschaftliche und kulturelle Erschliessung Sibiriens," in *Russlands Aufbruch ins 20 Jahrhundert* (Olten and Frieburg, 1970), 137-152. English translation in "The economic and cultural development of Siberia," in *Russia Enters the Twentieth Century* (New York, 1971), 138-151.

46. Martti Räsänen, *Versuch eines etymologischen Wörterbuches der Türksprachen* (Helsinki, 1969-1971). See a complete list of his publications by Paul Jyrkänkallio, "Die sprachwissenschaftlichen Veröffentlichungen von Prof. Dr. Martti Räsänen," *Studia Orientalia* 19:13 (1954), 1-14.

47. "The problem of Uralic and Altaic affinity," *Mémoires de la Société Finno-Ougrienne* 58 (1977), 221-225.

Chapter 11

1. Compiled by Arista Maria Cirtautas. Seattle: University of Washington, Institute for Comparative and Foreign Area Studies, 1977 (Parerga 4). She is the daughter of Professor Ilse Cirtautas and a talented graduate student at the University of Washington.

2. *Das Schriftmongolische und die Urgamundart phonetisch verglichen.* Helsingfors, 1902. 55 pp. (Journal de la Société Finno-Ougrienne 21, no. 2); *Über die Konjugation des Khalkha-Mongolischen.* Helsingfors, 1903. 143 pp. (Mémoires de la Société Finno-Ougrienne, v. 19).

3. *Mongolische Volksdichtung: Sprüche, Lieder, Märchen und Heldensagen. Khalkha-mongolische Texte mit deutscher Übersetzung, einer Einleitung und Anmerkungen.* Wiesbaden, 1955. 287 pp. (Veröffentlichungen der Orientalischen Kommission, Akademie der Wissenschaften und der Literatur, v. 7).

4. *Prakticheskii uchebnik mongol'skogo razgovornogo yazyka (khalkhaskoe narechie).* Leningrad, 1931. 180 pp. (Izdanie Leningradskogo Vostochnogo Instituta, no. 41).

5. *Khalkha-mongolische Grammatik: Mit Bibliographie, Sprachproben und Glossar.* Wiesbaden, 1951. 188 pp. (Veröffentlichungen der Orientalischen Kommission, Akademie der Wissenschaften und der Literatur, v. 1).

6. *Mongolian Language Handbook.* Washington: Center for Applied Linguistics, 1970. 175 pp.

7. Matthias Alexander Castrén, *Versuch einer burjatischen Sprachlehre nebst kurzem Wörterverzeichniss.* St. Petersburg, 1857. 244 pp.

8. A. D. Rudnev, *Khori-buryatskii govor. Opyt issledovaniya, teksty, perevody, primechaniya.* St. Petersburg, 1913-14.

9. *Alarskii govor.* Chast' pervaya: Fonetika i morfologiya. Leningrad, 1930. 130 pp. (Materialy Mongol'skoi Komissii, v. 11). Chast' vtoraya: *Teksty.* Leningrad, 1931. 216 pp. (Materialy Mongol'skoi Komissii, v. 13).

10. *Zametki o govore aginskikh buryat.* Leningrad, 1932. 23 pp. (Trudy Mongol'skoi Komissii, v. 8).

11. "Skizze der Phonetik des Bargu-Burjätischen," *Asia Major* 7 (1931), 307-378.

12. *Grammatika buryat-mongol'skogo yazyka.* Moscow-Leningrad, 1938. 268 pp.

13. *Buriat Grammar.* Bloomington, 1960. 129 pp. (Uralic and Altaic Series, v. 2).

14. *Dagurskoe narechie.* Leningrad, 1930. 176 pp. (Materialy Mongol'skoi Komissii, v. 6).

15. "Über die Sprache der Daguren," *Asia Major* 10 (1934), 1-32, 183-220.

16. *Materialy dlya issledovaniya tungusskogo yazyka: Narechie barguzinskikh tungusov.* Leningrad, 1927. 60 pp. (Materialy po yaficheskomu yazykoznaniyu, no. 13).

17. *Materialy po solonskomu yazyku.* Leningrad, 1931. 142 pp. (Materialy Mongol'skoi Komissii, v. 14).

18. A. O. Ivanovskii, *Mandjurica: 1. Obraztsy solonskago i dakhurskago yazykov.* St. Petersburg, 1894. xiv, 79 pp.

19. *Grammatika pis'menno-mongol'skogo yazyka.* Moscow-Leningrad, 1937. 196 pp.

20. *Grammar of Written Mongolian.* Wiesbaden, 1954. 195 pp.

21. *Uchebnaya grammatika yakutskogo yazyka.* Moscow, 1926. 120 pp.

22. Otto Böhtlingk, *Über die Sprache der Jakuten.* St. Petersburg, 1851. Reprint: Bloomington, 1964. (Uralic and Altaic Series, v. 35).

23. S. V. Yastremskii, *Grammatika yakutskago yazyka.* Irkutsk, 1900.

24. *Tatar Manual: Descriptive Grammar and Texts with a Tatar-English Glossary.* Bloomington, 1963. 271 pp. (Uralic and Altaic Series, v. 25); *Bashkir Manual.* Bloomington, 1964. 181 pp. (Uralic and Altaic Series, v. 36).

25. "Mongol'skie nazvaniya zhivotnykh v trude Khamdallakha Kazvini," *Zapiski Kollegii Vostokovedov* 1 (1925), 195-208.

26. "Das mongolische Sprachmaterial einer Leidener Handschrift," *Izvestiya Akademii Nauk SSSR* 1927, nos. 12-14, pp. 1009-1040; nos. 15-17, pp. 1251-1274; 1928, no. 1, pp. 55-80.

27. M. Th. Houtsma, *Ein türkisch-arabisches Glossar.* Leiden, 1894.

28. "Zur mittelmongolischen Kasuslehre: Eine syntaktische Untersuchung," *Zeitschrift der Deutschen Morgenländischen Gesellschaft* 103 (1953), 92-125.

29. "Eine viersprachige Zamaxšarī-Handschrift," *Zeitschrift der Deutschen Morgenländischen Gesellschaft* 101 (1951), 301-332.

30. *Istoriya mongol'skoi pis'mennosti.* Tom I. *Kvadratnaya pis'mennost'.* Moscow-Leningrad, 1941. Translated as *The Mongolian Monuments in ḥP'ags-pa Script.* Wiesbaden, 1957. (Göttinger Asiatische Forschungen, v. 8).

31. "The passive constructions in the language of the Secret History," *Ural-Altaische Jahrbücher* 36 (1964), 366-377.

32. "Die Sprache der mongolischen Quadratschrift und das *Yüan-ch'ao pi-shi*," *Asia Major* N. F., 1 (1944), 97-115.

33. See Ki-Moon Lee, *Geschichte der koreanischen Sprache* (Wiesbaden, 1977), 83.

34. See Hans Krahe, *Germanische Sprachwissenschaft*, v. 1 (Berlin, 1960), 24. (Sammlung Göschen, v. 238.)

35. "On some ancient Mongolian loan words in Tungus," *Central Asiatic Journal* 11 (1966), 187-198; "On some Mongolian loan words in Evenki," *Central Asiatic Journal* 16 (1972), 95-103.

36. "Jurchen and Mongolian," in *Studies on Mongolia: Proceedings of the First North American Conference on Mongolian Studies* (Bellingham, 1979), 30-37.

37. B. Ya. Vladimirtsov, *Sravnitel'naya grammatika mongol'skogo pis'mennogo yazyka i khalkhaskogo narechiya.* Leningrad, 1929. 448 pp.

38. Antoine Mostaert's major works on Ordos Mongolian include "Le dialecte des Mongols Urdus (Sud), étude phonetique," *Anthropos* 21 (1926), 851-869, 22 (1927), 160-186; *Textes oraux ordos* (Peking, 1937), and *Dictionnaire ordos* (3 vols) (Peking, 1941-44); his major works on Monguor (in cooperation with A. de Smedt) are "Le dialecte monguor parlé par les Mongols du Kansou occidental, Phonétique," *Anthropos* 24 (1929), 145-165, 801-815, 25 (1930), 657-669, 961-973; *Le dialecte monguor, parle par les Mongols du Kansou occidental, Grammaire* (Peking, 1945), and *Dictionnaire monguor-français* (Peking, 1933).

39. *Introduction to Mongolian Comparative Studies.* Helsinki, 1955. 300 pp. (Mémoires de la Société Finno-Ougrienne, v. 110).

40. "The primary long vowels in Mongolian," *Journal de la Société Finno-Ougrienne* 63 (1962), no. 2, 19 pp.; "On the long vowels in Common Mongolian," *Journal de la Société Finno-Ougrienne* 68 (1967), no. 4. 31 pp.

41. *Vergleichende Grammatik der altaischen Sprachen.* Teil I: *Vergleichende Lautlehre.* Wiesbaden, 1960. 188 pp. (Porta Linguarum Orientalium, n.s., v. 4).

42. *Introduction to Altaic Linguistics.* Wiesbaden, 1965. 212 pp. (Ural-Altaische Bibliothek, v. 14).

43. "Chuvashskii yazyk i ego otnoshenie k mongol'skomu i tyurks-kim yazykam," *Izvestiya Rossiiskoi Akademii Nauk* 18 (1924-25), 289-314; 19 (1925), 23-42, 405-426.

44. "Zur Stellung des Tschuwaschischen," *Central Asiatic Journal* 18 (1974), 135-147.

45. Ya. I. Shmidt, *Podvigi ispolnennago zaslug geroya Bogdy Gesser Khana, istrebitelya desyati zol v desyati stranakh, geroiskoe predanie mongolov.* St. Petersburg, 1836.

46. "Geserica. Untersuchung der sprachlichen Eigentümlichkeiten der mongolischen Version des Gesserkhan," *Asia Major* 3 (1926), 1-32, 167-193.

47. *The Twelve Deeds of Buddha: A Mongolian Version of the Lalitavistara.* Wiesbaden, 1967. 173 pp., 65 plates. (Asiatische Forschungen, v. 23).

48. "The Mongolian versions of the Vessantarajātaka," *Studia Orientalia* 30 (1964), no. 2, 92 pp.

49. *The Diamond Sutra: Three Mongolian Versions of the Vajrac-chedikāprajñāpāramitā.* Wiesbaden, 1971. 230 pp. (Asiatische Forschungen, v. 35).

50. *Letopisi khorinskikh buryat.* Vyp. 1. *Khroniki Tugultur Toboeva i Vandana Yumsunova.* Leningrad, 1935. 172 pp. (Trudy Instituta Vostokovedeniya, v. 9; Materialy dlya istorii buryat-mongolov, v. 2).

51. *Letopisi selenginskikh buryat.* Vyp. 1: *Khronika Ubashi Dambi Dzhaltsan Lombo Tserenova 1868 g.* Moscow-Leningrad, 1936. 55 pp. (Trudy Instituta Vostokovedeniya, v. 12; Materialy dlya istorii buryat-mongolov, v. 3).

52. Translation of note 50 in Trudy Instituta Vostokovedeniya, v. 33; Materialy dlya istorii buryat-mongolov, v. 4.

53. *Letopisi barguzinskikh buryat: Teksty i issledovaniya.* Leningrad, 1935. 75 pp. (Trudy Instituta Vostokovedeniya, v. 8; Materialy dlya istorii buryat-mongolov, v. 1).

54. "A fragment of the Bodhicaryāvatāra from Olon Süme," *Harvard Journal of Asiatic Studies* 17 (1954), 411-418.

55. "Eine mongolische Fassung der Alexandersage," *Zeitschrift der Deutschen Morgenländischen Gesellschaft* 107 (1957), 105-129.

56. Francis W. Cleaves, "An early Mongolian version of the Alexander Romance translated and annotated," *Harvard Journal of Asiatic Studies* 22 (1959), 1-99, 8 plates.

57. "Zolotoordynskaya rukopis' na bereste," *Sovetskoe Vostokovedenie* 2 (1941), 81-136, 24 plates. Reprinted in *Mongolica* (Farnborough, England: Gregg International Publishers Ltd., 1972).

58. "A Middle Turkic text of the Apostles' Creed," *Monumenta Serica* 24 (1965), 273-306.

59. *Yazyk i kolkhoznaya poèziya buryat-mongolov Selenginskogo aimaka.* Leningrad, 1934. 132 pp. (Obraztsy Narodnoi Slovesnosti Mongolov, v. 4). Reprinted by Gregg International Publishers Ltd. in 1972.

60. *Tsongol Folklore: Translation of the Language and Collective Farm Poetry of the Buriat-Mongols of the Selenga Region.* Wiesbaden, 1978. (Asiatische Forschungen, v. 55).

61. *Buryat-mongol'skii fol'klornyi i dialektologicheskii sbornik.* Moscow-Leningrad, 1936. 167 pp. (Obraztsy Narodnoi Slovesnosti Mongolov, v. 5).

62. *Mongolische Epen I, II, III, IV, V, VI, IX.* Wiesbaden, 1975, 1977, 1980. (Asiatische Forschungen, v. 42, 43, 47, 48, 50, 53, 65).

63. *Khalkha-mongol'skii geroicheskii èpos.* Moscow-Leningrad, 1937. 125 pp. (Trudy Instituta Vostokovedeniya, v. 26). Reprinted by Gregg International Publishers Ltd. in 1971.
64. *The Heroic Epic of the Khalkha Mongols.* Bloomington, 1979. (Mongolia Society Occasional Paper Number 11).

Chapter 12

1. Voznesenskii, in *Pamyat': istoricheskii sbornik* 3 (Paris, 1980), pp. 455, 458.
2. E. N. Nenarokova, *Ital'yanskaya tsvetnaya gravyura na dereve XVI-XVIII vekov.* Leningrad, 1962.
3. *Jangh"r, Khal'm"g baatarl"g duulv"r (25 bölgiin tekst).* Vol. 2. Moscow, 1978.
4. *Dzhangar, Kalmytskii narodnyi èpos.* Moscow, 1958.
5. *Wörterbuch des Chaladsch, Dialekt von Xarrab.* Budapest, 1980.

Person Index

Chugaev, Lev Aleksandrovich, 33
Churchill, Winston, 184, 192
Cirtautas, Arista Maria, 261
Cirtautas, Ilse   SEE Laude–Cirtautas
Clay, Lucius D., 193
Cleaves, Francis Woodman, 201, 275
Conze, Edward, 227, 228

Dagmar, Princess, 68
Dagva, a Mongol guide, 89
Dandaron, B. D., 135
Davies, Joseph E., 200
Deborin, Abram Moiseevich, 120
Deeters, G., 166
Denikin, Anton Ivanovich, 139
Denisov, a director, 139
Diederichs, Charlotte, 58
Diederichs, Max, 58
Diederichs, Wilhelm (Willi), 58, 59, 171, 189
Dilowa Khutuktu, 223, 234
Doerfer, Gerhard, 270, 271, 272, 293
Donat, Walter, 175, 179, 183
Donner, Kai (Karl Reinhold), 140, 258
Dorzhiev, Agvan, 130, 131
Dragunov, Aleksandr Aleksandrovich, 233
Drozhdzhinskaya, Ekaterina Nikolaevna (Kitti), 79
Duda, Herbert W., 230
Dumas, Alexandre, 136
Dunlop, D. M., 247
Dushan, Ulimdzhi (Ülimji) Dushanovich, 73
D'yakonov, Ivan Mikhailovich, 251
D'yakonov, Mikhail Mikhailovich, 251
Dyrenkova, Nadezhda Petrovna, 69, 70

Eberhard, Wolfram, 236
Ebermann, Aleksandr Aleksandrovich, 80

Goldshtein, an ear doctor, 92
Goltz, Gustav Adolph Joachim Rüdiger, von der, 37
Gomboin, Lubsan, 103, 234
Gombojab Mergen Gün, 89, 98
Gor'kii, Maksim, 107
Gosudarev, an instructor, 157
Gottlieb, a British officer, 175
Grinberg, Mikhail Davidovich, 61, 62, 91
Grishin, Dmitrii Vladimirovich, 178
Grónbech, Kaare, 248, 249
Grum-Grzhimailo, Grigorii Efimovich, 120, 121, 282
Gundelach, Mrs., a library employee, 114
Gylling, Edvard Otto Wilhelm, 138

Haenisch, Erich, 171, 172, 191, 201, 226, 253
Haenisch, Hans, 191,
Haenisch, Wolf, 172
Hahn, Otto, 192
Halén, Harry, 255
Haloun, Gustav, 191
Hamayon, Roberte, 256
Hamm, Frank Richard, 250
Hangin, John Gombojab, 244
Hannikainen, Karl Onni Gerhard, 25
Hattori, Shirō, 253, 275
Heissig, Walther, 240, 248, 249, 250, 255, 277
Helenius, Artturi, 24
Hilger, Gustav, 200
Hitler, Adolf, 115, 133, 134, 171, 179, 185, 189, 226, 227, 235
Hogness, John R., 203
Hoover, Herbert, 244
Hope, Earl R., 232, 233
Houtsma, M. Th., 266
Hromatka, major, 164
Hsiao Kung-ch'üan, 219, 227
Hultman, Frithiof H., 3

Person Index

Yumsunov, Vandan, 275
Yunusov, Gāzī 'Alī, 119
Yushchinskii, Andryusha, 49

Zajączkowski, Ananjasz, 253
Zakutnyi, D. E., 178
Zamatkinov, Bardym Man'yarovich, 72
Zehzahn, a refugee, 169
Zhamtsarano, Tsyben Zhamtsaranovich, 43, 75, 89, 132, 134, 276, 277
Zhebelev, Sergei Aleksandrovich, 141, 252
Zhilenkov, Georgii Nikolaevich, 184
Zhirmunskii, Viktor Maksimovich, 229
Zhukov, Dmitrii Petrovich, 135
Zhukov, Georgii K., 178
Zhukovskii, Valentin Alekseevich, 53, 54, 101
Ziegler, Edith O. SEE Poppe, Edith
Ziegler, Karl Vladimirovich, 216
Zinov'ev, Grigorii Evseevich, 139, 141
Zuckmayer, Carl, 137